CULTURE AND SOCIETY IN THE WEIMAR REPUBLIC

For RICHARD HINTON THOMAS   b. 12 August 1912

KEITH BULLIVANT *editor*

Culture and society
in the Weimar Republic

Manchester University Press

Rowman and Littlefield

Published by Manchester University Press
Oxford Road, Manchester M13 9PL

ISBN 0 7190 0689 9

USA

Rowman and Littlefield
81 Adams Drive, Totowa, N.J. 07512

ISBN 0–8476–6012–5

British Library cataloguing in publication data

Culture and society in the Weimar Republic.
  1. Germany – Civilization 2. Germany – History –
  1918–1933
  I. Bullivant, Keith   II. Thomas, Richard Hinton
  943.085   DD239

  ISBN 0–7190–0689–9

Computerised Phototypesetting by
G. C. Typeset Ltd., Bolton, Lancashire

Printed in Great Britain
by The Scolar Press Ltd.

CONTENTS

The editor and the publishers gratefully acknowledge the assistance of the Deutscher Akademischer Austauschdienst and the University of Warwick in making the publication of this book possible.

PREFACE

The fascination of the culture of the Weimar Republic derives partly from the fact that many areas of it still remain relatively unexplored and partly from the complex internal relations between writers and cultural groups during the life of the republic. Any attempt at surveying the panorama of this rich and varied period, the first truly modern cultural age in Europe, is faced, however, with the twin dangers of superficiality on the one hand and more detailed analysis of possibly less representative aspects of its cultural life on the other. This volume in no way pretends to offer the English reader the broad coverage he or she can find in Peter Gay's *Weimar Culture* or Walter Laqueur's *Weimar. A cultural history, 1918–33* but seeks instead to complement such excellent general surveys. In addition to two new studies of Thomas Mann there is an essay on another important conservative intellectual, Friedrich Sieburg, who is hardly known in this country. An important section of the volume examines various aspects of the vigorous left-wing cultural activity of the period that has until recently been so neglected by critics, and it is to be hoped that these essays will help to rectify an often unbalanced view of the era. The other contributions take a new look at two of the better known parts of the Weimar spectrum, 'Neue Sachlichkeit' and the operas of Brecht and Berg.

By the unanimous wish of the contributors this volume is dedicated to Richard Hinton Thomas, a pioneering scholar in the field of German studies and a much respected colleague, teacher and friend, on the occasion of his sixty-fifth birthday.

University of Warwick

KEITH BULLIVANT

ROY PASCAL

The Magic Mountain and Adorno's critique of the traditional novel

Theodor Adorno's little essay of 1954, 'The locus standi of the narrator in the contemporary novel', is often quoted and enjoys the prestige that attaches to his work.[1] It reflects the decisive dilemma of the modern novel, giving a characteristic Adorno-esque twist to similar views expressed by Jean-Paul Sartre in *What is Literature?* (1948) and much discussed since then.[2]

The closer one scrutinises Adorno's deliberately challenging essay – it was composed as the text for a discussion – the more questionable do some of the assertions and arguments appear. This is so even when the provocation is intensified by its form, as with the much-quoted 'Es lässt sich nicht mehr erzählen'. Actually this assertion is one branch of a paradox – 'It is no longer possible to tell a story, while the form of the novel requires a story'. The implication of this paradox is, as we can ascertain from what follows, not that novels are no longer possible but that a new model of story is required, and is in fact to be found in the most significant modern novels.

Adorno proceeds immediately to explain why the traditional type of story is now obsolete. The novel, he states, was the 'specific literary form' of the bourgeois age, from its beginning faced with the experience of 'a world bereft of enchantment' ('entzaubert'), and therefore centrally concerned with 'the mastery in art of bare existence'. That is, it was in principle realistic, realism was 'immanent' in the novel form. It is this realism that the modern age rejects, and with it the traditional story-model. It must be observed that the dependence of 'story' on 'realism' is only asserted by Adorno, not proven; but we shall return to this question in a moment.

Adorno then analyses the failure of realism, first from the point of view of the story-teller. Modern subjectivism undermines the 'epic requirement of "Gegenständlichkeit"'. By this term we are intended to understand, not so much 'objectivity' as devotion to things, respect for their spiritual significance, and hence for the concrete environment and appurtenances of the characters of novels. The novelist's traditional concern for tangibles, things and persons, was possible, Adorno argues, only in an age when the world was loved; and love, again, was possible only because the world seemed 'meaningful'.

Are these statements as self-evident as their dogmatic form suggests? Adorno mentions Stifter as an example of the love of things, but Stifter is not representative enough to bear out the assertion, and in the long history of the novel detestation, hostility, criticism have as often been the stimulus to realism as love. And what does 'meaningful' ('sinnvoll') mean? It cannot have a transcendental sense, since Adorno had defined the world of the novel to be 'bereft of enchantment'. So it must mean 'meaningful' in the secular sphere of personal life, in the sense that the objects and circumstances of daily life are felt to embody a spiritual value, to construct and contribute to the coherent identity, the purpose, the self-fulfilment of the individual, the 'hero'.

But does this conception of the world hold for the traditional novel? I think that much more substantially we see 'meaning' not as something inherently within the hero's world but as something frail and menaced, something that has to be imposed on a world of threatening or indifferent contingencies, and that may, of course, often enough elude him or her, as in *The Mill on the Floss*. There is no immanent 'meaning' for Tom Jones or Don Quixote or their like, nor in the world of Balzac, or Fontane, or even Dickens; the successful individuals can be thankful, to luck, chance, and their own efforts, that they have 'made it'. What clear-sightedness belongs to the opening words of the final chapter of *Mansfield Park*:

Let other pens dwell on guilt and misery. I quit such odious subjects as soon as I can, impatient to restore every body, not greatly in fault themselves, to tolerable comfort, and to have done with the rest.

Jane Austen is acknowledging that even the area of modest 'meaningfulness' that deeply engages her – the achievement of 'tolerable comfort' – is not accessible to all the world. It would seem that the realistic novel did not depend on love of things or the imputation of 'meaningfulness' to things.

When Adorno examines his contention from the other side, 'von der Sache her', we don't need to take exception to the claim that reportage and the media, the techniques of the psychologist and sociologist, have encroached on the novelist's terrain and driven him away from factualities and psychological analysis; nor to the statement that literature is less capable of developing abstract forms than painting because of its medium, language. But it is difficult to accept his assertion that we no longer know 'the identity of experience', i.e. 'a continuous and articulated life', not least because it is not clearly explained. His argument here is directed at the traditional 'narrator' of the novel, which implies, he states, a rigid ('unverrückbare') narrative perspective that cannot do justice to the multiplicity and discontinuity of the individual. Here Adorno simplifies greatly the function of the narrator in the traditional novel and does not recognise that the problematical relationship between fiction and reality is a recurring theme in the eighteenth-century novel.

The next point that calls for comment is Adorno's further argument that, while telling a story must mean that one has 'something particular' to say, this is impossible in the modern, bureaucratic world, the 'verwaltete Welt' of standardisation and 'sameness' – vague, unsatisfactory terms that would have been more acceptable in 1954 than they are today. 'Story', he goes on, is wedded to individuality, in the sense that the 'course of the world' is conceived to be essentially a matter of individual lives and that the given individual with his urges and feelings has almost the solidity of destiny, so that his 'inner self' makes an impact on the world. None of these presuppositions, Adorno maintains, is valid today.

There is no doubt that the position of the individual has changed in modern society, that his impact on society is very small, and the conception of a personal destiny seems illusory and, if presented in the novel, cannot have the force of a universal symbol. What I question in Adorno's formulations is his habit of turning differences of degree into absolute differences, so that he eagerly embraces despair in preference to seeking solutions. In regard to the novel, this situation is less new than Adorno states, since it has been a constant theme of the bourgeois novel to investigate how the individual may maintain himself, shape his life, despite the course of the world. A man's 'inner self' was always menaced; was it ever powerful?

Adorno goes on to argue that the modern novel must abandon 'surface realism' not only because this has been taken over by reporters, sociologists and psychologists but also because it falsifies the reality of modern existence. In the prevailing reification of all relationships, the 'universal alienation and self-alienation', all the human qualities of men are manipulated into becoming 'grease for the smooth running of the machinery of society'. If the novelist concerns himself with personal happiness, personal relations, self-fulfilment, etc, he reproduces only the 'façade' of life and deludes man as to his real being. Adorno introduces here a distinction between the empirical man and the essential man. Today the essence of man lies in his estrangement, and the peculiar impulse of the novel, which was always 'the elucidation of the puzzle of external life', must now abandon its traditional realism and turn to portray the human essence, which is alienation. This is the explanation of the 'anti-realistic' element in the modern novel, of its 'metaphysical dimension', that arises, as traditional realism once did, from the nature of its theme, social life.

Such phrases as 'the universal alienation and self-alienation' illustrate Adorno's habit of thinking in terms of absolutes. Though they belong to a Marxist tradition, their absoluteness seems to indicate rather a religious or existentialist source. They recall the early Marxism of Georg Lukács in *The Theory of the Novel* and *History and Class Consciousness*, in which terms like alienation, reification, totality, throb with the religious emotion that characterises his pre-Marxist work *Die Seele und die Formen*, in which he had sought 'redemption' in art from a God-forsaken world. It is strange, however, that Adorno should adopt such terms without the regulative model of a religious image, and even without the simple faith of the Marxist Lukács in a social redemption.

Still, few would challenge Adorno's criticism of the traditional realism of the novel, even though he himself acknowledges that the modern situation is not entirely new, since he observes that at least since *Tom Jones* the novel has always recognised its true theme to be 'the conflict between living men and petrified circumstances'. What I would question is the relevance of his thesis about realism to the main theme of his essay, the story structure and the function of the narrator. As I have already remarked, the implications of the one for the other are by no means clear.

From this point in his essay Adorno proceeds to consider the ways in which modern novelists have created new narrative forms, and he makes acute comments, critical and appreciative, on the work of Proust, Joyce, Broch, Kafka and others. These comments do not add up, of course, to a demonstration that 'it is impossible to tell a story', but contribute to the investigation of the ways in which 'story' has been modified in order to reflect our modern world and modern consciousness. Among the great innovators Adorno counts Thomas Mann particularly, with Gide and Musil, in respect to the embodiment of reflections within narrative, reflections that, as he puts it, break through the pure immanence of form ('die reine Formimmanenz') that characterises the traditional novel. Though this term seems very dubious, Adorno is right in observing that the embodiment of reflection within narrative produces repeated changes of narrative perspective that undermine the objective authority that the traditional story-teller with his unvarying perspective could assert. He makes the further helpful observation that the narrator's reflections in the modern novel are in principle unlike the moralistic authorial intrusions in the traditional novel, since they serve to warn the reader against the 'illusionary character' of the story, against the narrator himself, against 'the lie of descriptive narrative'. This has indeed, he sums up, become the essential theme of the modern novel, and today we can see in the late novels of Thomas Mann (*The Holy Sinner* and *The Black Swan*), says Adorno, the clue to the enigma of his irony, which is directed not at the characters but at the narrator himself; it is the 'gesture' with which Mann 'shakes off' the pretension of creating 'something real'. Under these circumstances, writes Adorno, the work of art re-acquires the character of 'higher fun' ('des höheren Jux') that it once had, before it presumptuously claimed to be an image of reality.

Despite the subtlety of the argument, it seems to me to be wrong-headed to claim these later works to be the apex of Mann's achievement; *The Magic Mountain*, and *Joseph* tetralogy, *Doktor Faustus* surely tower above them, so that they seem only a coda to a great achievement. But this is worth saying only because they tower above the latest works chiefly because they are not primarily concerned with form, with illusion, but all have an ethical motivation and theme, and in this as in other ways are not 'higher fun' but 'images of reality'. When I consider the various doubts I have expressed over Adorno's theses it would seem that they add up to the following question: is it not possible to modify the form of the traditional novel so that a modern story can be told, true to the subjective and objective characteristics of modern existence, but without abandoning the claim of realism and an ethical purpose, without becoming obsessed with the problem of narrative form? It is this question that the following analysis of *The Magic Mountain* is intended to answer. It centres upon the problems of the alienated individual and his relation to the social world, which include that of the ending, and the varieties of narrative perspective, especially in relation to realism or 'Gegenständlichkeit'.

The Magic Mountain – alienation and ending

Mann makes it clear from the beginning that the problem of his novel is what a later generation is accustomed to call alienation, and that this personal story also has a 'suprapersonal' significance. In a completely authoritative authorial comment, not subject to irony or any other qualification, he states that every man lives 'not only his personal life, but consciously or unconsciously also that of his epoch and contemporaries' (I, 58). [3] He goes on:

When the impersonal world around him, the times themselves, for all their superficial activity fundamentally lack hopes and perspectives, when they reveal themselves to him as secretly without hope, without perspective, and bewildered; when, faced by the question – posed consciously or unconsciously, but still somehow or other posed – what is the final, more than personal, unqualified meaning of all effort and activity, they answer with a hollow silence; then, with individuals of a more honest nature, such a situation will almost inevitably have a certain laming effect, which may extend through the spiritual and moral region even to the physical, the organic side of the individual.

Such is the profound alienation from which Hans Castorp suffers, the reason for his strange lethargy, that enables him so readily to drop out of the life in the Flatlands, which responds to his unformulated question with 'a hollow silence'. This life without commitment is intensified at the Berghof sanatorium (freedom at the price of 800 Marks a month!), which functions throughout partly as the opposite of the Flatlands, partly as their intensified mirror image. The sanatorium possesses, however, two advantages over the Flatlands. First, it offers a short-term answer to the question about 'meaning', namely health, the cure, the sanatorium routine. Second, it gives access to many thoughts and experiences, enthralling in their novelty, that in the main arise from the fascination of disease and death, the predominance of death over life, the perspective of life as a process of dying. These new experiences release Hans Castorp from his lethargy, for they challenge all the presuppositions of his life, and his lethargy, down in the Flatlands; they even promise an answer, even though a paradoxical one, to the great question. But, up here in the Berghof, though spiritually responsive and intellectually active, Castorp still remains 'lamed', only partly committed in his interests and his friendly compassion – not identified with the impassioned 'suprapersonal' faiths of Settembrini or Naphta, nor with Peeperkorn's frail vitalism, nor with Joachim's simple will to return, nor with the other patients' evasions or Behrens's medical dedication, nor even committed to erotic love.

But *The Magic Mountain* is a true 'Bildungsroman', not a clinical diagnosis.[4] Castorp's responses to the various facets of the life at the Berghof are at first lively but bewildered, but they are active, and soon betray the purposefulness of a search to which he ultimately finds a name – 'sich regieren' (II, 84). It is a complex term which means 'to direct oneself', but as a precondition 'to come to terms with things' and 'to come to terms with oneself'. In this sense he seeks experiences and ventures to 'experiment', begins to criticise his mentors, to challenge 'the uncanny' by his expeditions into the high mountains (II, 227). The enrichment from this life in death leads him swiftly to drop the claims and obligations of the old world, but his enquiries into disease and death also enhance his curiosity about life, so that the distinguishing peculiarity of his love for Clawdia Chauchat is his tenderness for endangered, diseased life. His mountain expeditions are motivated by his double drive, and it is in the 'Snow' section, when lured and threatened by death, that he makes his final decision for life – 'For the sake of kindness and love, man must yield death no dominance over his thoughts' (II, 260). It is a commitment.

But this is not the end of Castorp's uncommitted existence at the Berghof. Dr Swales had rightly put into sharp focus the fact that Hans Castorp does not act upon this resolution and actually almost forgets it.[5] He stays on for years, almost more detached and devoid of purpose than before, while the life around him (and in the remote Flatlands) grows more sour and empty, fuller of aggressiveness and hatred. It needs an external event, the outbreak of war, to bring him to act, to enlist with his compatriots, in a curious sense to fulfil his pledge. For Dr Swales the long delay before Castorp acts on the insight of the 'Snow' episode, and the disparity between the insight and the actual action (taking part in a disastrous war) indicates the fundamental disparity between contemplative insight and activity. I think another answer must be sought for this very real problem.

The commitment in the 'Snow' episode is indeed so vague and inconclusive that Dr Ziolkowski can write that Hans Castorp leaves Davos 'unpledged' 'not a whit richer in belief'. He argues, in agreement with Erich Heller, that Castorp has become fitted only to be an artist, and this means, as Professor Heller puts it, that he lives 'above the contradictions' of life, recognising the meaninglessness of life and responding to this meaninglessness by 'existing inwardly'.[6] Such a judgement, however, fails to recognise that the modest and diffident affirmation Hans Castorp makes is much more than a mere rejection of a systematic, confident faith or ideology. It is not a null. There is as great a difference between it and the 'hollow silence' as there is between a positive number and a zero; and a failure to recognise the positive commitment in Hans Castorp's formula and final action is as serious a misinterpretation of the book as would be a claim that it gives a confident definition of how the world is to be restored or redeemed.[7]

By relating the terms of Castorp's pledge to Thomas Mann's own evolution from his wartime ideology (much of which appears in Naphta's arguments, as in Hans Castorp's 'sympathy with death'), T. J. Reed has convincingly shown that what may seem to a modern reader a somewhat vague commitment to 'kindness and love' and to life is in fact, in its historical context, a decisive commitment to a whole humanistic tradition that involves democracy and tolerance. Contemporaries would recognise the terms as signifying a general political faith, as opposed to aggressive nationalisms as to the mystical authoritarianism or totalitarian doctrines. [8] It would, however, be difficult to claim that these implications are made clear in the context of the book itself, and equally difficult to find such a meaning in the decision of Hans Castorp to fight in the war. I believe the vagueness of his pledge and the inconclusiveness of his enlistment are deliberately there, and belong to the conception and the structure of the novel.

When Thomas Mann was completing the book in 1924 Germany had scarcely emerged out of the chaos of the post-war turmoil and the inflation. Coming painfully to terms with democracy, he could not at that time confidently prescribe a positive policy or even describe a positive hope. How much less could he allow such to his young hero in 1914! So Hans Castorp has no programme, no ideology, only the will to share in his nation's fate, and a vague hope for 'love', renouncing that once fascinating but now hollow freedom. [9] His belief and his act round off the story of his experiences. But, as he steps back into the Flatlands, he loses the central position he has enjoyed. Now he is only one of millions, and the war, the future, is the theme that usurps his place. The war will not be decided by a personal decision or commitment. So Mann does not exalt Hans Castorp with some rhetorical or tragic final gesture, with some faith that promises the world redemption (as so many Expressionist writers were prone to do). On the contrary he dismisses him from the scene, significant now, in the midst of nationalist and ideological forces, only as a faint hope.

Thus the ending of *The Magic Mountain* is peculiar, but its peculiarity lies in its modernity. It does not suggest that the hero's life is fulfilled, nor that this fulfilment has a general, symbolic significance. We do feel, however, that Hans Castorp has completed a cycle of experiences, such as his environment offered him, and has fulfilled the conditions upon which he entered upon the scene. That is, we have an aesthetic sense of completion, and are ready to dismiss him. But the generality, society, that created the world that answered Hans Castorp's unspoken questions with a 'hollow silence', now momentarily broken by his small voice, has found no conclusion and has not changed. The outbreak of war reminds us sharply of its potent presence, and because of this we can dismiss Hans Castorp and turn our attention to that world and its continuing problems. In this sense, therefore, the novel ends and must end with an open, unresolved future. This was Thomas Mann's answer to the problem of the ending set by Joyce or Proust.

In respect both to the theme of alienation and the problem of an ending, Mann's novel offers a critical comment on Theodor Adorno's theses. Mann seems to reject Adorno's system as decisively as Hans Castorp does those of Settembrini or Naphta. In Castorp's alienation there is nothing of the exalted, despairing absolutism of Adorno; it is deep in his whole being, but the possibilities of overcoming it are not dismissed. There is no arrogance in the hope of a cure, but the hope is not rejected. If Mann is not inclined to exalt an individual fate into a universal destiny, neither does he dismiss the individual life and effort as impotent and insignificant, since it may make itself a worthy self-purpose and may even have an effect on the whole.

The Magic Mountain – the narrative perspective

It is not hard to become aware that, as far as narrative perspective goes, *Der Zauberberg* does not belong to the tradition of the illusionistic, realistic novel that Adorno calls obsolete. The narrator is throughout prominent, as it were standing in the way of a naive reader participation in events; there is much reflection mingled with the narrative, breaking into what Adorno calls the 'pure immanence of form' of the novel. What we must be especially concerned to discover is whether these typical modernisms also necessarily involve the 'breakdown' of realism, the undermining of 'the lie of artistic presentation', a 'metaphysical element', and whether we find what Adorno considers to be the logical outcome of these, the replacement of practical and ethical issues by formal, artistic ones.

In a 'Nachwort' added in 1925 to an article of 1915, 'Objektive Erzählung', Oskar Walzel welcomed the return of the narrator in *The Magic Mountain*, after the long dominance of the Spielhagen conception of 'objective narrative'. It is a return, Walzel states, to the traditional form of 'oral narrative', a return to a descriptive epic style as opposed to a dramatic, dialogic one, presenting events only through the medium of the narrator, and drawing the readers into participation and collusion with the narrator. Walzel also notes how closely the narrator sticks to the perspective of the hero and 'describes almost everything as it is mirrored in the mind of the hero', though often separating from his fictional character to address the reader direct as 'we' or 'the narrator'. Walzel is not wrong in claiming that with this work Mann does contribute to the restoration of an ancient narrative tradition, and to the overthrow of the dominance of the illusionist-realist novel of Flaubert and the Naturalists. But he does not recognise the new functions that Mann's narrator develops. [10] The narrative perspective in *The Magic Mountain* is in fact most complex and requires a systematic analysis. I must limit myself here to what is sufficient for my present purpose. [11]

1. The narrator appears throughout as an external authority, i.e. authoritative in respect to the truth of facts and their interpretation. Thus

he appears in the preface, where he discusses his story and its 'pastness', and in the opening pages that describe Hans Castorp's arrival at Davos. The grounds of Castorp's detachment, alienation, are explained by this authoritative narrator (I, 57–9). On innumerable occasions this narrator reflects, in odd remarks or longer passages, on issues arising from his story, particularly on the lapse of time and the character of the environment – typical is the remark on the air in the high altitudes – 'Without the odour of dampness, without body, without memories' (I, 198), where the last substantive insinuates a large theme. The descriptive narrative itself is steadily narratorial, that is, it describes in the rather complex, sophisticated language of Thomas Mann the events and people and the thoughts of the characters; conversations are often given, at great length, in direct speech, but also the forms of indirect speech, normal and free ('erlebte Rede'), are employed, forms that imply a narrator and often bear his stamp of sympathy or irony. At times the narrator steps back from his involvement in events, as in the section 'Stroll by the sea', where a lonely stroll on some seashore gives him the distance and mood necessary to review the whole (II, 334–45). This authoritative narrator is impersonal and undefined, except that he allows himself a sort of avuncular sympathy with his 'hero', the 'simple young man', a sympathy which, he says, does not prevent him from being truthful and impartial (I, 57); the use of the editorial 'we' and impersonal 'the narrator' seems to guarantee this. At the same time this anonymous narrator establishes from the beginning an intimate contact with his reader, as Walzel noticed, a sort of collusion in concern for the tale and its hero, the 'problem child'.

He often plays with the reader, too, as when he anticipates the account of Peeperkorn's death with a series of questions supposed to be put by impatient readers; his rather cryptic evasions typically make us aware that this is a story and must observe the rules of story-telling; we must, he says, 'accord time at least as much honour as the peculiar nature of our story allows' (II, 391). This familiar, slightly jocular tone appears rather more frequently towards the end of the novel, reflecting the firmly established intimacy between narrator and reader. He even can call his readers his 'audience', as if they were all together participating in an imaginative experience – 'Who was Ellen Brand? We had almost forgotten that our listeners do not know, while to us, of course, the name is familiar' (II, 528). At the end he identifies himself with the readers: 'We shadowy onlookers by the wayside are in their midst' (II, 626), where the 'shades' observing the battlefield are in truth, as we know, the real persons viewing the imaginary beings of the story.

But this anonymous narrator is not always impersonal. Even in 'Stroll by the sea' he has something of a shape and gesture. His sympathy is in some degree personal, and so is his criticism. When he says, after reporting that Hans Castorp 'says to himself' that he hopes the couple in the next room will be quiet that night, that he was not being quite honest and indeed, 'to tell the truth', that he hoped for the opposite, he is introducing a choice or discrimination for the narrator which implies a person rather than a function (I, 153). At times he actually puts on a mask. He describes Hans Castorp's love for Clawdia Chauchat as 'a rather far-fetched and outlandish form of this folly', and recognises that this is a particular point of view when he continues, 'Like anyone else, we claim the right to make our own private thoughts on the.story being told here' (I, 387–8). The mask usually serves to ironise both the pseudo-narrator and his object, in this case Hans Castorp's love. A little later he again associates himself with other sober-minded persons, 'we level-headed ones', in mock consternation over the odd behavoiur of lovers (I, 398–9). He can even for a moment suggest he is one of the inmates of the Berghof – 'But every member of our circle knows that' (II, 355) – and jokingly pretends it is a 'true' story – 'We can only be grateful to a gentleman like Mr Settembrini, if on some occasion he very perceptively addressed the young man, whose destiny is engaging our attention, as a "problem-child of life" [...]' (II, 345).

These frequent if transient narratorial variations are among the great charms of *Der Zauberberg*. Their charm is playful, but not arbitrary, since a particular effect, tone, insight is enhanced through the assumption of a personal relationship, even more by that of a mask. If we consider this authoritative narrator with his personal modifications as a whole, we can discern a large and cumulative effect, and its chief import seems to be to remind us that we are reading an invention, a story, which requires the presupposition of a story-teller, who shows himself worthy of our trust by suggesting that a number of items might be told or interpreted in several ways. When, at times, he adopts the somewhat pompous tone of an old-fashioned moralising narrator – 'What is man, how easily does his conscience deceive him!' (I, 270–1) – he does so not in order to denigrate the substance of this narrator's remarks but to make fun of the note of parsonic certainty in them. Our task, as readers, is to become involved in the story, but imaginatively involved at an aesthetic distance, so that we can weigh it up, ponder on it, as we experience it.

2. This more or less 'objective', authoritative narrator is often termed 'omniscient'. This is almost always an unsatisfactory term, and in this case extremely so, as has already been indicated. We quickly realise that we are not told anything about the inner life of characters other than Hans Castorp, except as they make themselves plain to Castorp through

their words or actions, The narrator himself is never admitted behind the screen of Joachim's reserve, except when he reveals himself to his cousin; the narrator can only guess what is going through Clawdia Chauchat's head, except on the few occasions on which she speaks. He and we know Settembrini, Naphta, and Peeperkorn and the other characters only when Castorp is present with them. Indeed, the hierarchy of importance in which the characters are arranged corresponds exactly to their importance for Hans Castorp; their nearness to or distance from the narrative 'camera eye' is decided by him, our 'hero'.

The narrative perspective, in short, is closely aligned with Hans Castorp: we know only his experiences. This is not a simple identification of narrator and hero, for the narrator has also that independent, restricted, objective role we have already considered; both narratorial roles, the objective and the spokesman for Hans Castorp, are combined, interlaced. [12] Often what are ostensibly narrator's reflections may turn out to be the thoughts of Hans Castorp, and in many cases Mann makes this clear by adding to such a passage an explanatory comment like 'this was more or less what Hans Castorp thought to himself.' For instance, the fairly long 'excursus on the sense of time' concludes with the exculpation 'These observations are inserted here only because young Hans Castorp had something like them in mind' (I, 177). Sometimes a formula like this strains our credulity. The account of the earlier life of Naphta, told with a certain asperity, receives the explanation 'Hans Castorp learned these things in conversations from Naphta himself' (II, 165–77). It is highly unlikely that the wily Naphta would have laid himself open to such penetrating insight, and the comment is interesting only since it shows that Mann felt it to be desirable that the long account should be more integrated in the story than it would be as a narratorial contribution.

The relationship of the two, narrator and hero, is very intricate, and indicated in various ways. Though the popularity of the *Art of Seduction* book among the sanatorium inmates seems to be described in objective narrative, Hans Castorp's involvement is syntactically so merged in the account that one can believe that the whole description gives actually Hans Castorp's reaction. The apparently 'objective' statements lead up to the attitude of the young patients – 'After supper they would sometimes study it jointly in various rooms' – and then comes: 'Hans Castorp saw how the young man with the fingernail handed it in the dining-room to a girl patient, one of the less serious cases', as if this observation of Castorp's was the ground for the general remark preceding. When the narrator suggests that perhaps everybody except for Settembrini and Joachim and one or two others read the book, this is evidently Castorp's thought, since only he would not mention himself with the other two, and this is borne out by the addition 'Hans Castorp was inclined to believe so', thus suggesting that all the statements, including the uncertainty here and there, belong to Castorp (I, 460). Less explicitly, authorial comments may use characteristic turns of speech of Castorp's, or may assimilate the phrases of other characters as Castorp does (Castorp's borrowing and assimilating is one of the ways in which he learns). When the inmates of the Berghof are described in an ostensibly objective form, the phrase 'evidently a prime ass' ('ein kapitaler Esel offenbar') is clearly Hans Castorp's and we then ascribe the whole somewhat crude description to 'young' Castorp and not to the more sophisticated narrator (I, 187–8). The habit of the narrator at any time to use phrases already coined by some character must be attributed mainly to this intention to evoke the workings of Hans Castorp's mind, and hence to suggest that the passage is a sort of 'erlebte Rede'.[13] The close alignment of vision gives rise to the little joke the narrator allows himself when, after Hans Castorp has described to Behrens his impression of the newcomer, Peeperkorn, he writes: 'We have consigned to him the task of giving a rough sketch of the new, unexpected visitor, and he has carried it out not badly – we could not have done it essentially better ourselves' (II, 349). Here Castorp borrows the narrator's skills, while elsewhere the narrator borrows *his* experience and language. There are occasions, indeed, when Castorp is represented as thinking entirely in the complex terms and syntax of the narrator, notably in the extensive reflections, given as direct speech, when he half awakes out of his dream in the snow (II, 256–60). Such language must run the risk of being considered out of character and pompous for the 'simple' young man – thought of course it occurs at a moment of extreme danger and exaltation, and arises out of his vision, which itself surpasses his normal conscious grasp, so that it would be a mistake to take the passage for realistic prose.

The whole structure of the novel accords with this alignment of the narrator with Hans Castorp. We, the readers, accept the hero as our 'problem child', we experience what he experiences and nothing else, our sympathies are engaged in accordance with his. Yet at all times we are also distanced from him, provoked to critical reflection, by the fact that the narrator's perspective constantly diverges from his, in small and large ways. Sometimes in the simplest sense that, within a predominantly subjective passage of description, given from Castorp's viewpoint, his external appearance may be indicated as well, e.g. his inflamed eyelids; sometimes through moral comments, suitable only to an external observer, such as the comment that tells us his adventurous excursions in the high mountains were motivated by his 'courage', the challenge he issued to the meaningless immensity (II, 233–4). More specifically, the narrator may 'correct' terms that Castorp is said to use – for instance, 'to be happy' and 'affair' for his relationship with Clawdia Chauchat – and the correction serves to define Castorp's attitude to the 'affair' as well as to Clawdia (I, 235–7). Thus objective narrative can easily slip into indirect speech, which, especially in the form of free indirect speech ('erlebte Rede'), fuses the language and feeling of the character with the implicit comment of the narrator. The narrator describes the foolish lover's ecstasies after his path had happened to cross Clawdia's as they enter the dining room:

He stands in the breath of her passing person, idiotic with happiness [. . .] He follows her, he falters to the right to his table, and as he sinks into his chair he can observe that 'Clawdia' on the other side, also sitting down, looks round at him [. . .] O incredible adventure! O jubilation, triumph, and boundless rejoicing! No, Hans Castorp would not have experienced the ecstasy of this fantastic satisfaction over the glance of any healthy goose of a girl.

The form of the two exclamatory sentences is typical of 'erlebte Rede', which quickly gives way to the ironical comments of the narrator, though the exclamations themselves contain irony enough (I, 389).

These alternations of perspective and modifications of the narrator's role contribute greatly to the ambiguity that attends so much in *The Magic Mountain*. [14] In addition, there is one form of double perspective that is ever-present, and highly intricate in its form and effect. We have seen that the narrator often stands close to Castorp, doing little more than expand at length the visual and auditory perceptions, the fleeting and incomplete thoughts that Hans Castorp has. In this respect the narrator is very similar to the narrator of *Death in Venice*. But in this earlier story, the intellectuality, the sophisticated self-consciousness of the hero, Aschenbach, is of the same quality as the narrator's, and the narrator's reflections are such, we might venture to say, as Aschenbach would have made, if he had retrospectively been able to review his experiences. [15] In *The Magic Mountain*, if the perspective belongs to Castorp, the explanatory comment, the richness of observation, are such as Hans Castorp could never reach, either at that moment or in retrospect. This is one of the reasons why the ascription to Hans Castorp of the account of Naphta's early life is so forced. But normally this discrepancy between sophisticated narrator and 'simple young man' is a source of richness. We see Castorp's world, experience his experiences, but always with the help of a medium that makes us more aware, further-sighted, than the protagonist. It is this medium, the narrator's voice, that both enriches every event with ambiguities of meaning and at the same time builds a unity of experience out of the contingencies of events, and binds the ending to the beginning.

The complexity of the narrator's function shows how inadequate is Adorno's notion of the relationship of story and rigid perspective, particularly since in this respect, as Walzel observed, Mann belongs to a long tradition. 'Most novels,' writes Barbara Hardy, 'create tensions between narrators,' including in the latter term all characters who build their own story-image of their world. [16]

'Gegenständlichkeit' – the world of objects

The reader's first impression of *The Magic Mountain* is of an immense richness of objects, persons, facts; a richness of the persons connected with the sanatorium and of its appurtenances, its routine, the countryside and weather, a richness in the sensations, feelings, thoughts that this world stimulates, that culminate in the intensive preoccupation with the problem of health and disease, life and death, morality and self-centredness. This fullness is the concomitant of the lively attention of the newcomer, Castorp. But neither his attentive interest in these objects, nor their abundance, seems to have anything to do with 'love', nor in the first place even 'love of life'. Rather, both result from the massive actuality of this strange, artificial world that thrusts itself upon the morbid curiosity of a young man estranged from the values of the 'real' world. Those who, like Joachim, are there only to get well do not observe this world closely or with respect; ideologists like Settembrini and Naphta hardly notice their surroundings, so preoccupied are they with the life in the Flatlands. The wealth of this sanatorium world, its details and its problems, are evident only to Hans Castorp, the alienated and detached.

Already the first impression is modified. This world is not rich for everyone. It is immediately clear that its richness is not only something to which Hans Castorp is receptive but also something he in part creates. All literary realism is selective, of course, since the author must select from an infinite and teeming world what is of significance to his story. But the selectiveness in *The Magic Mountain* is different from that in Balzac, Dickens or Zola. Things are not described because they are important in themselves but because Castorp's attention singles them out. The attention of the narrator, like that of the reader, is guided by the hero's. At the same time the narrator offers, in some degree, his own independent observations, but his apprehension is dominated by Hans Castorp's experience, and all he does is to describe, expound, interpret this.

The opening paragraphs give a striking example of this relationship between narrator and character. They describe Castorp's journey from Hamburg to Davos, and the subjectivity of the account is clearly in evidence since the first part of the journey, through Germany, is told in an abstract way, as if Hans were bored and inattentive, while it livens up and becomes concrete only when he joins the mountain railway at Landquart. Only now is he too described, as if the reader's attention awakens with his. But if we look closer at the text we see much more than a journey told from the traveller's perspective. Not only does the disarming tone of 'A simple young man travelled' distance the reader from Hans. How strange is the description of the rail journey through Germany! There is mockery of provincialism in 'From Hamburg to up there, that is a long journey', for in 1907 it wasn't so far as all that. Then: 'You go through many principalities, uphill and down'. These are all deliberate anachronisms. Prussia, Thuringia, Swabia, Bavaria were no longer principalities, 'Herrenländer', nor felt to be so; and does one feel that a train goes 'uphill and down'? The narrator is evoking an older form of travel, coach travel, and an older time, as he does when he writes of the 'leaping waves' and the 'abysses that were once thought to be unfathomable' of the 'Swabian Sea' (the Lake of Constance, 'Bodensee'). With the third paragraph, the arrival in Switzerland, a really modern engine engages our attention, and the whole tone becomes modern. Hans, it is subliminally suggested, has moved from an old-fashioned provincial world to a modern one.

This is how the narrator builds his effects and his story. With some freedom regarding factualities, but a close attention to the hero's psychological situation, he presents the journey as one from a staid, closed world to a modern one, and thus prepares us for that ambiguity constantly adhering to the sanatorium, which is partly a place 'hermatically sealed off' from the great world, and partly the setting for its intensified presence. The opening does not, of course, establish a final interpretation; it directs our thought to provisional judgements which will be continually revised as the story unfolds.

In all that follows, the wealth of objects, persons, ideas corresponds to Hans Castorp's fascinated interest, to his unconscious search for an answer to his 'question'. The emptiness of the later years of his stay, that are shaken out of the timelessness of routine only by spasmodic events, corresponds to the torpor he falls into after the death of his last 'educator', Peeperkorn. It cannot be said that Castorp's interest in things arises from 'love' of this world, even less than with Balzac, Dickens, Flaubert, or Zola, who were fascinated by the existence of things but often forced by horror or indignation to write about them. There is little in the sanatorium that is lovable; Hans Castorp's hopes that illness might make people worthy of admiration or love are mercilessly dashed. Even if we are ready to accept the narrator's argument, when describing his hero's 'love' for Clawdia, that the word is, properly, vastly ambiguous (II, 433-4), it would be difficult to read into it anything of the affirmation of reality that Adorno implies by the term. When Castorp comes to his famous conclusion: 'For the sake of kindness and love man must yield death no dominance over his thoughts' (II, 260), he himself makes use of the ambiguity of the term 'love'. For surely he cannot here mean a personal love, nor a love of circumstances, the world, reality. Most clearly it means devotion to the opposite of death, love of life; and since it is allied with, secondary to, 'kindness' it must embrace a compassionate caring for mankind, a desire to help men against the destructive powers within them, and without, against the hostile indifference of the universe. It is a declaration of solidarity with mankind, but a love, not of the splendour of man, but of his mortality.

The fact that the 'Gegenständlichkeit' of *The Magic Mountain* depends on the state of mind of the hero has a curious result that also distinguishes the realism of its writing from that of nineteenth-century novelists. In one aspect the individual items, objects or persons, belong to the contingencies of daily life; in another aspect they acquire a representative significance, they tell us about him whose interest makes them significant; they are symbolical as the narrator defines the term, in a passage very reminiscent of Goethe. It arises out of his discussion of Hans Castorp's devotion to the Schubert song 'The linden tree' (II, 521):

A spiritual, that is, a significant object is 'significant' just because it points beyond itself, because it is the expression and exponent of some more general spiritual situation, a whole world of feeling and attitude that has found in it a more or less perfect image – and it is this whereby we measure the degree of its significance. Further, the love of such an object is likewise significant in itself. It says something about the man who feels such love, it indicates his relationship with that generality, the world that the object represents and that, consciously or unconsciously, is loved at the same time.

This representative, symbolic function, to which Hermann Weigand drew attention in his excellent study, *Thomas Mann's Novel 'Der Zauberberg'*, of 1933, governs all objects, persons and incidents in Hans Castorp's experience. Clearly Joachim, Settembrini, Naphta and Peeperkorn are such representative, symbolical characters, as also are Behrens and Krokowski. Those of the patients who emerge from the anonymous mass do so by virtue of some marked characteristic that makes them representative of a problem or attitude, like silly Frau Stöhr, or Hans Castorp's neighbours, with their excessive sexual vigour. Often the characters appear only in their symbolical role, and we and the narrator have no interest in their personal fate outside their function for Hans Castorp. This is so even with Clawdia Chauchat, who, one might observe with some asperity, exists by virtue of her Dostoyevskian 'Russianness', and hardly emerges to any fuller or more individual personality, drifting in and out of the pages of the book according to the role she fulfils for the hero. The whole structure of the novel obeys the same principle. The sanatorium is, among other things, a double symbol, of the world and of existence out of the world; the 'Snow' chapter is there for its symbolic function as the setting for Castorp's challenge to the indifference of the inorganic world. The suicide of Naphta, the anti-semitic brawl, Castorp's devotion to the Schubert songs (the fascination of death), are all clearly and almost explicitly symbolic. And Castorp himself defines his own symbolic reference when, in his reflections on his vision, he applies the epithet Settembrini had coined for him to mankind generally – 'The problem child of life, it is man' (II, 258).

The quotation above states not only that 'significant' objects are representative of something more general, but also that a person's love for them indicates 'his relationship to that generality, that world, that the object represents'. This must here mean that they all reveal the nature of Hans Castorp's relationship to the world. If the objects are loved, then so, consciously or unconsciously, is the world they represent. This might seem to be identical with Adorno's claim that 'Gegenständlichkeit' in an author implies 'love of the world'. But the immediate cause of the narrator's observation is Hans Castorp's love for the Schubert song, and the 'love' that is expressed through it is, we are told, his 'sympathy with death', so powerful and so disguised that, when he realises it to be so, he has 'pangs of conscience'. It is a reminder that when Mann used the word 'world' ('Welt') he gives it a meaning very different from Adorno's, for here it has no social meaning, it bears no affirmation of any form of social life, and scarcely goes further than an affirmation of life, of the organic world; and even so, quite distinct from any positive vitalism of the Peeperkorn variety, but simply a modest 'wily friendliness towards life'. This is the term the narrator finds for the meaning of his love for Clawdia Chauchat, 'sympathy with the organic world, the moving and voluptuous embrace of what is doomed to corruption' (II, 434).

Professor J. P. Stern has made the important point, in his discussion of Mann's *Doktor Faustus*, that while events and persons with symbolic meanings may lurk anywhere in Mann's novel they are never merely symbolic but overflow with private functions too.[17] The story is not a point-by-point allegory. The same is true of *The Magic Mountain*. The characters or events may perform a symbolic function, but they overflow it in their individuality. The character of Behrens is an example, or the many great conversations, or the snow scene; these and many more testify to an exuberance of interest in the particular and specific, into the varieties of being and of thinking, that we transfer to Hans Castorp, and that makes him and his experiences more than an allegory. This exuberance of interest can be accompanied by any response – irony, admiration, distaste, as well as love – but throughout it testifies to Castorp's avid curiosity about life. This we might call the realistic element in the book. But still, the general structure is symbolic. Fontane once said the test of a realistic novel was whether the characters go on living after the end of the book. But in *The Magic Mountain* we have no such concern, and the author switches our attention even ruthlessly away from the characters to the generality, to the general problem that brought the story into existence.

I have indicated in passing how Thomas Mann's 'Gegenständlichkeit' refutes some of Adorno's assertions. It does so partly because it arises from a more complex relationship to and evaluation of the 'world' than Adorno envisages, and partly because it is fitted into a symbolical frame, which gives the objects described a peculiar more-than-realistic function. Though there are elements in the Berghof world that reflect a situation, tensions, in the Flatlands, it is essentially not a mirror image of the world but a symbolic reduction of the warring interpretations and valuations governing the outer world. This peculiarity in a 'Zeitroman' has often been commented on, and has given rise to the searching question whether the concrete social world can find an adequate reflection in the form of mental attitudes. This question we have not to answer here. But we have to note that the objects and circumstances of this upper atmosphere are not there as representatives of concrete situations in the 'real' world, and we are not concerned whether Hans Castorp will acknowledge, respect, accept their reality – as Wilhelm Meister or Keller's Heinrich are to do. They are, on the contrary, the vehicle of another, spiritual story, in which all its elements are items, stages, and may even have a direct allegorical function. In this sense *The Magic Mountain* bears out Adorno's statement that realism is no longer sufficient, and it fits into a large tradition that uses realistic materials in the service of a spiritual problem or message. Even so, however, Mann does not fall into 'anti-realistic' methods and remains deeply attached to the varieties of human behaviour, just as he refuses to see alienation as modern man's essential being.

Story and narrator – contra Adorno

It was Adorno's contention, in respect to story-making, that the individual on whose 'articulated continuity' story depended could no longer experience the 'identity of experience' required for a coherent story, and that the traditional narrative perspective was too rigid to cope with the multiplicity of the individual. He claimed further that an individual life had no longer any general (practical or symbolical) significance. He concluded that the novel was no longer competent to tell a realistic story without paying homage to an inhuman pseudo-reality, and that its only theme can be the illusoriness of its own fictional form.

It is not clear whether Adorno would consider *The Magic Mountain* to be a modern or a traditional novel. What I believe this investigation demonstrates is that it is both, and that the existential problems that Adorno lists can be embodied within the scope of the traditional novel, i.e. within the structure of a story and in earthly, human dimensions. Adorno seems often to think of the traditional novel as a fixed form, whereas the tradition of the novel is the history of a changing form, changing even in respect to its essential features, story and coherence.

Adorno's criticism of story, as such, is made more plausible by his definition of the novel as a 'bourgeois' literary form. The same formula is used by Roland Barthes to justify his campaign against coherence and story. [18] This postulate not only leaves out of account that the novel form is much older than Western bourgeois society, but much more seriously it confuses 'story' with novel. For stories are as old as human society. This is not merely of literary or historical significance. When the possibility of writing a coherent narrative – whether of actual or imagined events – is denied, a most important and universal means of understanding is renounced. H. R. Jauss, in his highly intelligent discussion of the legitimacy of historical narrative, defines it as 'a basic category of historical apprehension '(Wahrnehmung')'. [19] W. B. Gallie makes a wider claim on behalf of 'the genus Story', to which he considers historiography to belong; story, the creation of connections with regard to an ending, while it cannot have the 'scientific' purpose of demonstrating the 'necessity' of actions and events, does make human behaviour significant and intelligible. L. O. Mink, supporting Gallie's recognition of the function of story, has stressed the uniqueness of this mode of understanding human actions, which no other mode of thought can provide. [20] If, as Adorno says, story is no longer possible, it would mean that man's self-understanding is grievously maimed.

How does *The Magic Mountain* refute Adorno? Instead of a fixed narrative perspective we have a highly mobile one, which allows events, persons, thoughts to be seen in various lights and invites us to ponder over them. It destroys Adorno's pseudo-concept of 'immanent form', since reflections are embodied in the structure, which is the story of the reflections. A hero with an intelligible coherence in his character and behaviour emerges in a world to which he gives meaning, although this coherence and meaning are not immanent. The world in which he moves, in this an image of the world of the Flatlands, is not only made up of contingencies, but like the Flatland world has a pseudo-order and a pseudo-purpose; Castorp himself is without marked features or purpose, puzzled, hesitant, modest. But out of the encounters with contingencies and pseudo-orders he constructs understanding and an obscure commitment which, even, is so slight that it needs the assistance of the great accident, war, to find realisation in action. The ending of the book is no fulfilment; it too is shrouded in accident, and it transfers the responsibility for some sort of fulfilment to the world, a world engaged in a conflict that we know to be savagely disastrous. The novel presents an ethical problem, both within the hero himself and for the world; serious as it is for Hans Castorp, it is presented in a way that evokes sympathy, irony, humour, not high pathos or tragedy. These last are reserved for our thoughts about the general outcome, since the role played by the individual in this general process does not qualify for them. We are not permitted to believe that the personal decision of Hans Castorp is of decisive importance or has symbolic representativeness for the generality. The irony that plays on so many characters, and on the narrator himself, however, never depreciates Hans Castorp's search and the possibility of finding a way. It is never that bitter irony that would turn a story into a self-absorbed game of mockery, 'higher fun'.

It would almost seem that Thomas Mann sets out to repudiate what Adorno also asserts must be repudiated – 'the pretension of the narrator, to assume that the course of the world is essentially one of individuation, as if the individual with his impulses and feelings approached the dignity of fate, as if a man's inner self was still capable of producing an immediate effect'. But Mann does so without giving up the possibility of composing a story, without depriving the individual life of substance and value, and without denying it the possibility, however faint, of acquiring a social meaning.

Notes

[1] 'Standort des Erzählers im zeitgenössischen Roman' was composed as a lecture, and its provocative, paradoxical formulations are partly due to this. I quote from the reprint in Theodor W. Adorno, *Noten zur Literatur 1*, Bibliothek Suhrkamp, 1965, pp. 61–72.

[2] Jean-Paul Sartre, *'Qu'est-ce que la littérature?'*, *Situations* 2, 1948. The criticism of the traditional novel form is anticipated in Sartre's novel *La Nausée* of 1938.

3 The references in brackets are to *Der Zauberberg*, 2 vols, Berlin, 1924.

4 T. J. Reed has shown very clearly how the ultimate 'Bildungsroman' emerged out of the earlier plans and drafts of the novel – *Thomas Mann. The Uses of Tradition*, 1974, pp. 226 ff. Mr Reed also sees the novel as much more of a true 'Bildungsroman' than a parody.

5 Martin Swales, 'The story and the hero (*Der Zauberberg*)', *DVjs*, 46, 1972, pp. 368–71.

6 T. Ziolkowski, *Dimensions of the Modern Novel*, Princeton, 1969, p. 88. Erich Heller, *The Ironic German*, 1958, pp. 213–4.

7 More justifiable, but still in my opinion a misinterpretation, is the term used by Ulrich Karthaus when he calls Castorp an 'ironist' ('Ironiker'), irony being defined here as 'the mode under which tolerance and humanity appear in poetry' ('*Der Zauberberg*, ein Zeitroman' *DVjs*, 44, 1970, pp. 304–5). Castorp's scepticism and irony are applied to the ideologies he meets, but his commitment is non-ironical, wholehearted, even if still resistant to the lures of theory (the term 'Zeitroman' is used for those novels in which the author seeks to define and interpret the distinctive character of his own times).

8 T. J. Reed, *loc. cit.* The 'confusions' that Karthaus (*loc. cit.*) alleges in respect to the period to which this 'Zeitroman' refers are not real difficulties, since all historical novels are written from the writer's perspective and embody a later point of view and judgement. Mann several times commented that this poetic account of the pre-war period presupposes his experience of and response to later events.

9 It is strange that Dr Ziolkowski can say that at the end of the novel Castorp is 'liberated from all bonds' and 'emerges in perfect freedom' (*op. cit.*, p. 77). Surely the reverse is true. He escapes from the hollow freedoms of alienation to accept the bonds and obligations of membership of a community.

10 Oskar Walzel, 'Objektive Erzählung', first published in *GRM*, 1915, and reprinted with additional comments on *The Magic Mountain* and other modern novels in *Das Wortkunstwerk*, 1926.

11 Helpful accounts of the narrative perspective in *The Magic Mountain* are to be found in the cited books of Th. Ziolkowski and T. J. Reed, and also in Winfried Kudsus's article referred to in n. 12 below. See also W. Hoffmeister, *Studien zur erlebten Rede bei Thomas Mann und Robert Musil*, 1965.

12 Winfried Kudsus has shown how this double narrative perspective – close to and distanced from Hans Castorp – promotes the reader's activity, both in identifying himself with Castorp and in reflecting critically upon his experiences. The descriptive methods employed, particularly the reticence, are also considered to activise the reader's imagination, since he is provoked to build a whole out of suggestive details. In this latter respect I do not think Mann's method is distinctive, nor does it always produce the effects that Winfried Kudsus claims – 'Understanding Media; zur Kritik dualistischer Humanität im "Zauberberg" ', *Besichtigung des Zauberbergs*, ed. H. Saueressig, 1974, pp. 59–67.

13 The many repetitions of fixed expressions with respect to Peeperkorn have been indignantly counted by Martin Walser, who sees in them only a self-indulgent mannerism of the author. Walser fails to see that these repetitions convey the baffled wonder of Hans Castorp at Peeperkorn's 'personality', his failure to fathom it. Generally, Walser seems determined not to distinguish between Mann's own opinions, as expressed for instance in his essays, and the views of his imaginative characters or his narrator. ('Ironie als höchstes Lebensmittel oder: Lebensmittel der Höchsten', *Besichtigung des Zauberbergs*, ed. H. Saueressig, 1974, p. 193.)

14 Many of these ambiguities are admirably presented in R. Hinton Thomas, *Thomas Mann. The Mediation of Art*, 1956, pp. 99–111. T. J. Reed makes valuable observations on ambiguities arising from the long process of composition of the novel (*op. cit.* pp. 226 ff.).

15 Some of the problems involved in this relation of narrator to hero in *Der Tod in Venedig* have been discussed in T. J. Reed, *op. cit.* pp. 173–8.

16 Barbara Hardy, 'Towards a poetics of fiction', *Novel*, vol. 2, 1968.

17 J. P. Stern, *History and Allegory in T. Mann's 'Doktor Faustus'*, inaugural lecture,

University College, London, 1975.

[18] Roland Barthes, *Le Degré zéro de l'écriture*, 1953.

[19] H. R. Jauss, *Literatur als Provokation*, 1970, p. 228.

[20] W. B. Gallie, *Philosophy and the Historical Understanding*, 1964; L. O. Mink, 'History and fiction as modes of comprehension' (*New Directions in Literary History*, ed. Ralph Cohen, 1964). Professor Gallie's investigation is of particular interest to students of the imaginative story. It is true that he starts out from a very simple model of story, and might have found his discussion of historical narrative easier had he taken modern novel forms into account. I find the following points of particular interest. Professor Gallie directs attention primarily to the question, how can and do we 'follow' a story? Not in order to discover that events demonstrate some general law, but to find profit in just following it; the story is inexhaustible, and every fresh reading adds to our understanding. The ending is and must be unpredictable. The factor of contingency (that 'matches that in everyday life') is essential to story – a story is 'about contingencies, not regularities' – and is made acceptable, and in this sense intelligible, by the story. The ending is the 'main focus' from the beginning, it corrects all the provisional conclusions we come to in the course of reading, and it alone establishes the unity of the story; the 'right place to stop' is 'where fullest understanding has been achieved'. Endings are often 'transpersonal', like the endings of historical narratives (and, we might add, like the ending of *The Magic Mountain*).

KEITH BULLIVANT

Thomas Mann and politics in the Weimar Republic

Amongst commentators on the political and cultural life of the Weimar Republic it has over the years tended to become one of the conventional wisdoms that Thomas Mann quickly left behind him the undemocratic, highly conservative position of the *Reflections of a Non-political Man* and consistently underlined his 'democratic conversion' (T. J. Reed) with a series of speeches supporting the increasingly beleagured republic. This sort of understanding of Mann's political writings at this time is seen at its most undifferentiated in Marianne Dörfel's claim that he 'moved completely away from a nationalistic romantic conservatism to positive rational republicanism',[1] ascribing to him an 'inner break with the past' which others did not achieve. Peter Gay, while finding Mann's shift 'a little late, and not particularly impressive', nevertheless writes of this 'conversion to the Republic and to democracy',[2] seeing in him the archetypal 'rational republican' ('Vernunftrepublikaner'), and T. J. Reed, in his recent searching and stimulating study of Thomas Mann, is clearly convinced by 'a known conservative's declared change of heart'.[3] Kurt Sontheimer, perhaps Mann's most eloquent apologist, manages to excuse the *Reflections* as being 'literary politics', not concerned with political reality at all – an argument which, as such, has much to recommend it – yet then claims that in the political essays of the Weimar period Mann had 'so clearly and decisively supported the Republic that there was no longer any doubt as to which side he was on'.[4] Hans Mayer, in a not always consistent analysis of Mann's political writings, takes the line that the real expression of a deeply felt change of position comes in the 'Joseph novels', but nevertheless notes a fundamental change in Mann's position in *The German Republic* (1922) from that in the *Reflections* (1918).[5] Roy Pascal, in *The German Novel* so definite about Mann's 'belief in the Republic', has more recently spoken with greater caution of his 'somewhat hesitant espousal of democratic principles'.[6] Against the chorus of the near-consensus on Mann's change from allegiance to authoritarian State to support for democracy one particularly prominent solo voice can be heard. In *The Ironic German* Erich Heller claimed that the *Reflections* left Mann with a sense of a political debt, which he tried to pay off in 'exceedingly paper currency', and in a more recent public exchange he has argued that Mann's so-called conversion to republicanism was 'much less profound than it seemed at the time'.[7]

Given the strength of the established view on Mann's political development in the '20s, it is perhaps surprising to find that the truly major objection to this interpretation comes from Thomas Mann himself. In the introduction to *The German Republic* he proclaimed, 'This affirmation of the Republic continues the line of the 'Reflections' exactly and uninterruptedly on into the present' (XI, 810) and in his actual speech he announced, à propos the earlier work, 'I retract none of it. I take back nothing essential' (XI, 829). These public utterances are matched by similar private ones, such as his letter of 8 July 1922 to Ernst Bertram. Perhaps more important than these statements made at the time is his review of this period of his life in *My Life and Times* (1950), written at a time when, given the hardly positive reputation of the *Reflections* and the proximity of the excessive nationalism with which it could so easily be associated, it might have been expected that he would then distance himself from his most controversial work:

A mere four years after the appearance of the *Reflections* I found myself the defender of the democratic republic, this feeble creation of the defeat, and an anti-nationalist, without being aware of any breach in the pattern of my life, without the slightest feeling of having to recant anything. The anti-humanism of the day made it clear to me that I had never done – nor wanted to do – anything other than defend 'Humanität'. I will never do anything else. [XI, 314][8]

We thus have a position where, as Hans Mayer has pointed out, scholars have tended to view Mann's literary work as a unitary system, seeing a clear continuity from the early works through into those of the Weimar period and beyond, whilst a 'clear political discontinuity' has been attributed to his political writings. Since the author himself has on a number of occasions disagreed with this reading of his development, there is further good reason to hold the established viewpoint up to critical scrutiny by a close study of the relevant works. Before proceeding to this, however, due consideration must be given to the most recent study in depth of Thomas Mann, by T. J. Reed, which contains the most detailed presentation of the case for seeing a clear break in Mann's political views after the first world war, a case based not on too uncritical an acceptance of his public declaration of allegiance to the republic but on a careful consideration of the implications inherent in the changes

made in the two versions of *Goethe and Tolstoi* (1921 and 1925) for
our understanding of this problem.[9]

Goethe and Tolstoi (subtitled 'Fragments on the problem of
"Humanität" ') is concerned with the tension between spirit and nature
('Geist' and 'Natur') and the achieving of a balance between these two
forces, a balance which, if attained, is the highest expression of the
essence of mankind; 'Effortless nature is crude. Effortless "Geist" lacks
root and substance. A lofty encounter of nature and "Geist" as they
mutually strive towards each other – that is man' (IX, 138). Mann sees
both Goethe and Tolstoi as embodying this tension: both were vitally
alive ('Geist') and yet had an 'intimacy with death' ('Natur'), both had a
humanist and a heathen side, the two forces being in constant dialectical
play, the balance continually shifting. In the case of Goethe the scales are
tipped, in the main, by his spirit of 'self-denial' which represses the wild
nature that had come to the fore in his early work, appealing through
'works imbued with a truly German and exemplary renunciation of the
Avant-gardes of barbarism' (IX, 124) such as *Iphigenie* and *Torquato
Tasso* for a redressing of balance in an age increasingly marked by
barbaric excesses. There is, however, Mann claims, a reassertion of the
other side of Goethe in *Elective Affinities*, in which is detected an
authoritarian, conservative note (*cf.* IX, 165). Similarly Tolstoi is seen as
demonstrating the same sort of duality, being a humane yet 'barbarous'
conservative. Both, therefore, embody the ultimate goal of mankind, the
synthesis of these antithetical forces which for Mann is true 'Humanität':

This reciprocity of sentimental longing . . . , the striving of the children of 'Geist'
for nature and of the children of nature for 'Geist', points to a higher unity being
the goal of mankind, which it endows with its own name, with that of *humanitas*.
[IX, 172]

Mann also clearly views both writers as national figures in the particular
sense of their articulating problems of pivotal concern to the cultural life
of the nation. Thus Russia is viewed as a cultural unit pulled between its
European self, exemplified in the rule of the tsars from Peter I onwards,
and its Asiatic self, which reasserts itself in the October revolution, and
of which one side of Tolstoi (his 'pedagogic bolshevism') was, according
to Mann, its prophet. The Russian revolution is further seen as indicating
a turning point for the whole of Europe:

The question is put today as to whether our Mediterranean, classical, humanist
tradition belongs to the whole of mankind and is thus coeval with it, or whether
it is only one form of intellectual expression of one particular age, the bourgeois
liberal epoch and will thus die with its passing. [IX, 166]

The apparent answer that Europe was giving to this question was clearly
reflected in a rejection of parliamentary democracy and a move towards

dictatorship and the rule of terror in Russia, Italy and Spain, with the threat of a similar move posed by German fascism (which Mann was so quick to identify as a threat and name as such). In this situation, particularly given the attitude of certain French politicians, Mann can see only one possibility for Germany:

> It is not the moment for Germany to go in for anti-humanist behaviour by following the example of Tolstoi's pedagogic bolshevism or by seeing Goethe's steadfast resistance to the hedonism of the ideal of general human education, his will to renunciation and self-limitation as ethnic barbarism. On the contrary, it is the moment to emphasise strongly our great humane traditions and to cherish them reverently – not only for their own sake, but also in order to show most clearly how unjustified the claims of 'Latin civilisation' are. [IX, 169–70]

The solution he propounds, one which is repeated a number of times in the ensuing years, most notably in *Culture and Socialism* (1928), is the development of a German socialism that would be a fusion of the ideas of Marx and Hölderlin, reflecting the cultural balance inherent in the role of the German people as the 'people of the middle way'.

In his analysis of this essay T. J. Reed points out that in the 1921 version of *Goethe and Tolstoy* there is a statement about the affinity – stressed in the *Reflections* – between Russia and Germany. This is omitted in the later version and the rejection of an 'anti-humanist' stance, quoted above, inserted. In this Reed feels that 'a total reversal in Mann's outlook and in the direction of his effort becomes dramatically clear',[10] and it is at this point that 'the measure of Mann's change of heart' can be judged. Such an interpretation, which is somewhat helped by the omission of the reference to Goethe in the quotation as given by Reed, ignores the fact that in both versions of the essay the value centre is the same. Mann posits as an ideal a balance between two forces, 'Natur' and 'Geist'; both Germany and Russia represent in their cultures the tension between these poles, between, as Mann would put it, East and West, and are as such both to be described as a 'country of the middle way'. By the time the later version of the essay was written a clear imbalance on the side of 'Natur', in the shape of irrationalism and totalitarianism, had manifested itself not only elsewhere in Europe but in Germany too, and Mann, therefore, in the interests of the ideal higher synthesis, finds himself forced to reject for the moment that side of Tolstoi he calls 'pedagogic bolshevism' and also the 'barbaric' side of Goethe. By definition, since his essay is concerned with demonstrating the way in which both these figures embody within them the dialectic of the two forces, he is affirming the humanist side of both of them – indeed, this aspect of Goethe is continually assented to during the following decades – as a means of redressing a temporarily lost balance, but Mann always, as we shall see, shows a sympathy for and understanding of the antithesis to the rational humanism he defends so eloquently during the Weimar Republic and the years of exile. Thus, even at a time when – in 1935 – it might have been politically more advantageous for him to talk of *Goethe and Tolstoi* as demonstrating a clear turning away from an earlier position and an unambiguous alliance with the forces of reason, Thomas Mann is at pains to point out its 'rejection of too hasty a decision in favour of either nature or "Geist" '; it and his later essays of the Weimar period are all characterised by the defence of his ideal in the face of excessive irrationalism:

These thoughts of mine serve the idea of 'Humanität' itself, as I understand it, namely that man's being embraces both nature and 'Geist' and is complete only in the union of the two. I represent the idea of balance and it is this that determines what might be called my tactical stance on the problems of the age. The position in my essays and cultural criticism for the last ten years or so has been expressly rationalist and idealistic, but I only adopted it under the pressure of that irrationalism and political anti-humanism now spreading over Europe, but particularly over Germany, that makes a mockery of humane balance.[11]

In the face, then, of an international, irrational 'depressive anti-humanism', 'obscurantism', as he called it, of which German fascism was the most significant manifestation, and concerned for 'the preservation of the cultural tradition of Western Europe, ... its defence against barbarism and political frenzy of all kinds' (XI, 940), Thomas Mann quickly reacted in an attempt to prevent a spiritual imbalance. As he said of himself in *Culture and Socialism*, both 'a cordial acceptance of life (the area of 'Geist') and 'sympathy with death' (the area of 'Natur') continued to constitute 'a legitimate part of his being' (XII, 640), but he now recognised that:

the moment has even come for Europe when a conscious overemphasis of the democratic idea of life over the aristocratic principle of death has become a vital necessity. [XI, 354–5]

Balance, contained in this and so many other similar formulations, remained the ideal. At the time of the *Reflections* the threat to the cultural tradition came from the Western world; it now came from a different quarter, and so Mann's stance had to be modified to take account of this. Helped in part by his reading of Ernst Troeltsch's *Natural Law and 'Humanität' in World Politics*, he saw both the need for and the possibility of German culture reabsorbing Western ideas 'without the need for any fundamental denial of our spiritual make-up' (XII, 627). As he stressed in *The German Republic* and a letter to Ernst Bertram, he had to overcome his objection to words that he had earlier rejected as having undesirable connotations, but his ideal remained that of true 'Humanität', the synthesis between aristocratic and democratic principles, life and death, 'Geist' and 'Natur'. To remain true to this, however, the stance he now took was 'in conscious self-correction' of the major emphasis of the *Reflections*, although he had already anticipated the possible need for the adoption of such a position in the earlier work:

The patriotic, opportunistic democratism, however wrong it may be from a spiritual point of view, does have a good, practical political justification. May intellectuals and artists who wish for Germany's political greatness out of a sense of attachment to the nation, far from being held back by this bond, be led by it to affirm a democratic political order in Germany. They should not, however, forget that one should not over-estimate the importance of legalistic matters in the life of the nation . . . [XII, 271]

The 'unpolitical' relativisation of the importance of a particular socio-political order contained in this last statement is something which is inherent in Mann's political speeches and writings in the Weimar era and beyond and which has been missed or ignored by many commentators. Thus T. J. Reed sees Mann progressing in the '20s from a 'Vernunftrepublikaner' into a devoted servant of the republic, whilst Kurt Sontheimer claims that he 'also did not hide which political forces and ideas he supported'.[12] A close study of Mann's work at this time suggests, however, that his allegiance to his ideal and his unpolitical stance remain constant, despite his apparent espousal of institutions and causes which would, normally speaking, have unambiguous political connotations. It might well be argued that the tragedy of the Weimar Republic derives in part from the fact that Thomas Mann and, most important, those who identified with him, thought that the sort of ideas he was articulating *were* political. This thus helped to foster a political vacuum in the centre which could be exploited by extremists.

In most of his early essays and speeches he reiterated a view expressed at some length in the *Reflections* whereby a 'mechanically democratic' view of the state – one which concentrates its attention on questions like universal suffrage and other legislative measures – is rejected. Both in correspondence to Ernst Bertram and in *The German Republic* he continued to emphasise that a particular social form was determined by the mood of the people, rather than by the establishment of particular institutions, and was essentially to be seen as the expression of a transcendent collective cultural consciousness. The result is an aestheticisation and despecification of the social institution he was claiming to recommend to his public. In *The German Republic* he set out to win German youth over to the republic, 'to what is called democracy and what I call "Humanität" ' (XI, 819). Given this shift at the beginning of his argument, he was able to present the republic not as a break with the past but as part of a cultural continuum that goes back to German Romanticism, and to Novalis in particular. The way in which Mann could accept the republic – having overcome his earlier semantic hostility to the word – is perhaps best illustrated in *The Spirit and Character of the Republic* (1923), in which it is viewed as 'the fulfilment of German "Humanität" ', as 'the unity of State and culture'. In it politics cease to be 'mere politics', 'it is thereby elevated to "Humanität" ' (XI, 853f.) The republic is translated into a purely conceptual entity, one of various near-synonyms for Mann's ideal of 'Humanität'. As Golo Mann has said, his support for the republic was 'literature, not reality'.

According to the ideas of critics like Reed and Sontheimer we could expect that, in the course of the life of the republic, these statements by Mann about the new State would become sharper, more precise, as his sense of allegiance to it grew. In fact the aestheticisation of the matter, the jump from a political problem to the realm of abstract ideas, is, with one major exception, constant. As in *Goethe and Tolstoi* he is concerned to strike a balance between antithetical forces which form part of the 'world polarity' (*cf. The Trees in the Garden* 1930), to proclaim, as in *Germany and Democracy* (1925) and *Lubeck as a spiritual way of life* (1926), the idea of the 'German middle way', 'which does not get carried away, but critically asserts the idea of "Humanität", of mankind and its education against extremes on both left and right' (xi, 397). His, in his own terms, sceptical attitude to left and right is part of the 'complex of ideas of "Humanität" ', a typically German non-fanatical attitude (*cf.* XI, 411 f.), an attitude which, as he told the Warsaw PEN club, prevented those Germans like himself from over-hasty and one-sided involvement in the debates of the day. His very act of making the connection, as he does a number of times, between the republic (too easily seen as merely the area of intellectuality) and German Romanticism (the embodiment of the chthonic) is in itself an act of redressing an imbalance that existed before 1914, is an establishment of the 'middle way'. In perhaps his most bizarre image of the time, Mann saw Stresemann himself as the physical representation of this quality; he was a man who was 'led and driven by a flexible embracing of life, which carried within it the physical seeds of death' (XI, 886). Even when the threat of the republic was overt, in his *Speech to Workers in Vienna* (1932) he saw it as the role of the moderate Right to hold on long enough for Germans to gain 'reflection . . . and understanding', whilst it was up to the 'embattled left' to see that they did not thereby infringe the basic rights of the people: the ideal of the middle way was still foremost in his mind. T. J. Reed claims that Mann 'continued to defend the Republic whose days were clearly numbered',[13] yet in this same speech he clearly stated of it that 'the history of this political and social order no longer seems to have much long-term credit' (XI, 899). In addition, in an important letter to the Reich Ministry of the Interior, written in 1934, not only did he again stress reservations about the importance of the political sphere for society, he was by no means anxious to identify himself with the republic. The impression, rather – and this is confirmed by later speeches such as *The Coming Victory of Democracy* (1938), in which his views seem unchanged from those of the previous decade – is of a temporary nominal association with the real republic, a vigorous championing of an ideal that he thought could be realised through his notion of a republic, and a turning away from this as he looked elsewhere for a means of achieving a social world suffused with the spirit of true 'Humanität'.

Closely linked with the established idea of Mann's so-called republicanism is that of his development as a socialist; Reed, for example, says that he was 'driven increasingly leftwards by the excesses of a "conservatism" he could not accept',[14] whilst Sontheimer labels him a conservative socialist. It is easy to understand, given the growth in strength of right-wing ideologies in this period, how Mann, in his consistent declarations of belief in his ideal, should appear to be moving ever to the left, but the implication behind, say, Sontheimer's description of Mann's 'decision for socialism' is that the espousal of (what he called) socialism was a new departure. Such a suggestion ignores the fact that even in the *Reflections* he had stated:

It is the peculiar feature of German individualism that it is compatible with ethical socialism, with what is called state socialism and which is very different from the Marxist kind that is obsessed with formal human rights. [XII, 280]

He returned to this in *Germany and Democracy*, where he rejected what he felt to be inferior materialist forms of socialism and proclaimed instead his own socialism, which he defined as 'regaining contact with that higher German essence, 'the soul of which has always been striving to reach the land of the Greeks' (XIII, 578). To fulfil its current role it was necessary – this a formulation that he repeated several times over the years and which itself contained the idea of the middle way – for Karl Marx to read Hölderlin. In the more famous *Culture and Socialism* he saw that the time had come for concessions to be made by the 'cultural idea' to the 'socialistic conception of society', but he rejected political radicalism (= Communism) for its fanatical, excessive faith in the power of the 'proletarian class'. He claimed that:

What would be needed, what could be quintessentially German, would be an alliance between the conservative cultural idea and the revolutionary concept of society; to put it bluntly, an alliance between Greece and Moscow. [XII, 649]

We are left with a highly rhetorical aesthetic construct, which yet again reflects the idea of the 'German middle way', but it is impossible to imagine what it could have meant to leaders of German socialists at the time. If we look closely at what being a socialist means for him (in *The intellectual position of the writer today*, 1930), then the formulations are reminiscent of statements made in the early '20s:

We affirm 'Geist' when the soul, having discredited itself, threatens to bring shame on mankind. When the needs of the hour call us, we speak out for the aims of decency and rationality. [X, 304]

His goal of working to redress an imbalance in the dialectical play of the forces that together constitute 'Humanität' remained constant; the medium was now to be a sort of socialism mediated not through activism but, in a way that is very close to Schiller, through art:

We reject activism. We believe in the seriousness involved in play and in the dignity of play. We still believe in mysteries, in the human mystery of art which mocks and will always mock socio-rational attempts to poison its conscience. [X, 302]

There is, however, a significant shift in Mann's stance between this speech, delivered on 13 September 1930, and his 'appeal to reason', *Deutsche Ansprache*, of 17 October. In the interim the elections to the Reichstag had shown a huge rise in the Nazi vote and an advance from twelve to 107 seats. He was now stirred briefly out of a position which he saw in this situation to be self-indulgent, and was driven to what he later called 'a political action dictated by the crises of the moment' (XII, 661). In his attempt to explain to the bourgeois public he continually strove to influence he produced, for the first and only time, a clear analysis of the factors working against the republic – the faults in the Versailles Treaty, reparations, the attitude of the French and internal doubts as to the 'Germanness' of the new State. Moreover he recognised that 'the political thinking and feeling of the masses are to a large extent determined by their economic condition' (XI, 871). However, after this clear opening Mann then went on to chart the intellectual and spiritual causes of National Socialism, which, as he had said right at the beginning of the era and now repeated, were given a particular impetus by their having a certain justification and necessity.

The continued affirmation of irrationalism at this time, whilst having its logical justification in Mann's speeches as one part of the dialectic examined in *Goethe and Tolstoi*, is not only disturbing but has the effect of weakening the criticism of National Socialism. In *The Trees in the Garden* (1930) he examined at length the way in which Germany continually reacted against ages of enlightenment, and protested against the weakening of mankind through reason and provoked a chthonic revolutionary change in human thought and experience of the world, a new injection of the fruitful emotional forces of night into thought and experience, which undeniably had gained on each occasion in fullness and profundity. [XI, 865]

In the *Speech to Workers in Vienna* he analysed, in much the same way as in *An Appeal to Reason*, the causes of Nazism, to warn his audience against it, and yet even there he talked of it as part of a justified counter-movement against liberal idealism, as aiming to lead society 'back again close to the fount of life, to the natural reality of things' (XI, 903). At another point in this speech, in terms so redolent of 'Blood and soil' literature, he described 'the ties with the village, the soil, the fatherland and folk culture as in the nature of things', as 'holy and indestructible'. He believed that 'the revolutionary movement in defence of the natural' was not only justified but was a necessary and progressive force. It was, however, wrong in its assumption that the aims of nineteenth-century liberal idealism had been fully achieved and in its consequent failure to recognise that the present age needed a fusion of the two movements. Mann stood then, by his own admission, as close to the supporters of irrationalism as he had at the time of the *Reflections*; what he objected to and protested against was the usurpation of it by those in the service 'of what is false and hostile to life', i.e. the Nazis. The at times undifferentiated distinction between 'true' and 'false' cultural conservatism must have been difficult for Mann's audiences to grasp; furthermore his opposition to the Nazis could easily have been misconstrued as the essentially aesthetic rejection of a mass movement, since the particular danger of National Socialism lay in its representing 'irrationalism as a popular mode of thought' (*cf.* XII, 670 ff.).

In Mann's view this popularising of a warped version of otherwise justified conservative cultural views produced a 'mankind that had run away from its true ideals', a grotesque political organisation. The enemy that Mann had been so quick to spot was now a real threat to the bourgeois cultural values he had always held dear and now again reaffirmed, and so – repeating a formulation he had used in *Culture and Socialism* and was to use more than once later – he now saw the need openly to express his affiliation with those who stood for the same ideals:

The socialist class, in direct contrast to the bourgeois cultural heart of the nation, is alienated from 'Geist' in its economic theory, but is friendly to it in practice, and – given the way things are today – that is what really matters. [XI, 884]

The call for the support of the Social Democrats is, as T. J. Reed has said, astounding from someone such as Thomas Mann, but this declaration itself shows how problematical Mann's alliance with them was. The clear implication is of support for socialism only in an extreme situation and then, as with earlier formulations quoted, the whole expressed with an astounding rhetorical opacity. The statement does, however, make it clear that Mann's so-called political conversion had little or nothing to do with socialism 'pur sang' but everything to do with the defence of bourgeois culture. Admittedly he argued in *Speech to Workers in Vienna* – a most difficult speech that must have caused its audience some trouble – that the great figures of German culture had produced work that was not class-specific and was at pains to point out that 'intelligent members of your class, those yearning for culture, reject the idea of opposing so-called bourgeois cultural values with so-called proletarian ones' (XI, 892), but elsewhere in the speech he said that the preservation of 'the spiritual heritage of the German burgher' compelled the bourgeoisie to line up with the Social Democrats. Later, in his letter to the Reich Ministry of the Interior, he clearly stated that the alliance he had propounded with Social Democratic workers, 'these people who are so well disposed to culture' (XIII, 103), would have meant 'the salvation of bourgeois culture'.

Whilst Mann's call to opposition to Hitler and the Nazis was unambiguous and bold and he deserves full credit for his continuous and consistent attack on them, that which he held up against Nazism was in political terms vague and lacking in conviction. Golo Mann, whose assessment of his father's political essays and speeches is so much more dispassionate than that of many other commentators, has rightly said that 'His "yes" had always been half-hearted, qualified by criticism and self-criticism'. [15] Just as his support for 'the republic' by-passed the reality and functioned instead with an ideal construct, so was his view of socialism either yet another term for his ideal or so vague as to be meaningless. Thus in *My Allegiance to Socialism* (1933), which is substantially a repetition of earlier statements made in very different political circumstances, socialism was described as

merely the dutiful decision no longer to hide one's head in the sand of ethereal things and avoid the most pressing demands of the material world, of collective social life, but rather to take sides with those who strive to give a meaning to the world, a human meaning. [XII, 681]

Moreover in these and later essays written in exile, such as *The Coming Victory of Democracy* (1938), we find an aristocratic view of 'true' democracy, unchanged from the *Reflections*, which is difficult to square with a professed socialism. There is, in fact, much in a Nazi attack on *An Appeal to Reason* by Rudolf Ibel, which held that Mann was trying to convert workers to his 'support of bourgeois civilisation' by extending the hand of friendship to Marxism 'after appropriately purifying it in a way that leaves little of its original substance'.[16] This is true of all the famous later essays embracing 'socialism' and of earlier ones too, including the *Reflections*, in which the value centre is constantly Mann's ideal of true 'Humanität' ('Kultur', 'the German middle way', etc).

Whilst apologists of Thomas Mann distort the substance of his essays by claiming that he became a sincere republican and/or socialist, there is a danger of distortion through over-personalisation of the argument and of it too easily becoming an attack on Thomas Mann, resulting in bizarre excesses such as that of Walter Muschg in *Tragische Literaturgeschichte*. These political writings should be seen rather as representative of the tradition in which Mann was rooted. T. J. Reed has claimed that he 'remoulded and used those traditions in a process of re-education, for himself and his contemporaries, that ran counter to the course of national disaster',[17] but the facts of the matter are scarcely as simple as that. Firstly there were, as he repeatedly said, very real affinities between some of his own ideas and those expressed in a base form in Nazism, but in addition this statement implies that Mann overcame the problems inherent in the German tradition. That he was very much aware of the problematical aspects of the tradition of personal development ('Bildung') in the existing situation is admirably demonstrated in the relatively early and perceptive essay *The Spirit and Character of the Republic* (1923), in which he rightly pointed out that it was 'a sphere of pietistic, autobiographical, confessional and personal culture, within which the objective world, the world of politics, is felt to be profane and is rejected as irrelevant' (XI, 854). Mann saw the way in which the exclusion of politics from the notion of 'Bildung' – to which he first drew attention in the *Reflections* (*cf.* XII, 270) – created a tremendous difficulty for the German bourgeoisie in the '20s and tried very hard to extend his own intellectual range to accommodate this in the essays and speeches of the period. Despite this consciousness he was unable to become a more political animal; thus he urged support for the republic on the grounds 'that the Republic, *taken in an ideal sense and ignoring the shortcomings of the existing reality*, is nothing other than the political name of "Humanität" ' (XI, 857; my italics). In the latter days of the republic he said that its weaknesses stemmed essentially from the fact that 'it too faint-heartedly failed to speak up for an ideal that was regarded as dead and contemptible' (XII, 677). T. J. Reed implies that Mann, unlike those intellectuals drawn into proximity to National Socialism, succeeded in distinguishing between art and politics in other than aesthetic terms, whereas these quotations, and indeed all his commendations of the republic and socialism, show that this was not so. The result is the setting up of a constant ideal which, though completely admirable in itself, was presented in such a way that there either appeared to be in many utterances an implicit criticism of the institution Mann was claiming to support, or that this ideal is seen as existing in an almost autonomous aesthetic sphere outside or above that of politics. Despite all his critical awareness of the shortcomings of the German idealist tradition he could, as Käte Hamburger so perceptively observed as early as 1932, 'only judge the political life of the State according to the yardstick of the supranational, unpolitical Idea, which for him is always recognisably active amidst constantly shifting political phenomena'.[18]

Another complementary aspect of the German tradition that is relevant here is the belief, going back to Schiller's *Aesthetic Letters*, in an aesthetic education of the nation by intellectual writers, an education which by definition was seen as being outside and above the political world. In two speeches above all, *In the Warsaw PEN Club* (1927) and *The intellectual tendencies of present-day Germany* (1926) Mann declared his faith in the persuasive abilities of these people – who are uncannily similar to the silent intellectual minority ('die Stillen im Lande') of the Conservative Revolutionaries – with whose important activities he would undoubtedly have classed his own political pronouncements:

it is not going too far to claim that, generally speaking, nothing now can happen in Europe against the quiet, indirectly effective will of the intellectuals: this is not a formalised position, and its effect presupposes that the 'intellectual' (der Geistige) – using this term for the type of higher, more knowledgeable, freer, well intentioned person I mean – does not allow himself to be carried away again by the passions that he is called upon to watch over and moderate through his criticism. It presupposes too that he opposes them in the strongest possible way, and it is this pressure that is, in my opinion, of such decisive importance today. [XIII, 583]

Although this was stated to be an 'incontrovertible fact, given the present-day distribution of power' (XI, 404), there was, however, a perhaps unconscious anticipation of the failure of the intellectuals ('die Geistigen') to stem the tide of Nazism in one of these speeches when Mann said of the PEN club, which was to have provided a unifying focus for their activities, that its job was also to be 'a haven and a refuge for 'Geist'. There is no doubt that, at the time, he was by no means alone in his optimistic faith in the potency of 'Geist'. Moreover, despite the defeat by Nazism of the humane liberal tradition that Mann supported, this notion is far from dead in Germany. Thus a recent essay on the occasion of the hundredth anniversary of Mann's birth gives positive emphasis to the fact that terms like 'republic' and 'democracy', as used by Mann, were not political but rather 'poetic definitions, in no way based on tangible political realities, but rather seeking to imbue these realities with

a poetical element that would consolidate them spiritually . . .'. The secret
of his contemporaneity is, we are told, his realisation that 'the longings
of poets really can change our lives'.[19]
Mann himself, looking back in exile on his political writings of the
Weimar period, admitted that there was, between his self-awareness as an
artist and his political activities, a contradiction which necessitated
'overcoming of self' (*cf.* XI, 465 f.) and in his letter to the Reich Ministry
of the Interior he recognised that 'my real leaning was and is to the area
of the spiritual and the artistic, not the political' (XIII, 101). Given this, it
is not surprising that he wrote to Harry Slochower that it was in his
literary works that 'my true self, which demands balance in human
affairs, expresses itself far more clearly'.[20] Mann's self-assessment is
surely right here: the true embodiment of his ideal was contained not in
his political works but in *The Magic Mountain*, a work which
thematically and structurally is suffused with the idea of the 'the German
middle way'. But it would be wrong to see too great a gulf between the
novel and the speeches and essays. These too were concerned far more
with the striving for balance between the forces of the world dialectic
than with concrete political problems, their ideal is that synthesis
contained in the 'Snow' chapter, and they too, despite all Mann's
strivings, in their steadfast allegiance to the ideal of true 'Humanität'
were as ineffectual in the true political arena as Settembrini's crusades
from Davos. They remained on a magic mountain of ideas, leaving the
Flatlands to the real political combatants.

Notes

[1] *Kurt Tucholsky als Politiker*, Mainz, 1971, pp. 102–3.
[2] *Weimar Culture*, London, 1969, p. 74.
[3] *Thomas Mann. The Uses of Tradition*, Oxford, 1974, p. 293.
[4] *Thomas Mann und die Deutschen*, Frankfurt a.M., 1971, p. 43.
[5] *Der Repräsentant und der Märtyrer*, Frankfurt a.M., 1971, p. 75.
[6] *Encyclopaedia Britannica*, 15th edn., London, 1974, vol. II, p. 456.
[7] 'The uses of literary scholarship', *Times Literary Supplement*, 11 October 1974, p. 1105.
[8] I have found it impossible adequately to render in translation two key terms Mann uses and therefore have given them in German throughout. 'Geist' is often translated as 'spirit' or 'intellect', both fail to convey the way in which the German word is shot through with a quasi-religious faith in the power of 'Geist', which imbues cultural life with a coherence transcending particular social and political phenomena. 'Humanität' means much more than the English 'humanity' and conveys, as I hope this essay will bring out, the sense of the highest essence of mankind, the synthesis of its finest qualities.
[9] An attempt to extrapolate Thomas Mann's political position from his imaginative writings of the period would, of course, be substantially complicated by the factor of irony, although it could be argued that irony in these writings corresponds in literary terms to Mann's notion of the 'middle way', which I delineate in this essay. In the political

speeches and essays analysed in this study, which were intended in the main as statements on politics that should have exemplary value for their audience, it is fair to assume – as other commentotors on them have done – that Mann's irony is here absent.

[10] Reed, *Thomas Mann*, p. 287.

[11] Letter of 1 September 1935 to Harry Slochower, *Briefe, 1889–1936*, Frankfurt a.M., 1962, p. 398.

[12] Sontheimer, *op. cit.*, p. 66.

[13] Reed, *op. cit.*, p. 310.

[14] *Ibid.*, p. 288.

[15] *History of Germany since 1789*, London, 1968, p. 371.

[16] Quoted by Thomas Mann in *Die Wiedergeburt der Anständigkeit*, XII, p. 666.

[17] *Times Literary Supplement*, 11 November 1974, p. 1230.

[18] 'Romantische Politik bei Thomas Mann', *Morgen*. Monatsschrift der deutschen Juden, 8, 1932, p. 115.

[19] Peter de Mendelssohn, 'Der Schriftsteller als politischer Bürger', *Thomas Mann, 1875–1975*, Bonn and Bad Godesberg, 1975, pp. 26 and 32.

[20] *Briefe, 1889–1936, ed. cit.*, p. 398.

All references in the text are to Mann's *Gesammelte Werke in dreizehn Bänden*, 2nd edn., Frankfurt a.M., 1974.

GODFREY CARR

'A sudden and passionate revulsion towards Germany': Friedrich Sieburg's concept of political thought

An Englishman browsing through the lists of recent publications in 1929 might well have been puzzled and intrigued by a work with the title *Is God a Frenchman?*[1] written by a German journalist, Friedrich Sieburg. If he had bought the book, hoping perhaps to encounter new heights of eccentric speculation, he would have been surprised and disappointed to find almost nothing about God in the whole work. If, however, he had recovered from this setback sufficiently to look at a further work of Sieburg's which appeared four years later in English translation with the title *Germany: my country*[2], he would have found not the nationalist theology suggested by the title of the first work but a lengthy theology of nationalism. In the open letter to the English publisher of *Germany: my country*, which serves as an introduction to the work, Sieburg asserts that 'nationalism is, consciously or unconsciously, saturating the life of every individual German, saturating his every thought and every emotion and revealing itself in the whole conduct of his life.' (*GMC* p. 15). He himself is happy, he states, to be considered an evangelist of the Third Reich, and he praises Adolf Hitler for freeing Germany from an 'evil spell' through the 'magic formula' of National Socialism. Sieburg writes of Hitler's 'prophetic quality', his 'mysterious driving force', and argues that in contrast to the heads of state of other countries a German leader's authority 'must be illuminated by a radiance from above, however inexplicable its origin'. Anticipating the difficulty foreign readers might have in accepting this nebulous statement, Sieburg attempts to justify it by appealing to the authority of the world of literature, pointing out that 'our great poet, Stefan George, has in his visions again and again beheld the saviour in this light' (*GMC* p. 14).

The style of this second work is remarkable for its repetitiousness and its endless generalisations, full of exaggerated pathos. It is doubtful, for instance, whether an English reader would make any sense of sentences such as the following:

> The German has buried his treasures of mute tenderness and modest joy deep in the earth and a fierce torrent is washing over the spot ... The black waters of time sweep on and not one star is mirrored on their awful melancholy surface. [*GMC*, pp. 190–1]

And yet Sieburg was an experienced journalist, having been the foreign correspondent of the *Frankfurter Zeitung* from 1923 in a variety of European capitals, including London and Paris. *Is God a Frenchman?* had been translated into both French and English and had been praised for its lucid and informative evocation of French life, though at least one Frenchman had had reservations about Sieburg's attitude to France. Bernard Grasset, the editor of the French version, confessed to being surprised at finding Sieburg 'so near and at the same time so far from us – so near in your perfectly spontaneous surrender to the charm of France, so far in the way your intellect opposed that surrender' (*IGF*, p. 294). Grasset is disturbed by a dualism which runs through the book and which he feels is not simply a reflection of Sieburg's attitude to France but is typical of the attitude of the majority of Germans. In fact, of course, Grasset is referring to the majority of Germans who had published comparisons between the two countries, in other words German writers.

The dualism or inherent ambiguity in Sieburg's thinking forms the common factor between his much-praised book about France in 1929 and the incoherently nationalistic account of Germany of 1933, and it presented the translators with very great problems when they tried to render Sieburg's original German titles into English or French. *Is God a Frenchman?*, for instance, sounds ridiculous, but it is the best the translator could manage when faced with the original *Gott in Frankreich?* a phrase which depends for its effect on knowledge of the German proverb 'leben wie Gott in Frankreich' (to live like a king, like a lord, to live in the lap of luxury). Automatically, therefore, the German reader, on seeing the title, associates France with an enviable state of material well-being. At the same time the same reader is encouraged to be suspicious of this state, for Sieburg turns the phrase into a question. In just three words the title conveys a complex of contradictory emotions and attitudes, feelings of admiration and envy on the one hand, and superiority and revulsion on the other. In his later work, *Germany: my country*, Sieburg maintains that this is the attitude of all Germans towards France and that the individual German is either 'so impressed by the social refinement and cultural stability of the French, and so ashamed of his own instability, that he succumbs to indiscriminate enthusiasm and sometimes even longs to impose the French national form on himself or his own people; or the French complacency and self-sufficiency repel him, and he proudly compares their torpor with the dynamism of his own antion' (*GMC*, p. 69). It is this second attitude which prevails in *Germany: my country*, but the English title, a cliché suggesting conventional patriotism, totally fails to reproduce the dynamism of the German original title, *Es werde Deutschland*, which might be translated as 'Let the real Germany emerge'. Had the full force of the German verb 'werden' (to become) been conveyed in English it would have been obvious at once that the work was directed against the existing German State, the Weimar Republic, and was a demand for its replacement by a totally different form of society. As France was the country which supplied the model for the Weimar Republic's constitution, the difference between Sieburg's two books is therefore clearly one of degree rather than kind, and the violent rejection of France which fills *Germany: my country* has already been signalled to the German reader by the curious German title *Gott in Frankreich?*.

Even with its French title, however, there was still enough in Friedrich Sieburg's first book to alarm a French reader, and Bernard Grasset sums up its effect on him in a line from La Fontaine's version of the fable of the goose that laid the golden eggs: 'We do not doubt your love, but it may cost us our lives' (*IGF*, p. 296). Behind every declaration of affection for France in the book there is a hidden threat, and this is immediately obvious in the strange introductory section which bears the title 'Why I have written about France'. It consists of some thirty clauses, each beginning with the word 'because'. In each of these Sieburg describes the love he feels for France when he thinks of the possible alternative – a soulless, technologically advanced, philistine Europe. His love of France is conveyed, however, in terms which are at best patronising and at worst contemptuous. 'I am writing about France,' he claims, 'because I am weak enough to prefer to remain in an old-fashioned and untidy paradise rather than in a spick-and-span, dreary model world' (*IGF*, p. 9) and again, 'because I want to perpetuate the tear with which I take leave of an obstinate, superseded France, before I enrol without enthusiasm but against my worser [sic] judgement to becoming an active member of the European community' (*IGF*, p. 9). The whole of this introductory section is written in a self-indulgent confessional manner, and what is more it is terribly confused. Sieburg evidently loves and respects French culture, but cannot quite respect himself for doing so, as the society which has produced that culture is outmoded and founded on suspect values. Sieburg declares, for instance, that the Germans cannot live without the French, despite the 'questionable position of France from a national, political and social point of view (*IGF*, p. 12). What, then, is there left of France that is so lovable? Only her culture, and this, Sieburg suggests, should be preserved and absorbed by Germany, a country with a real future ahead of it. No wonder Grasset suspects his love. In a response to Grasset, however, Sieburg, obviously hurt by these suspicions, expresses his love for France in the words of Philine, one of the characters in Goethe's novel *Wilhelm Meister's Apprenticeship*. Addressing the hero, Wilhelm, she asks tartly, 'If I love you, what is that to you?' (*IGF*, p. 302). The analogy is revealing, for Philine, a charming but totally self-centred creature, wants to possess Wilhelm but is not prepared to change her own way of life in order to create a lasting relationship. She always seeks the easy way through life, is essentially frivolous and can be either generous or malicious according to her whim. She is at home in the world of the theatre, for she loves illusion and is for ever in love with her image of herself. Similarly Friedrich Sieburg is not so much in love with France in its entirety as with those parts of France which provide him with aesthetic pleasure. He desires no reciprocation of his love and tells Grasset that he is 'amply rewarded by the imperishable treasures which your country offers to every mortal eye and spirit' (*IGF*, p. 302). Love of this kind is totally egoistic, and Sieburg is really only interested in those aspects of French life which as a cultured German he feels should interest him. In response to Grasset's criticisms he even goes so far as to argue that his book should not in any case concern a Frenchman, since it is 'at bottom a book about Germany, France being merely the mirror in which Germany is intended to recognise herself' (*IGF*, p. 302). This remark pre-empts further discussion but raises two important questions. Why should Sieburg prefer to write about Germany indirectly instead of devoting the whole of his book to this subject, and what sort of Germany is it that he describes in this way? In order to begin to answer these questions it is necessary to examine closely the structure of the book on France.

Is God a Frenchman? is divided into five sections, and the first is devoted to an account of the importance of Joan of Arc. Sieburg considers her to be the founder of the French nation and its constant inspiration to the present day. He portrays her as a leader receiving inspiration from heaven and yet never losing contact with the peasant world from which she came. Without her charismatic leadership and fierce patriotism there would be no French nation, he concludes. The second section is devoted to aspects of contemporary French civilisation, and here we detect little of the enthusiasm that could be felt in the first section, for Sieburg has important reservations. The French concept of freedom, for example, is described as being freedom to act against the laws of nature and lacking any element of 'évolution créatrice'. Sieburg believes that the French experience nature only as part of themselves and are never prepared to accept that the reverse might also be true. He admits that this has been a source of strength in the past, but argues that it is now becoming a serious threat to the continued development of the French people. An equally critical attitude is also taken to other characteristic features of French life, such as politeness, tact, provincial life, travel, the spoken word and finally literature. Throughout this section Sieburg has been trying to identify differences between France and Germany, and this last aspect of French civilisation enables him to establish a sharp contrast:

There is as little distinction in France between the language of social intercourse and the language of poetry as there is between poetry and civilised manners. The country of Hölderlin and Stefan George cannot help thinking that this fact, of which the Frenchman is justifiably proud, indicates a weakness, or at any rate a lack of distinction of rank. Once more we are faced with the great gulf fixed between two different natures, the depth of which shows up particularly clearly in French literature. [*IGF*, p. 140].

French literature is not a retreat from the realm of public life, but is on the contrary part of it. Whereas Germany has isolated examples of individual genius, in France literature is part of the furnishings of life.

With this discussion of the literary world Sieburg might well be thought to have concluded his survey, but the third section of the book makes it clear that there are other aspects of French life which do not quite fit into this dualistic scheme. Called 'Intermezzo', it consists of a number of vignettes of French life and contains some of the most vivid and realistic writing of the whole book. Here Sieburg describes those idiosyncratic customs of the French which obviously both delight and exasperate him. They include the French telephone service, the activities of the concierge, the French passion for hunting and the regular motorised exodus from Paris at weekends and holidays. Throughout the section one is conscious of a note of wistful admiration, even envy, for the French because they are able to find happiness in such simple pleasures as the obligatory mid-morning breakfast. The final image of French happiness is that of the tramp happily eating his crust of bread dipped in red wine and sitting contentedly in the sun on the banks of the Seine.

A continuing preoccupation with the question of happiness seems to be the only possible reason why this section should close with a series of personal reminiscences which otherwise seem oddly out of place. Displaying the same penchant for ambiguity that we have noted earlier, he calls these few pages 'The search for the lost war', and then goes on to explain that by this he means not the war 'which the generals lost' (*IGF*,

p. 192) nor the sordid reality of the war, but instead a number of unforgettable moments during those four years which have haunted him ever since. All these experiences are connected with that point in the year when the fullness of summer is giving way to the first signs of autumnal decay, and they include standing in an orchard in the middle of an offensive; contemplating a rotten apple; pressing close to the earth in tall grass whilst under fire and hearing his mother's voice calling out to him; and standing looking at neglected French gardens full of decaying asters. On each of these occasions he experiences a sense of infinite happiness of a kind, though from his description it seems to be a mixture of relief and pleasant melancholia, as he feels himself slowly losing his individual identity and merging into nature. The thought of being able to return to the earth or the womb is irresistibly seductive, and he yearns to be able to repeat the sensation, trying to capture its essence in paradoxical phrases such as 'desolate joy' or 'I was perfected, finished and therefore eternal – I was a human being' (*IGF*, p. 194). After the last of these moments he even admits that he no longer desired to live, and they represent, he believes, a glimpse of happiness far superior to that afforded by the material pleasures of French life. On the strength of these brief but intoxicating sensations of release from the self he claims that 'the Lost War will not be found and buried along with the rest of the dead till Life teaches us the same lessons as the nearness of Death did once' (*IGF*, p. 197).

Since Sieburg is obviously obsessed with a desire to reduce his interest in life, and indeed his will to live, to a minimum, it is hardly surprising that he was so disturbed by his stay in France. Wherever he went there would be countless reminders of the conflicting desires and ambitions of men. All around him men were doing their utmost to stimulate and satisfy human appetites and in so doing to affirm their enjoyment of life. In any civilised society, however, such pleasures are not the only things in life, nor necessarily the most important. Institutions are set up and measures taken to ensure that the individual's pursuit of happiness does not threaten the stability of the whole and prevent the further development of society. As a result the individual is able to enjoy the pleasurable activities of life in a meaningful and creative way. To a detached and often uncomprehending observer like Sieburg, however, French society could easily seem to consist of endless opportunities for the dissipation and fragmentation of the self.

Certainly Sieburg concluded that in the light of his wartime experiences France was now hindering the emergence of more exalted forms of human awareness which Germany alone could give to the world. With an abruptness which takes the reader completely by surprise

the tone of the book now changes, and the fourth section has the brutal
and aggressive title 'France as an obstacle'. It opens with an insulting
comparison between present-day France and the land of the Incas before
the arrival of the Spaniards. The French leader Poincaré is used to
epitomise all that is backward, limited and isolationist in France, and the
book ends with a short fifth section extolling Germany as the natural
successor to France. Only Germany can decide the future, Sieburg
argues, for only Germany has produced 'formulas of universal validity'
which form a real alternative to those of France. The examples he gives
are the categorical imperative, Hegel's philosophy, Romanticism, the cult
of nature, music and finally and significantly German militarism, or, in
Sieburg's words, 'the youthful muster of the blond 'barbarians' and 'the
armies that poured over the gardens, fields, and vineyards of the fair land
of France three times in a hundred years' (*IGF*, p. 259). Only Germany
has learned the deadly truth of the modern world which must eventually
replace the ideals of French civilisation, and this truth, according to
Sieburg, is best expressed in Dostoyevsky's command 'Seek thy
happiness in sorrow and labour unwearyingly' (*IGF*, p. 262).

The emergence of this gloomy philosophy is prefaced in *Is God a
Frenchman?* by Sieburg's return to his emotional condition of the war
years. In his later work, *Germany: my country*, however, it is evident
from the beginning that this period is more real for him than the present,
and indeed the book opens with an account of a conversation with a
friend who is just about to go on leave from the western front at a time
when the war is obviously drawing to a close. The anonymous friend,
referred to as M., is excitedly looking forward to returning home and
taking up his civilian life. Sieburg loathes the idea and says defiantly, 'I
am glad I am not going home on leave too. I should like to walk along
these roads all my life, to explore this sky, to measure the world by map
grids, and judge the time of day by the violence of the gunfire' (*GMC*, p.
32). In *Is God a Frenchman?* Sieburg had already described the effect of
his military training as being akin to a disordering of the eye. It was not
possible to look at a landscape without assessing its military potential,
because there had been a 'period in one's life when one did not see but
'observed', did not lie down but 'took cover', 'moved off' instead of going
away, 'marched' instead of walking' (*IGF*, p. 195). Clearly the effect of
this poisoning as far as he was concerned was to give a meaning to life
which was not previously there, and in *Germany: my country* he recalls
with nostalgia the challenges of the sentries as they sounded in the night.
He even tells M. that he has never really known Germany before the
outbreak of the war:

I admired her [Germany's GRC] scenery, her air, and her men of genius, but it never occurred to me that she was something to be cared about. Only lately have I realised that. But my Germany begins when the rockets mount to the sky and ends here where the train starts for Cologne. [*GMC*, p. 33]

When Sieburg talks of 'my Germany' he means simply his new interest in life during the war, for then everything had a meaning and purpose, and as a result he experienced for the first time a sense of his own worth to the community. By 'Germany', therefore, he understands a feeling of personal fulfilment which he knows cannot survive the coming of peace. He dreads the return of normality:

Out here I have been alone with Germany for the first time. I have whispered to her and she has answered me. I cannot go home and take up the old life again. All sorts of people will get in the way. Germany will once more be what she was before, so pleasant, so comfortable, no, so . . . [*GMC*, p. 33]

and at this point his friend adds, 'so uncompelling'. In other words, Germany would turn into that state of challenging confusion which Sieburg encountered later in France, which provoked the dualities of *Is God a Frenchman?* In that book he is prepared to admit that the French have a surprising ability to unite instantly in a moment of national crisis, despite their fierce individualism. Nevertheless Sieburg believes that he has discovered in the trenches superior and essentially German concepts of unity and individuality. He rejoices in the fact that 'there were thousands of us, yet we were alone' and that there was 'nothing left in the world, neither home nor career' (*IGF*, p. 193). Indeed, this combination of total isolation and submergence in the mass is presented as constituting a more worthwhile form of freedom than that afforded by the democratic institutions of countries like England and France.

So powerful is the impact left on him by his army service that it acts as a permanent yardstick by which to judge the post-war world, and as a result Sieburg totally rejects the Weimar Republic and is unmoved by the collapse of its political institutions. In the course of a further conversation with M., some twelve years after the first, Sieburg returns again to images of the war when M. tries to persuade him that humane values are being ruthlessly destroyed in Germany. At this point Sieburg sees himself once more tramping along a dark French road in those last days of the war, having said farewell to M. Disturbed by M.'s inability to share his enthusiasm for Germany, he remembers calling out the number of his brigade in the darkness 'like a child for its mother' (*GMC*, p. 39). When the second conversation also ends in a complete breakdown of communication Sieburg, with a huge sense of relief, retreats once more into his wartime self:

Once more I was alone with Germany, communing with her softly and caressingly, and the words we exchange I write down as a confession to the world that she is my country whom I love, and for whom I have suffered and still suffer. [*GMC*, p. 42]

Sieburg never actually admits that Germany is nothing more than a reflection of his own self. Only in response to Grasset's criticism did he acknowledge that the book about France was really about Germany, but in *Germany: my country* he concludes that 'anyone who wants to describe Germany today can, in the first place, describe only himself' [*GMC*, p. 261]. That there can never be a 'second place' is something Sieburg will not and indeed cannot concede. He feels that he has captured the 'elements which dwell in the soul of every individual German and distinguish him from other citizens of this world' (*GMC*, pp. 11–12). Germany, therefore, does not consist of unique individuals but is a unique macro-individual, and Sieburg maintains that in his book he was seeking 'more than the man; it was the German' (*GMC*, p. 12). In order to enlighten English readers as to the nature of this superhuman entity Sieburg quotes with approval a letter he has received from a French friend who 'did not know whether it was the picture of Germany or only the picture of a tragic soul' (*GMC*, p. 11).

On the surface there appears to be no obvious reason why Friedrich Sieburg should want to portray his nation and himself as a tragic soul. His nation had provided him with an excellent education, and he had obtained one of the most attractive posts in the whole world of journalism, which was in its turn one of the most important institutions in society. From 1923 onwards he had been the foreign correspondent of the *Frankfurter Zeitung* and did tours of duty in London, Paris and Copenhagen. Yet despite his success in his chosen career he remained fundamentally dissatisfied. The first world war gave definite form to this mood and thus brought such relief that Sieburg dared not abandon the attitudes which evolved then. It is important to note, however, that the feelings of dissatisfaction were there before the war and were the product of his student days, and in particular of his time at the University of Heidelberg immediately before the war. In an article[3] in the *Frankfurter Allgemeine Zeitung* to commemorate what would have been Friedrich Sieburg's eightieth birthday Karl August Horst quotes from a letter written by Sieburg in July 1963 in which he tries to capture the magic of this particular period in his life. He describes the intellectual life of the university as being 'the late blossoming of the nineteenth century, that is, Weber, Troeltsch, Friedrich Gundolf and many others', and recalls the frequent appearances of Stefan George and the 'marvellous atmosphere of intellectual curiosity and reverence' which filled the lecture theatre when Gundolf gave a course of lectures on Klopstock. Despite the passage of time he is 'often moved almost to tears' when he thinks back to these occasions, which 'cannot be reproduced and which no German will ever experience again'. There can be no doubt that they left a deep impression on him, but one is forced to wonder quite how genuine the emotion experienced here really is. He is not, after all, really 'moved to tears', and there are thus grounds for believing that the emotion has been sustained artificially and is little more than sentimental nostalgia. Sieburg himself, however, is convinced that his life has never been as enjoyable again as it was then, for 'it was a paradise, and he who has tarried in it must afterwards feel very often that the world is colourless and dry, and as though made of ash'.[4]

Heidelberg thus awakened an idealism which found practical fulfilment not in normal life but in the trenches and later the Flying Corps. The two periods merge in Sieburg's mind, and he writes about the war with exactly the same nostalgia he feels for Heidelberg. Both periods in his life enabled him to escape from the everyday world, the world of commerce and politics, of jobs and careers, of ambitions and successes. He believes this world to be inferior and that only as a soldier can a German find scope for 'his best and noblest qualities' (*GMC*, p. 92). Civilian life must be filled with the 'spirit of the front', and he agrees with Max Scheler's view that 'German militarism is more like a work of art than a tool'. (*GMC*, p. 93). This must be true, Sieburg maintains, because Germans have always cultivated militarism for its own sake. The war simply provided that longed-for greater cause to which all personal ambitions could be sacrificed. Sieburg never seems to have noticed that many of these same ambitions survived and flourished in the military world. On the contrary, he is convinced that the war has brought about a great revolution in German society, and it transpires that he means by this the end of Prussian dominance and the emergence of a new loyalty to the nation as opposed to the Kaiser. Officers were no longer representatives of a particular class in society and loyal servants of a particular ruler; instead they, and the men under them, were all servants of the national idea. This state of affairs Sieburg calls 'autonomous militarism', and he believes that the army has been 'politicised' by this new spirit. The revolution about which he writes so enthusiastically is certainly not a social one, for the Prussian officer caste did not lose its grip on the higher posts in the army. With the expansion of the army and the heavy casualty figures many newly created junior officers fought side by side with officers from the professional army, and in defending the nation they may indeed have experienced a new sense of unity, but the revolution is one of sentiment rather than substance. This is not to say, however, that it was without effect.

So powerful was the impression left on Sieburg that he was totally unable to face the reality of defeat. Instead he chose to see it as a conspiracy on the part of the Western powers to prevent a truly German revolution establishing itself. In the shape of the Weimar Republic the Western powers had imposed their own outdated values on Germany and in so doing they had given free reign to commercialism, materialism and the pursuit of trivial and vulgar pleasure. Sieburg just could not accept a Germany which fell so short of the aesthetic ideals awakened in Heidelberg and which seemed to make à mockery of those feelings of fulfilment and purpose which he had had during the war. In *Germany: my country* he announces that 'Things cannot go on like this any longer' (p. 166), though what he cannot tolerate is the fact that they have gone on at all! What he really desires is a return to the atmosphere of the years 1914–18 and an agreement on the part of his fellow Germans that they will behave as if they were at war. Those who like him are capable of sustaining this fantasy make up what Sieburg calls the 'secret Germany', which is characterised by its impossible contradictions. It involves a readiness to exist in a condition of 'permanent mobilisation' (*GMC*, p. 155), and throughout the book states of mind such as a belief in fate and a glorying in sacrifice and suffering, which arise as a result of the impermanence and abnormality of war, are combined with images and metaphors based on stars, anchors and stones, suggesting permanence and stability. The desperate attempt to pretend that fragmentation is a newer, more profound form of unity is clearly revealed in the following analogy:

We are shifting sand, yet in every grain there inheres the longing to combine with all the rest into solid durable stone. [*GMC*, p. 159]

Sieburg is compelled to produce such absurd formulations because he believes both conditions to be equally valid and equally German, and he can find no way of effecting a transition from one to the other except by a belief in magic formulae and by doing violence to the ordinary usages of language:

What many people today regard as a revulsion against the world, against reason, indeed against man, is in reality a revulsion towards Germany. [*GMC*, p. 16]

By Germany, therefore, Sieburg means a State in which the advantages of advanced industrial society are retained, but which rejects the social and intellectual changes that accompanied industrialisation. Thanks to the particular course of his life, his student days in Heidelberg, his life as an officer in the war and then his career as a foreign correspondent and freelance writer, Sieburg had never been forced to confront the problems faced by an individual who tries to play a full and active part in a particular society. His idealism had remained absolute, and he had never learned the satisfaction to be gained from achieving that which is limited but feasible. Those who achieve this sort of success, be they individuals or nations, are in his eyes an obstacle, and their efforts must be absorbed into the great dream which he cherishes and which goes under the name of Germany. He asks, for instance, whether the concept of the nation is capable 'of growing out into the universe and filling it[5], and insists that the German is engaged in rethinking the world and that, having started by 'analysing the foundations of his own existence, he has now reached those of his nation and will probably next proceed to analyse the foundations of the rest of the world' (*GMC*, p. 174). This process of rethinking the whole of modern society means the repudiation of the Enlightenment and of all the procedures by which ideals and values are articulated in public discussion. In their search for the most rational ways of organising human activity men were forced to create institutions facilitating and guaranteeing public debate, and any new concept had to be subjected to public scrutiny. Sieburg, however, replaces the glare of publicity with the glow of inner conviction, and suggests that 'the German community will shape for itself a body of hitherto unknown type which instead of depending for its light on universal ideas shall be illumined as it were from within' (*GMC*, p. 52). He presents this possibility as a spectacular leap forward beyond the ideas of the Enlightenment. Unfortunately for Sieburg, he is still forced to use a language which has been shaped by the Enlightenment and which is full of the universal values which he now finds redundant. His solution is to reduce them to one common denominator – his own attitude to life. Progress therefore becomes a defiant resignation to one's destiny, happiness is turned into an exultation in suffering for its own sake, critical thought is replaced by a deliberate refusal to see that which might contradict one's opinions, and public discussion gives way to brooding silence. All the distinctions upon which modern civilisation is based are destroyed and society itself returned to an inchoate mass. In the process, of course, human nature itself has been eliminated, and Sieburg is so trapped in his web of language that the world 'German' can even veil this appalling consequence:

There are to be no more private Germans; each is to attain significance only by his service to the State, and to find complete self-fulfilment in this service. Thus, to express it in more emphatic terms, there are to be no more mere human beings in Germany, but only Germans. [*GMC*, p. 13]

Sieburg would rather abolish human beings than give up the super- or rather sub-human ideal which he has nourished since the end of the war.

All Germany, he believes, wishes to live in an advanced industrial society inhabited by people whose thoughts and feelings are those of *a* pre-industrial world, thought not *the* pre-industrial world, for Sieburg is obsessed with a Romantic dream. His Germany is a virginal coquette, a fascinating witch, pure and yet seductive.

Such a creature exists only in the realm of fairytale, and in order to produce her he has to conjure two powerful genii back into their respective bottles – the machine, and the worker who operates it. These two elements present the major threat to Sieburg's dream, and he renders them harmless by a process of alchemical conversion. The inanimate machine is turned into a living natural force and the worker into an inanimate machine. We are told that the machine has delayed the achievement of German unity, but this in turn will enable the Germans to become the only true masters of the machine in the world. Because of their lack of unity they have been able to comprehend the machine not as mere matter but as a spiritual force. Once united, therefore, the Germans will be masters of the machine. By means of this totally circular argument he persuades himself that even slaves are really in their heart of hearts masters. The real slaves are, of course, the German workers, who, according to Sieburg, inhabit 'a world in itself' which 'seems to obey laws of its own, hidden beneath the smooth, gleaming surface' (*GMC*, p. 90). What is more, he is determined that the German worker should stay under that 'gleaming surface', for 'if once the outside world encroached upon this magic circle, all his calm and concentration would be scattered at one stroke'. A desperate desire to prevent the worker sharing in the wealth he produces is dressed up as a lofty moral and aesthetic ideal, and Sieburg declares that 'the German assigns to human labour an absolute significance' (*GMC*, p. 86). The German 'is able to engage in it for its own sake', for work is 'a game with its own rules and its own meaning'.

As a consequence of this ideal the German worker is 'akin to the artist' (*GMC*, p. 45) and at the same time by virtue of his Germanness he is 'a soldier by nature' (*GMC*, p. 92). It is thus by converting all Germans into soldier-artists that Sieburg hopes to square his circle and produce a modern society without stimulating pressures for social change. Cromwell's army was, he believes, the embodiment of such an ideal, for its unity was derived from the patriotism and puritanism of all its members. His choice of model is important, since he is particularly anxious to point out that the role of the officer in such an army had taken on a new significance. Instead of being 'the father of his soldiers' he had become the 'custodian of an idea', and his role was henceforth 'to a large extent pedagogic' (*GMC*, p. 97). It is now possible to see what Sieburg has in mind when he claims that the Germans, once united, would become 'masters of the machine and a spiritual Volk' (*GMC*, p. 53). A military State would be established, controlled by a class of pedagogues who would define the moral and aesthetic climate. Sieburg's obsessive concern with unity would result in the creation of a Germany permanently divided into two classes, but the language he uses blinds him to this painful consequence.

One of the chief reasons for his confusion is the inherent ambiguity of the German world 'Volk', which, like Sieburg's titles, is not fully translatable into English or French. Its peculiar connotations originate in its use in the late eighteenth century at a time when middle-class values were first beginning to spread to Germany. Although their society was woefully backward both politically and economically, German writers took a keen interest in literary developments in England and France, and were deeply depressed at the lack of a comparable literary public in their own land. Since there were few ways in which they could ascertain the desires of those who bought and read their works, they were forced to write for their own concept of the ideal reader. In other words, they were forced to write for themselves and to assume that their ideals were echoed by their readers. This inevitably led them to distinguish between the backward world in which they actually lived and an ideal world existing behind that reality which needed to be guided and encouraged. To such writers this ideal world was more real than their surroundings, because it was both sympathetic to their aspirations and very similar to the literary public of England or France. For these reasons Herder was able to write with vast energy and enthusiasm about 'das Volk'. The concept incorporated forces latent within himself which were desperately trying to find an outlet in the real world. Because the reason for his frustration and that of his fellow writers was the existence of so many tiny and backward states in Germany the word 'Volk' came to represent all that was lively and vigorous and beyond the grip of the stiflingly petty state bureaucracies. 'Das Volk' is therefore the alternative 'unpolitical Germany'.

Writers were not faced only with the problem of not knowing for whom they should write; in the conditions that prevailed in the eighteenth century it was also extremely difficult to know what to write about, and once more they were forced to concentrate on themselves. To have written about the world around them would have presented great artistic and political problems. A realistic reflection of their world would have been incoherent and aesthetically unconvincing by European standards, since German society was still largely feudal. What is more, such realism would almost certainly have resulted in censorship or even imprisonment. As a result writers turned to their own situation and described the problems faced by a talented individual trying to prepare himself for life, or, perhaps more accurately, trying to adapt to the conditions of society. Since it was impossible to resolve these problems, there could be no satisfactory ending to the many 'Bildungsromane' or novels on this theme, and they come to a halt just as the hero is about to take up a position in society.

The concept of 'Bildung' is thus a symptom of a social problem rather than any solution to it, and it is in any case a curiously anachronistic ideal, since the elaborate process of self-education which is described would be possible only for an aristocrat with unlimited resources of time and money at his disposal. It is in fact a way of life rather than a preparation for life, and represents an attempt by German writers to achieve social change in the only way which seemed feasible to them. A political revolution was never a serious possibility in Germany, especially after the revolution in France, which shocked German writers deeply, though it is hard to say whether they were appalled more by the bloodshed or by the release of so much apparently anarchic and egoistic energy. They contented themselves, therefore, with acquiring a wide general education and a high level of culture. By this means they hoped to be taken seriously by the aristocrats in power and to influence them, believing that if the process could be extended to all Germans it would be possible to unite the nation in spirit. This, they felt, would be infinitely preferable to political changes inspired by demands for an improvement in the material conditions of life of the sort they had seen in France.

The most detailed and influential exposition of this attitude is to be found in Schiller's *Letters on the Aesthetic Education of Man*. Starting from a conviction that the political institutions of society are like the mechanism of a clock, Schiller argues that it is folly to consider any modifications to the design as a result of external intervention, for this would involve stopping the mechanism, and it is obviously impossible to stop society in order to improve it. His alternative proposal rests on the belief that each of the components of society – the cogwheels, as it were – is capable of improving itself if given sufficient encouragement. As they improve so too will the whole mechanism work more smoothly. The basic flaw in this conception is, of course, the impossibility of knowing whether the wheels have in fact improved or whether they have just become better adjusted one to another. Schiller, however, recommends an aesthetic education for all, convinced that the creation and appreciation of works of art liberates the human being from egoistic desires and thus gives him a far more worthwhile freedom than that afforded by democratic institutions. In so doing he confuses psychological balance with political stability and ignores the creative function of political institutions, which are products of the human mind at least as remarkable as works of art. Like a book or a painting, a political institution has a life of its own when brought into being and continues to provide a meaningful focus for a variety of contradictory forces. By reducing the State to a mere machine – and in Germany at the time it was nothing more than a machine for carrying out one man's wishes – Schiller not only gives the individual total significance, he also accords new prestige to the role of the writer, who becomes the pedagogue of the nation.

The two concepts of 'Volk' and 'Bildung' are thus interlinked, and together they obliged the German writer to think of himself as the voice of the nation, though in fact his experience of the nation was usually extremely limited. With this important responsibility weighing on his shoulders the writer feels he has to say something but can communicate only his own feelings. He is certain, however, that in so doing he is presenting a political analysis. Perhaps conscious that English readers may be unused to this sort of analysis, Sieburg expresses in the introduction to *Germany: my country* the hope 'that a man may best explain the mystery of his Fatherland by trying to disclose the dark and mighty powers which have gone to shape his own character and destiny' [*GMC*, p. 11]. Immediately after the first world war he became a freelance writer in Berlin, and must have developed this ambition as a result of his studies in Heidelberg. There he would certainly have been filled with a sense of the writer's importance to society, and Karl August Horst describes the effect on him:

He was likely to have been affected long afterwards by the thesis put forward by the George circle, with whom he came into contact in Heidelberg, that the poet must be a representative public figure.[6]

The war gave Sieburg a vision of a nation united culturally under a class of officer pedagogues. As the problems of life in peacetime returned, he grew more and more sure that this alone could provide fulfilment for himself and Germany. It was a vision so compelling as to undermine his grasp of reality, to make normal life seem unbearable even, perhaps especially, when he was enjoying it. The uncomplicated pleasures of the average Frenchman are thus an intolerable provocation, for they both fascinate and repel him. Karl August Horst is puzzled by the apparent conflict between Sieburg's intense longing to achieve a state of total indifference to life itself and his feverish attempts to experience as much of it as possible. He was, for instance, a constant traveller. The conflict is inherent, however, in the concept of 'Bildung' and thus in Sieburg's understanding of his role as a writer. Reality is a threat to one's concept of oneself; therefore that self, like an infinite balloon, must be inflated constantly to encompass reality. All that remains is the problem of supplying the wind, and an examination of *Germany: my country* shows that this is solved by constant repetition.

Since the reason for this constant expansion of the self is, of course, a desire to stay the same, it is a paradoxical enterprise:

I wish to stay for ever the same. I wish to see the world in the same fixed condition. At the same time, however, it increases my sensation of life when I think that all things are in a state of flux and that my being will itself never attain its final form.[7]

Sieburg admits that it would be easier for him and for those around him if he could make a decision between the two attitudes, but finds it impossible to make such a decision and declares that the whole predicament is 'the real Either–Or of our times, which cannot and should not be decided'.[8] It is certainly the real Either–Or for those German writers who share Sieburg's attitudes; even far more significant figures such as Thomas Mann and von Hoffmansthal found themselves involved in similarly endless chains of dualistic thinking when they tried to comment on the political situation and to establish the fundamental differences between Germany and France. Towards the end of *Germany: my country* Sieburg concludes that the true essence of Germany can perhaps only be captured in deeds or poems and thus virtually admits that he has failed totally in what he set out to do. In effect he is admitting that he does not possess a language to describe the Germany in which he is living – the Weimar Republic. Friedrich Sieburg was a foreign correspondent long before he left Germany.

Notes

[1] Friedrich Sieburg, *Is God a Frenchman? or the Gospel of St Joan. A German study of France in the Modern World* (trans. Alan Harris), London and Toronto, 1931. Future references will be to this edition and will be given in the text as *IGF*, with page numbers. The German edition is *Gott in Frankreich? Ein Versuch*, Frankfurt a.M., 1929.

[2] Friedrich Sieburg, *Germany: my country* (trans. Winifred Ray), London and Toronto, 1933. Future references will be to this edition and will be given in the text as *GMC*, with page numbers. The German edition is *Es werde Deutschland*, Frankfurt a.M., 1933.

[3] Karl August Horst, 'Innerer Dialog', *Frankfurter Allgemeiner Zeitung*, 19 May 1973. (My translation).

[4] *Ibid.*

[5] *Es werde Deutschland*, p. 43. (This passage does not appear in the English version).

[6] 'Innerer Dialog', *op. cit.*

[7] *Ibid.*

[8] *Ibid.*

HERBERT SCHERER
Translated by PETER and MARGARET LINCOLN

The individual and the collective in Döblin's *Berlin Alexanderplatz*

The decline of the individual as an historically powerful figure had – owing to the conditions of production within large-scale capitalist industry – previously affected intellectuals for the most part only as observers, but with the advent of the first world war it became their own existential experience. As conscripts they too were made slaves of the machine in a war where battles of attrition allowed no room for individual heroism and where technological equipment alone was the decisive factor. Against this background the subjective outcry of Expressionism can be understood as a final impotent rebellion by an intelligentsia which was no longer willing to communicate its problems to a wider public, but was in the process of retreating into its own circle. This is one side of the coin.

The other is supplied by the reception of the Russian revolution. Here the claim was made that it was possible to erect a new social order in which collective interests should be allowed to assume absolute predominance over the separate interests of the individual. The reaction of the bourgeois intellectuals was ambivalent. Fascinated on the one hand by what they felt to be a utopian offer of an optimistic answer to the historical pessimism that had already overcome them, they could not on the other hand identify with a model of society geared to the class interests of the industrial worker while promising themselves as a group no perspective of their own.

Throughout the entire period of the Weimar Republic German writers were attempting to establish their position within the framework set up by these initial points of reference. Their stances range accordingly between individualistic escapism (Hesse's *Siddhartha*), the formation of elitist groups (the George circle), and the ready enrolment in the collective (League of Proletarian Revolutionary Writers, BPRS). The longer and more contradictory the process of self-definition is for an author, the greater chance there is that the problems associated with this process will be made into a theme within his work. A prominent example of this is Bert Brecht, who, having chosen to adopt a collectivist position and to align himself with the Communists, was nevertheless unable to leave behind the Expressionist individualism of his early works without a certain sense of quiet sadness,[1] and for whom the question of the relationship between the individual and the collective occupied a central position even in his extremely partisan didactic plays ('Lehrstücke'). In contrast to Brecht, who, although he continued to reflect this problem, had in fact unequivocally made up his mind, Alfred Döblin felt unable to reach a decision. This becomes apparent in *Berlin Alexanderplatz* (1929)[2] even more than in his theoretical writings, and it is thus our aim to study this novel as an example within the context of this viewpoint.

The title of the novel is intended to suggest that it is not the depiction of an individual destiny which is here at issue, but rather the representation of a 'milieu' which leaves its decisive imprint on the fates of the characters who are active within it. Yet it is an individual destiny which takes the central position. The one-time convict Franz Biberkopf, with whom the novel is concerned, is depicted very much as an outsider. In contrast to most of the other 'people around the Alex', who are part of the masses and whose life is almost exclusively determined by their milieu, Biberkopf possesses strong individual peculiarities. When it is said of the ordinary mass of people that 'To reckon them all up and to describe their fate is scarcely possible – it could only succeed with a few' (p. 147) it appears to be precisely Biberkopf's role as outsider which provides the precondition enabling a novel to be written about him. This supposition is confirmed at the end of the novel, during the course of which all Biberkopf's peculiarities have been systematically and at times violently driven out of him, with the result that he is now merely 'an insignificant worker'. It is now said of him; 'After the trial Biberkopf is offered a job as an assistant porter in a factory of average size. He accepts it. We have nothing further to report here about his life' (p. 409). The novel does not describe the collective fate of those around the Alexanderplatz, but rather the tortuous path of an individual's destruction which leads to his final integration into the collective. The life of the collective man himself is not suitable literary material.

Although one may already detect a certain contradition at this point between the alleged intention and its realisation, Döblin's position does appear at this level to be still quite unambiguous. Closer inspection shows that it is more complicated.

In a letter written to the literary critic Julius Petersen on 18 September 1931 Döblin reports that he originally intended to write a second novel, a continuation of *Berlin Alexanderplatz*, dealing with the transformed Biberkopf. Biberkopf was here to have developed from a passive sufferer into being an active participant:

In *Berlin Alexanderplatz* I really intended to bring Franz Biberkopf to a second phase, – I did not succeed. Against my will the book ended in this way simply due to the logic of the action and the plan; it was beyond hope – the dice were loaded against me.[3]

Döblin was unable to resolve the problem he established here, either in his novels or subsequently in his theoretical writings. Strictly speaking, this does not really concern an isolated problem but rather a whole bundle of contradictions which can be traced back to Döblin's ideological and political position.

While it is true that Döblin ostentatiously rejects the genre of the bourgeois 'Entwicklungsroman' (the novel of an individual's development or progress) both through the title of the novel as well as through other formal techniques such as the process of 'picking out' (there are, for instance, scenes in the novel in which the narrator observes the surroundings of the Alexanderplatz from a bird's-eye view in order to pick out individuals from the crowd apparently at random and briefly to sketch their life story[4]), yet the ideological experience of environmental conditioning and of the relative impotence of the isolated individual which underlies this rejection is to be found only intermittently in Döblin's work. On the one hand he accepts this as a general insight, but at the same time he proclaims his intention to disregard it when he informs us of his attempts to make an 'active man' out of Biberkopf in the end.[5] Against his will these attempts were not to be realised. Proof that Döblin was here faced with a real *aporie*, and was not merely flirting with a mock failure in the manner of an ironist, which he also was, may be deduced in two ways. Firstly, the conclusion of the published version of the novel differs considerably in its intention from the so-called 'Marbach manuscript version'[6] – showing that Döblin had intensively chiselled away at the conclusion – and secondly there is the statement which he made in a letter to Petersen. Here Döblin writes that in *Berlin Alexanderplatz* the 'self within nature' has prevailed over the 'self above nature', or in other words '... a more passive, receptive element with tragic colouring over an active element which is more optimistic. ...'.[7] With this formulation he is alluding to the train of thought pursued in his 1927 piece on natural philosophy entitled 'The self above nature', in which he propagated the idea that the active overcoming of the world provides the possibility of resolving the contradiction between the self (subjectivity) and nature (objective determinative factors). The successful synthesis is here denoted by the formula 'self above nature', already referred to in the title and taken up again in the letter to Petersen. This synthesis, which also encompasses that of the individual and the collective, corresponds to the harmonious reconciliation of self and world towards which the 'Entwicklungsroman' had aimed. Thus there arises for Döblin an irreconcilable contradiction between his insight that it is no longer possible to write an 'Entwicklungsroman' in the old sense of the word and his adherence to its ideal presuppositions. In *Wissen und Verändern* (*Knowledge and Change*), written in 1931, Döblin's thoughts are still revolving around the idea of the 'active man', who would overcome the dualism of spirit and nature through the reciprocal interpenetration of these two poles. It is in this sense of the word 'active' that Döblin here proclaims the utopian 'new man':

The new man is above all active. One can see this above all else. Indeed, it is only his activity which makes him a real man – for he stands within the ongoing thrust of a spiritual nature and is a responsible participant in the process of its completion. In the spiritual realm of nature and society man is only real as one who is active and who responsibly changes himself and those around him. But here we also recognise a change in the concept 'active'. In this sort of spiritual-natural world 'active' can no longer mean simple mechanical action; it also means involvement, empathy and permeation; yes, life, enjoyment and existence itself attain new values – the new value of *activity*. Man is now no longer divided into two halves – the spiritual and religious as against the natural, political and bourgeois. In this nature and society there is only the whole man, his existence made whole through activity.[8]

The use of a formulation such as the 'whole man' to describe his goal leads one to suspect once again that Döblin, like the 'Entwicklungsroman', is concerned with the perfecting of the *single* person as an individual. This tendency can be inferred even more clearly from a circular written by Döblin shortly afterwards to the friends and acquaintances he had gathered around him in 1931–32 in the form of a literary-political circle. Here, after a short analysis of the political and ideological situation, the maxim is established: '*The liberation of the individual* for the purpose of dissolving old forms of restraint which impede true consciousness and activation'.[9]

It is becoming clear why Döblin is forced into insoluble difficulties at the end of the *Alexanderplatz* novel: the fact that he has once turned away from the 'Entwicklungsroman' and has directed his attention towards representing a milieu which determines the individual has consequences for the way in which the novel's figures are drafted. It is through these that the dependence of the individual upon external factors is demonstrated, and one cannot simply reverse the process of this demonstration at the end of the novel. This is partly due to the fact that the novelist has placed at the centre of his book a hero through whom he is able plausibly to put forward the thesis of dependence upon milieu, in other words a non-intellectual, a man who, although given to reflection, is not in a position to arrive at a conscious evaluation of his own difficulties. In contrast to this the 'Entwicklungsromane' usually have intellectual heroes with whom the novelists are bound by a strong sense of identification. These novels have, to a greater or lesser degree, the function of progressively building up the ideal self of their authors, whereas Döblin depicts a hero from whom he is somewhat distant. For this reason he is not governed by the need to achieve the goal which would correspond to his ideal self. As may be inferred from the discussions held in 1931–32 in the Berlin Döblin circle, Döblin formulates his general notion of the 'active, whole man' as at present being a directly attainable daily goal only for the 'spiritual' ('die Geistigen'), that class of intellectuals among whom he counts himself but not the hero of novel, Biberkopf:

The development of mankind is borne by those who, as a witnessing element, are treading new paths. These are the spiritual from all peoples and all classes.[10]

In a certain sense, then, the conclusion of *Berlin Alexanderplatz* does not contradict Döblin's ideological position, which is orientated around the bourgeois ideal of education and development. His general ideal for humanity is not refuted by the fact that it is in the first instance realisable only for a minority.

The story of Franz Biberkopf is the story of an individual who is made to realise that he must first give up his ideals if he wants to get along in the world. These ideals take the form of his highly strained resolutions at the beginning of the novel to be 'respectable' from then on. He cannot put into practice that which is referred to as his 'aim in life' when confronted with the reality of 'Berlin Alexanderplatz' as a place.

A summary of the story is already outlined in the preface: 'Franz Biberkopf is forcibly subjected to a course of treatment. At the end we see the man once again standing on the Alexanderplatz, very changed, battered, and yet twisted into line' (p. 7). The process by which Biberkopf as an individual with a will of his own is made into a merely average sort of person accrues a negative value in the eyes of the author. This becomes apparent not only symbolically in the fact that Franz Biberkopf, or 'the fat one' as he is called at the beginning of the novel, loses an arm during the course of the story and thus becomes a partial cripple, but also in the way in which the narrator broadly summarises Biberkopf's resolutions in the preface – 'demanding more from life than one's bread and butter' (p. 7). At the end Biberkopf is one who 'demands no more than his bread and butter' and who therefore, along with his individual expectations of happiness, has also lost the individual traits which distinguish him from the average sort of person. He has become one of them. Even when the fictitious narrator evaluates this process in rather more positive terms, we are led to conclude that the novelist Döblin regards it as a negative one when we think of his positive goal of the 'whole, active man', which is the exact opposite of what Biberkopf has become by the end of the novel. This takes us right to the heart of Döblin's social-critical standpoint, for here in his evaluation of the relationship between the individual and society and in his confirmation of their incompatibility it becomes clear exactly which trends of social development Döblin surmises and how he responds to them.

The main point is the one which had already caused Döblin to depart from the old form of the 'Entwicklungsroman' – the recognition, that is, that the time when the individual was the driving force of history is past, and that a process has begun in which the collective and the masses take the leading role. In this respect it is important to bear in mind the further point that he wishes to see this trend as being only a transitional phase. He looks forward to the dawn of a new, non-egoistic, individualism. In a circular written on 22 December 1931 to the members of the Döblin circle on the theme of 'Society, the self and the collective' he sharply denounces any incorporation of the individual into collectives, whatever their structure, and suggests the following alternative to collectivism:

The individual comes to himself and in coming to himself he comes to the community [. . .] This is not a question of an individualism which aims at making the single person egoistic. Egoism is caused by the bad society itself, one which has broken the connection between man and man.[11]

Döblin sees no possibility in the collective for the self-realisation of the individual. He does not even go so far as to see the incorporation of the individual into the collective as being a necessary historical transitional stage through which one must pass in order to find in collectivism the basis of a new individualism. To this extent Döblin opposes trends of development whose cogent material basis is to be found in the development of technology. His social criticism has a basically conservative character. Such an assertion seems to be contradicted by Döblin's repeated profession of socialism,[12] and yet it is clear on closer inspection that he has worked out his own concept of socialism which is compatible with the anti-collective tenor of his ideas. In his *Wissen und Verändern* (1931) he propagates an 'ethical and utopian socialism' whose content should revolve around 'freedom, spontaneous human fraternity, rejection of all forms of coercion, rebellion against injustice and coercion, humanity, tolerance, peaceful disposition'.[13] For Döblin socialism is the ideal crystallisation of 'former bourgeois ideas of freedom'. In accordance with socialist tradition he challenges the 'spiritual' to ally themselves with the 'working class', which he describes in this context as 'the bearer of the former bourgeois ideas of freedom'.[14]

Even the reversal of a concept cannot simply set aside the meanings which resonate within it. The most important meaning contained within the concept of socialism, however, is precisely the idea of socialising the individual and the consequent shift of emphasis from individual to collective freedom and fulfilment. Thus, if Döblin does see himself as a socialist, it is not sufficient for him that the question of collectivisation be dismissed with a few polemical tirades. From this angle one could even see the abrupt vehemence with which he defends individualism in his circular 'Society, the self and the collective' as evidence of the direct way that Döblin felt affected by the problem of 'individual or collective?'. He does not seem to be in a position to arrive at a balanced viewpoint and so he becomes more and more entangled in the contradiction of wanting to be an individualist on the one side and a socialist on the other. Two passages from the circular mentioned above may be cited to illustrate the vehemence of Döblin's polemic:

False assumptions are being circulated about the role of society, the state, the community and the collective. It is being asserted with differing degrees of intensity that society, the State, the community and the collective are everything and that you are nothing [...] They form organisations, parties, hordes of various kinds, get themselves uniforms and weapons just like the despots and absolutists of former times, and they demand that you join up with them – otherwise you are nothing, or even a semi-criminal.

You must guard yourself against these masses. They are the evil of today and a real hindrance to a human existence. They are arrogant and disrupters of the peace and above all they are despots and absolutists appearing in a new and indestructible form. Whether they call themselves the emperor, the State or the collective do not be deceived, they all mean the same – they want to swallow you up.

Whoever wishes to remove from the self, the single person, the individual, his obligation to existence, the responsibility for his life, whoever makes such demands of him or even shamelessly maintains that it is only in these collectives and institutions that the self becomes self, that the self is fulfilled, and that I myself need not worry – whoever does this is practising a malicious act of deception and falsification.[15]

The fact that behind these sentences expressing an unequivocal rejection of collectivism the forcibly suppressed antithesis of this rejection is secretly making its claims felt, can, to be sure, scarcely be deduced from the sentences themselves. Such an assumption does suggest itself, however, when the claim it makes is once again compared with the conclusion of *Berlin Alexanderplatz*. There it becomes clear that this unequivocal position cannot even be realised through the playful, fictional command of reality that is possible for a novelist. (How much less, then, one would wish to add, in the world of political reality itself.) In the last pages of the novel *Berlin Alexanderplatz* Döblin's contradictory relationship to collectivism finds conspicuous expression when he allows Biberkopf to reflect upon his new situation, which is determined by the fact that as 'a simple worker' he is no longer an outsider but rather moves according to collective patterns. Döblin allows Franz Biberkopf on the one hand to be totally sceptical of the collective, when for instance he writes:

I don't swear that quickly by anything in the world. My dear fatherland, you can rest assured that I have my eyes open and will not fall in that quickly. They often march with flags and music and singing past his window, but Biberkopf looks coolly out of his door and remains quietly at home for a long time. Shut your mouth and step in line, march with the rest of us and you'll be fine. If I march then afterwards I'll have to pay with my head for what others have thought out for themselves. For that reason I reckon everything up first, and when it comes to the point and it suits my wishes I'll act accordingly. With his mind a man is skilled, asses form themselves into a guild. [p. 410]

The end of this quotation clearly echoes the wording of the circular of 22 December 1931 mentioned above (for example, 'They form organisations, parties, hordes of various kinds'). Here Döblin is expressing a part of his own opinion through the mouth of Biberkopf, although this résumé is relativised by the fact that, as a result of the development of the novel, it is not an 'active individual' but rather the broken, former individual, Biberkopf, who is here speaking. Whereas in Döblin's own discussion of this problem the renunciation of the collective is bound up with its positive counterpart, the strong individual, for Biberkopf it remains a negative renunciation, a sceptical destruction of the last hope of happiness which remains to him as one who has become one of the masses – the hope that one might free oneself together with the mass of other men and create new power as part of the collective.

On the other hand Döblin allows the assistant porter Franz Biberkopf to be gripped and influenced time and time again by this hope of happiness in the face of great scepticism, so that at the end one is left with an impression of inconclusiveness. For Franz Biberkopf the rejection of the collective does not unequivocally outweigh his hopes for it. It is rather the cause that each side of this contradictory situation serves to relativise the other. Prior to the passage last cited there are also passages in the novel such as these:

At the end he is an assistant porter in a factory of average size. He no longer
stands alone on the Alexanderplatz. There are some to the right of him and to
the left of him. Some are walking in front of him and some are walking behind
him. It causes a lot of unhappiness when one walks alone. When there are
several it is already quite different. [p. 409]

He is an assistant porter in a factory. What then is his fate? One is stronger than
I. When there are two of us it becomes more difficult to be stronger than I. When
there are ten of us even more difficult. When there are a thousand of us and a
million, then it is extremely difficult.
But it is also much finer and better to be with others. For then I feel and know
everything just that much better. [p. 409]

The sceptical retraction of hope in the community which was quoted
above is then followed in the first place by a consideration of the
necessity of individual alertness, but this is reversed again a little later on
into thoughts about the collective:

Be alert, be alert, something is going on in the world. The world is not made out
of sugar. [. . .] Be alert, be alert, you are not alone. The heavens can hail and
pour, you can't protect yourself against that, but there are a lot of things you can
protect yourself against. [. . .] Be alert, open your eyes, at the ready, thousands
belong together, and whoever does not wake up will be ridiculed or done away
with. [p. 410]

The inconclusiveness extends right to the last sentences of the novel. The
first of the two sentences in the concluding apotheosis which is especially
made to stand out through the use of italics takes up the theme of militant
collectivism as follows: 'Freedom is on its way. Onward to freedom. The
old world must collapse, wake up to the dawn' (p. 411). This is then once
again retracted in the next sentence in so far as the optimistic mood is
reversed into what is basically a gloomy presentiment of catastrophe, in
spite of the fact that it is mitigated by irony ('march, march, we're off to
the war') (p. 411). The collective destiny is once more dissolved into
numerous individual destinies whose community consists only in their
relative arbitrariness: '[. . .] one has it easy, the other gets done, one gets
the rain, the other gets the sun, for the one resounds the trumpet, for the
other rolls the drum, tara*rum*' (p. 411). These are the last sentences of the
novel. In keeping his evaluation of the collective in the balance right to
the end Döblin does not completely eliminate the hope of a collective
form of self-realisation for those like Biberkopf who do not belong to the
'spiritual', for whom the author postulates the strong individual as a
possible means of solution.

    Although the development of the novel had frustrated the intention of
making Biberkopf himself into an 'active man', preventing the idea of the
'self above nature' from being propagated at the level of the novel's

content, there is nevertheless another level at which this intention is partially realised: the *form*. In the role of the omnipotent epic writer Döblin reserves a place for himself beyond the world of the collective. The conflict between the collective and the individual appears in the form of the novel as a conflict between objectivity and subjectivity. Through the very title *Berlin Alexanderplatz*, denoting not a fictitious but a real place known to all his readers, or through the technique of montage, that is, the insertion of direct snippets of reality,[16] the author suggests a particular objectivity of representation. Diametrically opposed to this is the playful irony with which he constantly shifts the narrative perspective, with which he uses various associations to involve himself in the plot, or with which he demonstrates his creative omniscience through firm statements that span decades of the future destiny of the novel's subsidiary characters. Döblin tackles this problem theoretically in his essay 'The construction of the epic work' which he wrote at the same time as the novel *Berlin Alexanderplatz*. Here he writes: 'I demand that the epic form be made a totally free one, so that the author is able to follow all the possibilities of representation which his material demands. If his subject is intent upon lyrically dancing, he must let it lyrically dance.'[17] The necessity of liberating the epic form is here established from the angle of the subject; the reality with which an epic work is concerned should not be violated by formal constraints but, following its own regular pace, should be allowed as far as possible to infiltrate into the work. Yet with his next breath Döblin oversteps the scope of what he has already established by going on to argue:

From all sides authors experience the urgent call for actuality, for a literature of the present. Today, if we were quite honest, we would even say that we do not want any literature at all – it is a thing of the past, art is boring, we want facts and more facts. To this I say bravo and three times bravo. You do not have to parade your phantasy in front of me. [. . .] *The real poet has at all times been a fact in his own right.* The poet has to demonstrate and to prove that he is a fact and a part of reality [. . .].[18]

It is here that the logical transition from objectivity to subjectivity can be firmly located. His own subjectivity is referred to as that objective reality which the poet should allow to permeate his work the most fully. In the same essay Döblin describes the steps which he himself took to reach this position. Firstly, with reference to the 'so-called objectivity of the narrator', he had taken pains to incorporate facts directly into his poetic work; he had thereby felt something resembling a desire 'to transcribe complete official documents without alteration': 'Yes, I sometimes sank back in admiration among these documents and said to myself that I would not be able to do it any better'. There was a tendency with this procedure for his own self to become 'quite superfluous'. He had been unable to maintain this position, just as it cannot be consistently held in general. In other words, there necessarily comes a time when one discovers 'one's self' amid all the facts: 'I myself – that is the craziest and most confusing experience that an epic writer can have. At first it looks as though this is the experience which will be the death of him. But he sees himself in danger and in difficulties only until he sees that the work of art is the concern of the artist, that it is not the past which provides the laws but rather it is I who provide the law, and thus the epic work means something quite different for me.'[19] From this train of thought Döblin infers that it is permissible, or even vitally necessary, for the author to be present within his work: 'May the author speak within the epic work, is he to leap into this world? Answer: yes, he may and he should and must.'[20]

He follows this principle in *Berlin Alexanderplatz*. He does not merely recount a story but allows himself the liberty of indirectly commenting on it and presiding over it by means of parallel images from the Bible or concurrent plots, as in the slaughterhouse scenes. The most perfect form of this epic freedom is reflected by Döblin in those places where he uses the formal means of the inner monologue or free indirect speech ('erlebte Rede') as a way of apparently merging himself totally with the novel's characters and tracing their train of thought, and then suddenly, without any great transition, switches from the inner monologue of the characters to chains of association which cannot possibly be those of his characters, since they presuppose an entirely different cultural background – they are associations made by the epic writer himself. An example of this is when Biberkopf is standing in front of Minna's house, the sister of his former fiancée, and in an inner monologue is reflecting whether or not he should go to her:

Off he went. He strolled up and down in front of Minna's house. Mary sat alone upon a stone, quite alone. What do I care about her. [. . .] She should be happy with her old man. [. . .] The cats stink the same here as they do anywhere else. [. . .] Am I going to hang around here miserably looking at the house. And the whole bunch go cock-a-doodle-doo. Cock-a-doodle-doo. Cock-a-doodle-doo. Thus spoke Menelaus. And, without meaning to, he made Telemachus' heart so melancholy that tears rolled down his cheeks. [pp. 116–17]

The associations of the educated author continue, circling for a time around the Homeric figures, then turning to the subject of different types of hen.

Here the way in which the author is present in his work is directly deducible from the content. It would, however, be too shallow an interpretation if one were to limit the subjective tendencies of *Berlin*

Alexanderplatz to passages such as these. It is rather a basic structural feature of the whole novel, in as much as it casts off traditional forms and in this way allows the author to give free expression to his individual view of the world. This tendency in *Berlin Alexanderplatz* clearly stands in the tradition of Expressionism and Futurism, which, particularly in the plastic arts, developed a montage technique similar to that used by Döblin in his novel. In this way the subjectivity of the artist is supposed to achieve a direct form of expression in which elements of reality are arranged.

In *Berlin Alexanderplatz* fact is mounted next to non-fact. Döblin writes about this in his essay 'The construction of the epic work':

We are presented with the fact of marvellous, unbound, free invention. What do we mean by invention – the audacious, un-restrained reporting of non-facts, of notorious non-facts? It is the play with reality – in Nietzsche's words, a superior laughter over the facts, yes over reality as such.[21]

This play with reality is particularly ingenious wherever the novelist himself seems to disappear completely in order to see the world from the perspective of the characters he has created. In reality the apparent self-denial of the author is more like a playfulness which is carried to extremes. This playfulness is not an end in itself but also has a function within the content of the novel. In spite of his intention to give expression to his own self within the novel, the author nevertheless takes great pains to remain elusive. We can see this best in the way in which the figure of the narrator is brought to the fore. In *Berlin Alexanderplatz* a first-person narrator appears on the scene from time to time whose role is notable for the fact that firstly he neither introduces himself at the beginning of the novel nor does his character gain firm outlines later on, and secondly that he cannot be identified with the novelist himself. In other words he himself observes the events of the novel from a limited perspective, through which he acquires something approaching 'individual contours'. This phrase comes from Albrecht Schöne, upon whose thorough and pertinent description of the narrator figure in *Berlin Alexanderplatz* these remarks are largely based.[22] The individual contours of the narrator, which are still visible in those places where he appears as a type of ballad singer between each chapter, continually disappear, however, whenever he gives up the difference of language, for example, which separates him from the novel's characters and begins to speak their jargon and dialect – which also signifies a specific world view.[23]

That the character of the narrator should not be made responsible for the whole text of the novel, and that he should not be identified with its author, is clearly shown by the fact that his moral code is different from that of Döblin. One has only to think of the preface, in which the narrator represents Biberkopf's transformation as being in one sense a positive process, an evaluation which is diametrically opposed to that of Döblin:

At the end we see the man once again standing on the Alexanderplatz, very changed, battered, and yet twisted into line. To observe and to hear this will be rewarding for many who, like Franz Biberkopf, live in a human skin and who happen, like Franz Biberkopf, to ask for more from life than one's bread and butter. [p. 7]

The figure of the narrator inserted between the author, and the reader is used by the author as an additional, at the same time ironical, undermining of the novel's declared purpose, as a further playful means of evading a commitment.

Like the constant changes in the narrator's perspective, it aims at a position which represents the absence of all positions. This also has a political side which, for instance, is apparent in the novel when both Communists and National Socialists are depicted as being equally ludicrous types. The author's ironical unwillingness to take up a position leads him to see the unyielding commitment of both these movements as being tarred with the same brush, despite their fundamental differences. This clarifies a stance which Döblin in 1932 – in the so-called 'Döblin circle' – seriously upholds as being politically practicable. In a circular of 4 July 1932 he justifies his refusal to compose a political manifesto as follows:

In the light of the enormous tension of the present day and the confrontation between two powers, any manifesto must contain specific and unequivocal words minted for this situation. To step forward with only one viewpoint, without having tested it in a particular situation, would be feeble. It is wrong at this time publicly to put forward one front at the expense of other fronts. Whoever steps forward at this time and wishes to make an appeal, must make his appeal so as to lead to a decision for one of the two sides. This, however, is not the purpose governing us at the moment.[24]

Döblin's social critique is concerned, in the final analysis, not with the criticism of specific ills within the social framework, having as its goal the intervention in political events, but rather with maintaining a critical position which affirms the place of the powerful individual on the other side of political polarities and the totality of social contradictions. Because the individual acting as an individual no longer carries any historical weight, the sphere of his power may be located only on the other side of the real contradictions. With this we come back once again to the problem of the individual or the collective.

In reflective intellectual activity a sphere is found where, even in the twentieth century, despite all development towards collectivity the individual can hold his own. For himself as a novelist Döblin sees beyond this to the possibility of being not merely contemplative in this attitude but creative. In the essay 'The construction of the epic work' he places the poet, who allows his creative fantasy free play, at the side of the 'creator of the world'. Thus Döblin sees the creative act of the artist as being an act of highest self-realisation. To those who are not artists the reception of the work of art brings with it the possibility of participating in this act of rising above the pressures of reality:

Here one [the poet] competes with this stony, firm, and solid reality, and conjures away at it, blowing soap-bubbles from that same substance with which the creator once made the whole of this heavy earth, the heavens, and all animals and their destinies. We are on the very proud and very worthy territory of free fantasy.

[. . .] There everything that may be thought of becomes possible.

[. . .] Poetry is more than a dream. The dream also plays with reality, but for our emotions it is still fatally and tediously bound up with reality. In poetry the levity, the mockery of reality is complete. This is the fantastic gain in pleasure which the art of inventive writing assures, for the author as well as for the listener.[25]

This way of thinking is conventional if viewed within the framework of the German artistic tradition since the Romantics. That which one strives for in reality, in Döblin's words the 'self above nature', is seen to be realised in a utopian way in the work of art, although its realisation admittedly is limited to the form. The heavy weight of reality within the novel's content successfully resists Döblin's attempts to overplay this formally. It is precisely the unreconciled contradictory ending, contradicting its programmatic aims, which constitutes the realism of this novel. Döblin remains honest in that he does not use the novel's fiction to bring an over-hasty, illusory solution to the dilemma in which he feels himself to be caught.

This does not mean to say that we accept Döblin's position. In the end it lets him down when brought before real historical demands. In the face of increasing fascism it would not have been sceptical individualism but only a militant decisiveness to act collectively which would have been able to achieve anything. With the emigration into which he was forced a few years later Döblin had to pay bitterly for omissions which were also his own. But at this point political criticism of Döblin's position and literary criticism have to part company. It would be wrong to expect a solution to the novel which in reality the author was not in a position to give. If one accepts this premise one can again direct one's attention to the decisive quality of the novel, which is that through its realistic content and unconcealed demonstration of the problem it comes nearer to a solution – even a political one – than Döblin's illusory theoretical pronouncements.

Notes

[1] Garga's last words in *Im Dickicht der Städte* run significantly: 'The chaos has been used up. Those were the best times.' (B. Brecht, *Gesammelte Werke* I (Werkausgabe), Frankfurt a.M., 1967.)

[2] Alfred Döblin, *Berlin Alexanderplatz* (dtv edn), Munich, 1969, All page references for *Berlin Alexanderplatz* given in the text are to the dtv edition, Munich, 1969.

[3] Alfred Döblin, letter to Julius Petersen of 18 September 1931. Quoted from Leo Kreutzer, *Alfred Döblin, sein Werk bis 1933*, Stuttgart, 1970.

[4] Döblin, *Alexanderplatz*, p. 46, pp. 105 ff.

[5] Letter to Petersen, quoted from Kreutzer, p. 114.

[6] The manuscript version is named after the place where it is being kept, i.e. the Schiller-Nationalmuseum in Marbach. On this point see also Helmut Becker, *Untersuchungen zum epischen Werk Alfred Döblins am Beispiel seines Romans 'Berlin Alexanderplatz'* – diss., Marburg, 1962, pp. 156–77.

[7] Letter to Petersen, quoted in Kreutzer, p. 114.

[8] Alfred Döblin, *Wissen und Verändern (Knowledge and Change)*, Berlin, 1931, p. 87.

[9] Alfred Döblin, circular relating to discussion of 29 October 1931, quoted from Kreutzer, p. 150.

[10] *Ibid.*, p. 159.

[11] Döblin, circular of 22 December 1931, quoted from Kreutzer, pp. 153–4.

[12] *Cf.* Leo Kreutzer, p. 141.

[13] Döblin, *Wissen und Verändern*, p. 27.

[14] *Ibid.*, p. 58.

[15] Döblin, circular of 22 December 1931, quoted from Kreutzer, pp. 152–3.

[16] As, for example, tramway maps, telephone directory pages (*Alexanderplatz*, pp. 40–1), newspaper announcements (*Alexanderplatz*, p. 69), or a letter which he himself received from a patient (*cf.* Becker, *Untersuchungen zum epischen Werk Alfred Döblins*, p. 171, the manuscript version of the novel, p. 388, and *Alexanderplatz*, pp. 275–6.)

[17] Döblin, 'Der Bau des epischen Werkes' (The construction of the epic work) in *Aufsätze zur Literatur*, Olten and Freiburg, 1963, p. 115.

[18] *Ibid.*, p. 115.

[19] *Ibid.*, p. 114.

[20] *Ibid.*

[21] Döblin, 'Der Bau des epischen Werkes', p. 109.

[22] *Cf.* Albrecht Schöne, 'Döblins *Berlin Alexanderplatz*', in Benno von Wiese, *Der deutsche Roman*, vol. 2, Dusseldorf, 1963, pp. 322 ff.

[23] *Cf.* Döblin, *Alexanderplatz*, p. 194.

[24] Döblin, circular of 4 August 1932, quoted from Kreutzer, p. 160.

[25] Döblin, 'Der Bau des epischen Werkes', pp. 109–10.

STEPHEN LAMB

Ernst Toller and the Weimar Republic

The name of the writer Ernst Toller is still today most readily associated
with the period referred to as late Expressionism, or Activism, a fact due
in no small measure to the preponderance in research published both in
German and English[1] of attention paid to Toller's first two works, *Die
Wandlung* (1919) and *Masse Mensch* (1921), and above all to the
interest both contemporarily and subsequently aroused by his active
involvement in the abortive Munich Räterepublik of the spring of 1919.
Indeed, when critics do move outside this early formative period it is
invariably to consider those works produced during the Weimar
Republic which cast further light on the experiences of the November
revolution. These works include in the dramatic sphere *Hinkemann*
(1923), which examines the problems of reintegration into post-war
society experienced by an emasculated soldier returning from the battle
front, *Hoppla, wir leben!* of 1927, where again the theme is that of the
alienation of the individual disillusioned by the reality of post-war
Weimar society, and *Feuer aus den Kesseln* (1930), a dramatic
reconstruction, based freely on historical documents, of the events
leading up to the judicial murder of the two main protagonists in the Kiel
mutiny of 1917, considered by many historians to be the turning point of
the Wilhelmenian era.

This emphasis on Toller's early period, both directly and indirectly,
must be evaluated both positively and negatively. Positively in the sense
that it establishes the important fact not only that Toller's view of the
political reality of the Weimar Republic was conditioned by his
experiences in the immediate post-war years (he was for ever contrasting
the actuality of political social and intellectual life during the republic
with the expectations he and many others had shared at its inception) but
also in the crucial sense that Toller's own development in many ways
exemplified the belief of a generation of writers and intellectuals that the

failure of the republic was due precisely to its inability to break with the traditions of a past which represented their own formative years.

Negatively in the sense that this emphasis has meant a neglect of Toller's significant contribution to the intellectual and political life of the Weimar Republic, with the result that only a partial, if not distorted, picture of Toller as intellectual and dramatist has emerged. It is the intention in what follows to show that this picture has suffered not only as a result of such neglect but also as a result of the inability of the two predominant, and indeed often conflicting, schools of critics to come to terms with someone whose whole approach to questions such as the role of the writer in society largely defies attempts at categorisation. The spectrum of criticism ranges from assertions such as 'Toller would have aligned himself with the West'[2] through the metaphysical assertion that his real preoccupation was 'the age-old question as to the reality of life'[3] to the dismissal of all claims by Toller himself to merit the appellation 'socialist writer':

As an artist he was incapable of portraying the problems which were important to him and vital to the proletariat. It is therefore wrong to characterise Toller as a socialist writer. He never progressed beyond the stage of a bourgeois revolutionary democrat.[4]

Before progressing to a discussion of Toller's attitudes as mediated by his publications and speeches during the Weimar Republic, in which hopefully the severe limitations of such categorical approaches mentioned above will be revealed, it would seem useful to outline the biographical facts of his activity during the period in question.

The time of his active involvement in the affairs of the republic did not in fact start until the pattern of events had already been well established, since he was not released from prison until 15 July 1924, after serving the whole of his sentence for his participation in the 'Räterepublik'. 'Active' is used here in the wider sense, as Toller, no doubt as a result of his disillusionment with party politics, did not align himself with any particular party after his release from prison. Whether he would have rejoined the Independent Social Democratic Party on his release must remain a matter for speculation, since the USPD had merged with the majority Social Democrats during his period of imprisonment. The only record of any organised activity is his membership of the 'Gruppe revolutionärer Pazifisten' (Group of Revolutionary Pacifists), led by Kurt Hiller, which he joined in 1929. Otherwise he preferred to carry out a freelance role, as is evidenced by his extensive travels to Palestine, Egypt, the Soviet Union, England, France, Mexico, the United States and Spain. However, his decision to renounce party politics did not mean an aversion to politics as such, merely a wish to retain what he considered complete independence of thought and action, a question to which we will return later when discussing the precise nature of Toller's political views and his understanding of himself as a writer and intellectual. Although it would have been more than understandable if Toller had, as a result of the failure of the 'writers' revolution',[5] become disillusioned not only with party politics but also with the very justification of a writer's assuming any public role whatsoever, all the evidence indicates an increasing if more detached concern with public affairs. This is revealed not only in the thematics of his dramatic work, which will be considered presently, but also in the frequency of his public appearances. Only a month after his release from prison, for instance, he was guest of honour at a trades union festival in Leipzig, where his 'Massenfestspiel' *Erwachen (Awake)* had its première. His work *Quer Durch*, published in 1930, contains, apart from reports of his travels in the USA and the Soviet Union, transcripts of various speeches made between 1925 and 1930, together with articles previously published in newspapers and periodicals. He was a frequent contributor to the left-wing periodical *Die Weltbühne*, which carried a series of his articles called 'Documents on Bavarian justice'. These documents were intended to demonstrate the class nature of justice in Bavaria – obviously a major preoccupation of Toller's, since he and many of his comrades were victims of it – and were published in book form in 1927.[6]

This concern during the republic with an issue whose origins lay in the period of limbo immediately after the first world war is indeed a clear example of what was referred to earlier as the positive aspect of literary criticism's emphasis of Toller's early life, since it exemplifies the essence of the writer's general response to the reality of the Weimar Republic, which is best summarised as a belief that little of substance had really changed from pre-war Germany, that the social and economic structure was qualitatively the same – in other words, that the immense personal sacrifices of the war and the revolution had largely been in vain. This general response had already been formulated in gaol in 1921:

My German motherland is not on the path to spiritual and intellectual recovery. Military barbarism, the plague of corruption, the disease of servility are eating away at the body. Horrifying splits in the labour movement. Sectional hatred of every other point of view. The battalions of reaction are growing in strength. And every measure taken by the Allies which is governed by the contemptible old ideas of revenge and suppression is guaranteed to encourage them.[7]

This belief that the forces of militarism and nationalism, forces which had dominated the political life of Wilhelminian Germany, were again representing a real threat to the spirit of the new republic finds repeated expression in letters written in prison. In the summer of 1922 he was particularly struck by an article in *Die Weltbühne*:

See how the nationalist battalions and the 'Fehme' [extreme right-wing assassination squads] have been getting together! What hope is there? I can't get this article out of my mind. What it describes is a symptom. As it was, as it is, as it ... as it surely soon will be again in Germany. The work of Sisyphos. Or maybe not? Perhaps we ought not to ask such a question? Is the question itself not already a sign of lack of faith? We must do what is necessary. And even if we were to struggle in vain, there will be others to follow us. A struggle against centuries will not be decided in a few years.[8]

Toller's "struggle" against restauration at this early stage took the form of a play, *Der entfesselte Wotan* (*Odin Unchained*), which was first published in 1924.[9] This play, which has gone largely unnoticed by critics, represents a remarkably perceptive satirical critique of incipient National Socialism, and it is to Toller's credit that he was sufficiently aware of the movement to warn of its dangers at such an early stage in its development.

Toller's didactic purpose becomes clear in the brief prologue, in which the god Wotan warns the audience against the temptation of taking the play too much at its face value, that is, simply as a comedy:

O audience! Laugh not too soon!
For once you laughed too late
and paid for your blindness with living corpses.
Laugh not too soon! But – laugh at the right time! [p. 8]

This is further underlined by the dedication ('To the ploughmen'), a reference to the bitter remark in Act I of the disillusioned young worker that 'every field of corpses is fertile territory for the ploughman' (p. 17). The ability of the demagogue to exploit dissatisfaction amongst wide sections of the population (significantly the working class is excluded from this, although it can be argued that the exclusion is motivated not so much by ideological reasons as by a desire for historical accuracy) is exemplified in the play by the remarkably rapid success which the petty-bourgeois barber Wotan experiences in attracting recruits to his 'Office of the Co-operative for Emigrants to Brazil'. For Wotan, the frustrated idealist with delusions of grandeur, Brazil is a symbol of the Promised Land. He sees himself as a Messiah who will rescue Europe from its impending decline and fall. But to his backers, retired army officers, an out-of-work salesman, members of the aristocracy and a banker, he represents much more. They see in his apparent charisma and ambitions a potential power base, a means of regaining the political power and influence they looked like losing with the collapse of the monarchy in 1918. Schleim, whose credentials seem to Wotan impeccable ('A member of the League of Teutobold, I organised the Fehme'), impresses on Wotan the need for 'Realpolitik', by which he means a cynical appeal to all sections of the population, and the scrupulous avoidance of specific plans or strategy. (In reply to Wotan's question 'Shall I elaborate any content?' Schleim warns Wotan: 'You must be extremely careful! There are always people about who can read. Just describe the advantages and the splendour of it all' (p. 41).) This, together with Wotan's professed rejection of any ideology ('No party, no parliament, no communism can rescue Europe!') bears a striking resemblance to significant features of incipient National Socialism, above all the calculated exploitation of legitimate grievances and the scrupulous eschewing of a consistent and coherent policy.[10]

Indeed, it would be impossible within the confines of this short paper to detail and document all the characteristic features of National Socialism to which Toller draws our attention in this work. We must content ourselves with an enumeration of the most striking. These include the contradictory relationship with organised capital (on the one hand the professed anti-capitalist stance: 'We extend a welcome to all whose wings have been sucked under by the pestilential mire of servitude to interest rates ['Zinsknechtschaft'], the mire of the reddest materialism' (p. 40) and on the other bitter opposition to the Communist Party: Schleim reassures the American journalist, 'Any hankering on the part of members of the co-operative after communism is forestalled by the contract . . . Self-administration . . . democracy . . . our ears are closed to that kind of talk' [p. 50]). As was the case with National Socialism itself, this anti-capitalist stance is contradicted by the actual reliance on financial support from banking circles and industry. Added to this is the emphasis on expansion: Wotan explains that Brazil, the original focal point of his plans, was really only a means of attracting initial interest:

Brazil can only be a stepping-stone for me. A step on the road to the totality of the world. I will divide up the world into four areas . . . Each area will be divided into sub-sections, each sub-section into allotments . . . The whole will be organised by a central office. My plan will include the building of an army and navy, which, equipped with all the advances of modern technology, will become a formidable weapon at my disposal. [p. 51]

Apart from the obvious anticipation of the doctrine of 'Lebensraum', it is remarkable how Toller at such an early date prophesies with such accuracy the vast programme of rearmament which Hitler undertook a decade later on his accession to power, and without which the enactment of the policy of 'Lebensraum' could not have been achieved. One of the mainsprings of this policy was, of course, anti-semitism, and again it is remarkable how Toller highlights this as a central aspect of National

Socialism. Like Hitler, Wotan finds the Jews a convenient scapegoat:

The Jews are to blame! The three hundred elders of Zion! I could have achieved my European, indeed my world mission but for them! See how they cover their hooked noses with gold! See how they drag the blue-eyed Germanic heroine into their filthy bed. [p. 15]

This portrayal of the political and ideological aspects of National Socialism is accompanied by some incisive insights into the nature of the authoritarian personality, although it must be stressed that Toller avoids the weakness of other more famous satires on the phenomenon,[11] in that he refuses to focus exclusively on the charismatic personality as such, preferring to highlight the political and social circumstances which provided the preconditions for such 'false Messiahs' to exercise such fascination for wide sections of the population.[12] It is this contextualisation which makes Toller's approach so compelling. At a time when Hitler was attending his 'university at the State's expense',[13] Toller's Wotan was proclaiming slogans ('In work joy and pain we are united') which are ominously reminiscent of Nazi phrases such as 'Work is freedom' and 'Strength through joy', and warning the world, shortly before his imprisonment as a result of the initial failure of his plans, that he will write his memoirs, prophetically entitled 'The stab in the back shortly before the goal', which will serve as a 'final warning to Europe'. This book will be the salvation of Europe from collapse . . . I will achieve my mission' (p. 61).

Having looked at *Der entfesselte Wotan* and observed Toller's acute perception of the dangers of right-wing reaction, we can turn to what is perhaps Toller's most differentiated statement on the complexities of political life in the Weimar Republic, namely *Hoppla, wir leben!*[14] For it is here that Toller draws on his first-hand experience of events in the '20s, and manages most successfully to give dramatic shape to the whole spectrum of political life, which includes, for example, the location of nationalism within its wider social context. The use of related media, for example film, an increasingly potent force in Weimar culture,[15] means that Toller is able to invest his examination of issues with a degree of specificity which was not always evident in his earlier, more abstract works. The Filmic Interlude, for example, with its use of a screen on to which is projected a list of decisive steps in the development of the republic, allows him to surmount the problem of how to draw the audience's attention to the significance of internal and external political events without overburdening the work with information and thereby sacrificing the predominant conviction which he believed essential in any work of art. Indeed, it was this guiding sense of inner conviction

('Gesinnung'), which raises the work above the level of pure mimetic realism and thus separates it from the dominant contemporary trend of 'Neue Sachlichkeit' which Toller found so weak.[16] The key to Toller's approach to the Weimar Republic is indeed contained in the very title of the work in question, a reference to a popular song of the period often played on the wireless. The song encapsulates an attitude prevalent in Weimar Germany, namely the sentiment that life is as it is, that one should resign oneself to it and not seek to change it. It is the expression of a superficial cultural gaiety, which concealed and even repressed a confused, complex and highly contradictory political reality characterised by Franz Neumann as a system of pluralism.[17] The use of the term 'pluralism' by Neumann is by no means original, for, as R. Hinton Thomas and Wilfried van der Will have pointed out,[18] the first attempt at a definition was made as early as 1904, albeit from a philosophical point of view. What is interesting about Neumann's use of the term however, is that for the first time it is used to describe the political, social and economic structure of the Weimar Republic as an ideal type, that is to say, in accordance with the aspirations of those who drafted the constitution of the republic:

Compromise among all social and political groups was the essence of the Weimar constitution. Antagonistic interests were to be harmonised by the device of a pluralistic political structure, hidden behind the form of a parliamentary democracy. Above all, there would be an end to imperialistic expansion. Republican Germany would find full use for its productive apparatus in an internationally organised division of labour. [p. 18]

As Neumann says, the rationale of this pluralistic conception was the reduction of the role of the State in the regulation of social affairs to that of a mediator in all conflicts between various groups with conflicting interests. 'Pluralism conceives of the State not a sovereign unit set apart from and above society but as one social agency among many, with no more authority than the Churches, trade unions, political parties or occupational and economic groups' (p. 19). Underlying this aim of depriving the State of the power to promote any factional interests was the desire to re-establish in the individual a feeling of importance, a belief that it is possible to influence the course of events, either as an individual or as a member of a political party or pressure group:

Underlying the pluralist principle was the uneasiness of the impotent individual in the face of the all-too-powerful State machine. As life becomes more and more complicated and the tasks assumed by the state grow in number, the isolated individual increases his protests against being delivered up to forces he can neither understand nor control. [p. 19]

The pluralist theory of social organisation is therefore the response of 'individual liberalism' (p. 19) to the increasing isolation and alienation of the individual in an industrial society which threatens to become more and more anonymous as a result of increasing rationalisation of the forces of production and distribution. However, as Neumann has pointed out, this theory contained a serious flaw, a flaw which was to be of decisive influence on the eventual fate of the republic: a fundamental premise of the theory was the existence of a wide degree of understanding between all social groups involved concerning ultimate goals, together with a relatively equally distributed degree of power and influence. In other words, the society needed to be basically harmonious. In the case of the ill fated Weimar Republic this was manifestly not so. In the first place, the crucial article 165 of the constitution, which aimed at guaranteeing 'workers' representation to supervise production, distribution and the economic life of the nation' (p. 20) was never realised in practice, even though this was supposedly a cornerstone of the consensus between industry and organised labour and as such indispensable to the successful achievement of a truly pluralist society. Indeed, as Neumann suggests, it is reasonable to assume that this concession was made only to prevent further moves in the direction of socialism. The reality of Weimar Germany was a long way removed from the ideals of pluralism: enterprises such as Krupp, Stinnes, Siemens, etc, were far from equal partners in a national compact; the army, although nominally reduced in strength by the terms of the Versailles treaty, was still dominated by autocrats hostile to the republican ideal, and the judiciary was far from impartial in its treatment of political offenders.[19] In other words the political idealism of the founders of the republic foundered on the reality of its economic structure, and as long as the republic remained such a class society the harmony essential to the pluralist ideal was to remain a utopia. Far from allowing the individual a greater degree of influence in determining the course of events, the reality of the republic merely increased his isolation and feelings of impotence.

It is precisely this kind of problem which Toller thematicises in *Hoppla, wir leben!* The reality that confronts the revolutionary Karl Thomas, re-emerging into society after eight years of incarceration in an asylum, is that of a bewildering and amorphous multiplicity of possibilities which offer themselves to him. He feels so overwhelmed by the diffuseness of a society which differs fundamentally in structure and appearance from the one which he had struggled to achieve back in 1919 that he is forced to conclude that he is still in the lunatic asylum he thought he had left.[20]

Wilhelm Kilman, the former revolutionary turned Social Democrat Minister, embodies many of the bewildering contradictions of Weimar pluralism which characterise the society with which Karl Thomas seeks vainly to come to terms. In his first meeting with his former comrade Kilman emphasises his belief in his role as a government Minister mediating between capital and labour, whilst at the same time insisting that his disagreement with Karl Thomas is over means and not ends.[21] His commitment to a policy of gradualism, his pleas for moderation, which mask an underlying conservatism and the cynical emphasis on the need to avoid violence at all costs,[22] involve him necessarily in an antagonistic attitude towards the working class whose interests he sought to promote eight years earlier and claims to promote now. In a way which in many respects is reminiscent of *Masse Mensch*, Toller maintains a careful balance between the respective ideological approaches, scrupulously eschewing an elevated moral condemnatory stance. Increasingly in the '20s his primary concern was the highlighting of the complexities of the political situation as manifested in an immediate conflict between individuals. That this in itself did not mean a resigned acquiescence in the mere recording of such complexities is an aspect of Toller's world view we shall turn to presently. For the moment we must simply observe that for Toller drama became less and less the vehicle for the propagation of alternative approaches[23] and increasingly the means for an imaginative examination of as wide a spectrum as possible of Weimar Germany. In this specific sense Toller's approach to drama in the period after his release from prison merits the label 'realism', and it is this willingness to confront the reality of life and the issues it raises without resorting to simplistic solutions which characterises the depth of his development since the early utopianism of *Die Wandlung* and which indeed earned him the disapproval if not the resentment of many of his colleagues on the left.

This confrontation with certain unpalatable truths manifests itself in many other facets of *Hoppla*, not least his sober awareness of an unhappy congruence of interests between the left and the right in their attitudes to the Weimar Republic. The fact that Karl Thomas is pre-empted by a nationalist student in his attempt to shoot the 'traitor' Kilman and that Thomas automatically addresses the student as 'Comrade' is not just an ironic comment on the part of Toller, for he is here developing a theme whose treatment we have already observed in *Der entfesselte Wotan*, namely the very real threat which völkisch ideology poses in a situation of profound unrest. It is not coincidental that Pickel, the innocent from the country, who wanders on and off stage vainly seeking an audience with the Minister, Kilman, and who feels totally perplexed by the sheer anonymity of urban life, is an ex-soldier and a loyal member of his local League of Old Soldiers (Kriegerverein).

He represents, in other words, precisely the kind of disaffected and displaced ex-soldier from whom the Nazis were already in the early '20s drawing considerable support. The fact that the reason for his visit to the metropolis is a desire to register a protest against the building of a railway through his village is also not without significance: the Nazis were quick to exploit a profound distrust of all manifestations of urban industrialism amongst the rural proletariat.

Another aspect of the impersonality of the republic, which, as we have observed, contradicted the intentions of the designers of the Weimar constitution, was the irrelevance of parliamentary democracy to the man in the street. This is revealed in Act II in the action of the old woman whose only reason for voting at all is the fear of punishment, and who eventually makes her mark against the names of all three candidates, just to placate their respective advocates. Again Toller is not asking us here to accept uncritically the snap judgement of Karl Thomas that parliamentary democracy is simply an election fraud ('Wahlschwindel'), he is more concerned to register its considerable shortcomings and deficiencies.

The role of intellectuals in the Weimar Republic is subjected to equally sharp scrutiny. Behind the grandiose plans of the self-professed 'intellectual workers' ('geistige Kopfarbeiter') for 'spiritual redemption of the proletariat'[24] Toller reveals at best a deep-rooted elitism, and at worst a more sinister form of Social Darwinism latent in their attitude to the common man, on whose behalf their deliberations are supposedly being conducted.[25] That there is here more than a suspicion of self-criticism characteristic of all Toller's work is no doubt self-evident.

Toller, however, is no less critical in his assessment of the revolutionary potential of the proletariat. His sober (many would say defeatist)[26] attitude to the traditional subject of revolutionary change is, of course, a facet of his work which has its origins as early as *Masse Mensch*, although it does not become crystallised until *Die Maschinenstürmer* and *Hinkemann*. In the second of these works, written during his imprisonment, Toller's careful analysis of the response of workers to the introduction of industrial techniques in the specific case of Luddism in the early nineteenth century in Britain reveals a characteristic refusal to glorify the working class in the interests of proletarian solidarity. The didactic purpose of the work lies not only in Toller's warning against the contemporary facile anti-industrialism of works such as Georg Kaiser's *Gas* trilogy[27] but also in the appeal to the working class to guard against potential regressive tendencies manifested above all in the all-too-easy readiness to ascribe the causes of alienation to the process of industrialisation itself rather than to its real cause, namely its specific form of capitalist organisation.

This critical examination of the foibles of the individual worker as well as the proletariat as a social class, all the more surprising in view of the explicit dedication of *Masse Mensch* to the 'proletarians', is especially prominent in *Hinkemann*. Perhaps the most revealing example is a scene which in many ways anticipates the tenor of *Hoppla, wir leben!* As is always the case with Toller's dramatic work, the stage directions play a crucial part in the interpretation of the scene, since it is directed to be played 'like a nightmare for Hinkemann'. Hinkemann is depicted as surrounded by war cripples who at one and the same time appear to be closing in on him and yet remain distant from him. Their first action is to chant a military song from the first world war, but this is soon replaced by a revolutionary chant ('Down with the dogs of reaction'). However, the threat of police intervention immediately causes them to change their tune, and they revert to their original refrain, whilst significantly marching in different directions. This 'militärische Kehrtwendung' (military about-turn) is not 'counter-revolutionary' either in its intent or its essence, as has often been claimed.[28] Toller is here drawing our attention to an undeniable facet of recent political history, namely the divided loyalties of the labour movement at all levels – divided, that is, between loyalty to class and loyalty to country. Toller himself had experienced this conflict at first hand and had sought to articulate it in his semi-autobiographical first work, *Die Wandlung*, in which Friedrich comes to renounce his blind commitment to war – an attitude typical of the chauvinism of wide sections of the population in the early months of the conflict – in favour of a call to international revolution. The obligation to present a balanced view of the proletariat was for Toller a fundamental aspect of a politically committed writer's duties, and in his retrospective glance at the course of German history he interpreted the failure of 'vulgar Marxists' to take seriously the vulnerability of the working class to nationalist propaganda and ideology until it was too late as a decisive factor in the 'collapse of 1933'.[29] With more than a hint of the bitterness and disillusionment that led to his suicide in New York in 1939 he accuses contemporary writers of presenting an 'exaggerated image of the worker in his struggle' and of resigning in 'despair when confronted by the worker as he really is in all his weakness and strength, his pettiness and greatness'.[30]

It would be tempting to conclude from Toller's apparent concern for the fate of the individual in the complexity of post-war pluralist society, and from apparent disaffection with party politics resulting from his experiences in Munich, that he turned to solipsism or at least a philosophical individualism which denied the potential of any

collectivising political, social or economic doctrine to satisfy even
partially the aspirations of the individual. Indeed, if one were to focus
exclusively on *Hinkemann* such a conclusion might well be justified. Here
Toller's target is not only the customary one of the inhumanity of
capitalism but, more significantly, the inadequacies of its heir apparent,
Communism. The Communist Party functionary Michael Unbeschwert's
casuistic rationalisation of Eugen Hinkemann's personal problem of loss
of sexuality as a result of his war service, together with his profoundly
inhuman response of derision when told of the details of the case, leads
Hinkemann to reject both capitalism and Communism, since as far as he
is able to judge both forms of society appear unable to guarantee
fundamental human dignity. For Hinkemann the individual 'Seele' (soul)
is inviolate, and Unbeschwert's perplexity when confronted by the
concept is symptomatic of a wider deficiency in the ideology of
dialectical materialism, namely the bland assertion that in a future ideal
society a problem such as Hinkemann's will not exist, since its objective
cause, namely war, will have been abolished. The party functionary's
constant emphasis on the need to change social circumstances is for
Hinkemann meaningless as long as the individual propounding that
ideology is unwilling or unable to change his own morality and his own
attitudes to other individuals. This explains why Hinkemann appears
almost obsessed by the derision to which he is subjected. The fact that
Unbeschwert almost immediately regrets his laughter at Hinkemann's
plight is irrelevant: the contradiction between theory and practice has
been revealed. It is this failure, characteristic not only of Communism
but also of similar panacean doctrines such as Christian Socialism and
anarchism, to confront sympathetically even the most extreme case (and
Hinkemann's case is far less extreme in the immediate post-war years
than would appear at first sight) that leads Hinkemann to despair at the
possibility of any form of renewal whatsoever:

You fools! What can you know of the torment of a pathetic creature? How you
must change before the new society can be built ... You speak words, beautiful
words, pious words about eternal happiness. Words that are fine for *healthy*
people! You fail to see your limitations ... There are people to whom no State,
no society, no family and no community can bring happiness. It is precisely at
the point where your cures end that our torment begins.[31]

Whether the position of Hinkemann here is to be equated with that of
Toller is ultimately impossible to establish absolutely. It is, however, clear
that the very posing of the question, together with the way in which it is
subjected to such searching examination, at least suggests a profound
disquiet on Toller's part concerning the potential and above all the
limitations of dialectical materialism. To suggest, as Wolfgang Frühwald

does,[32] that *Hinkemann* also reveals the tragedy of a socialist society is surely to do Toller an injustice. Despite his scepticism concerning the materialist fixation on 'circumstances', Toller himself makes it abundantly clear that the causes of Hinkemann's demise are to be found in the *war*. It is the lack of understanding among self-professed socialists, not socialist society as such, which in any case did not exist in Germany at the time, that so profoundly disturbs Toller.

To elucidate this point further, it is important to introduce here a distinction which is crucial for a balanced discussion of Toller's political position. This is best described as a distinction between materialism as a school of critical thought which provides a methodology for the structural analysis of capitalism (essentially a descriptive or diagnostic process), and materialism as a form of antithetical thought which seeks to devise alternative systems (essentially a prescriptive or prognostic process). In ideological terms this is best expressed as a distinction between Marxism and Leninism. Many would doubtless claim – and this is indeed the line taken by East German critics of Toller – that the latter is the necessary consequence of the former, and that awareness of contradictions involves commitment to their removal, by whatever means necessary (including violence and the temporary renunciation of individual will), but this was not Toller's own view. Indeed, the *orthodox* Marxist approach to Toller, its insistence that he loses all right to the epithet Marxist or materialist simply because he failed to 'venture on to the ideological platform of the proletariat'[33] and to acknowledge the leading role of the (Communist) party, would itself provide fascinating material for a study in the reception of Toller, which above all would reveal that many of his own misgivings about the nature of orthodox Marxism are themselves substantiated precisely in its undifferentiated rejection of him. Characteristic of the approach of critics such as Reso is the assertion that all Toller's considerable insights into the highly complex relationship between the individual and his social environment lose their validity simply because of these alleged ideological shortcomings. To claim that 'the abstracting of all real causalities and the personification of schematics made [Toller's] deficient standpoint appear in its crassest form'[34] and that he failed to take account of the social ramifications of the predominantly individual problems which his dramatic work exemplifies is to ignore the real materialist basis of such observations as the following:

Millions had become unemployed. The slogan 'Freie Bahn den Tüchtigen' was a mockery. Two and a half million young people in Germany had no opportunity to assert themselves through work, and neither could they expect to in the foreseeable future. All that young people were learning to do was go on the dole.

Unemployment benefit was too much to die and not enough to live for. He who suffers from stomach pains and who does not know where he will sleep tomorrow is incapable of distinguishing between right and wrong.[35]

This materialist approach is more clearly articulated in an important statement made in one of Toller's letters from prison which in many ways marks a crucial turning point in his development, from the predominantly idealistic intellectual of youth to a more reflective, balanced position characteristic of his work in the '20s:

> For months I have been working intensively on 'real issues' and concerning myself with works on economic, political and sociological questions. This is because I realise more and more clearly that politics demand more from us than 'beliefs' ['Gesinnung'] 'a spiritual sensitivity' ['seelische Grundstimmung'] and 'ethics' ['Ethos']. Fundamental factual knowledge is necessary to enable full command of the laws of political action.[36]

It is important here to establish clearly what Toller understands by the term 'politics'. For him it is more than what is normally connoted by the term 'Realpolitik'. The activities of the politician should be imbued with a sense of ethical mission, that is, he is ideally a 'fighter for social formations, which provide ... the preconditions for a higher form of living ['Lebenserhaltung'].[37] In a letter to Stefan Zweig Toller develops this further, at the same time intimating why for him socialism was the only morally justifiable form of political theory:

> Progress in the process of autonomous organisation of social structure (from an economic point of view the most important aspect of socialism) implies the overcoming of social disorder by the application of socially constructive forces. This does not mean that the 'mystical' and 'irrational' side of life is completely rationalised, as some dogmatic socialists claim, but rather that it is 'limited'. It withdraws, and yet remains in all its incomprehensibility.[38]

Only in the light of such a statement can we really grasp the true import of a work such as *Hinkemann*: it is not the theory of dialectical materialism as such which is being attacked, but rather the way in which 'dogmatic socialists' apply the theory to all situations in the arrogant assumption that *all* mysteries, contradictions and complexities can be 'resolved'. To decry this as idealistic and hostile to the spirit of socialism is to do Toller a profound injustice, since his primary concern was always the struggle to remove all *anthropomorphic* irrationalities, foremost in which was the gross injustice of capitalism's distribution of wealth and the concomitant deprivation of the producers of that wealth, namely the proletariat. As Toller stresses in the above statement, the autonomous reorganisation of the *economic* structure of society was a necessary precondition for the achievement of a morally just society, although this in itself would never result in a removal of all irrationalities and anomalies. For Toller utopia would always remain an unattainable absolute:

The absolutely perfect 'Paradise on Earth' will never be put into practice by any social system, it is simply a question of struggling for relatively the best possible system which man can devise and put into practice. A system based on injustice, inequality and unfreedom cannot stand up to the scrutiny of reason.[39]

Here again we recognise a quality in Toller's thought which many critics have been reluctant to concede: far from being the romantic utopian revolutionary, Toller was in many ways a realist, always prepared to confront the limitations of human endeavour and above all of theory. It is this spirit of realism which forms the basis of the work that represents the dramatic treatment of Toller's reflections in prison, namely *The Machine Wreckers*.

It was this scepticism vis-à-vis the potential of intellectual theory rather than simply a profound abhorrence of violence that provided the impetus behind his misgivings about Leninist revolutionary tactics. For Toller the absolute equation of the interests of the working class with the aims and tactics of the Communist Party (KPD) was not only morally and philosophically untenable but also implied a degree of authoritarianism which he was constantly striving to overcome.[40] (It is interesting to note here that Reso, in his critique of Toller's 'inconsistency', fails to provide any satisfactory justification of this critique, preferring instead to rely simply on assertion and extensive quotations from Lenin.)

These misgivings do not mean, however, either that Toller rejected the need for radical change or that he failed to perceive that radical change would need more than mere rhetoric to ensure its success. In a speech to Berlin workers made in November 1925, some fifteen months after his release from prison, he reflects on the mistakes and failings of 1919, included in which is the naive belief that the ruling class could be convinced by the power of words alone to renounce its position of political and economic power.[41] Action too was necessary, and it is in this speech that Toller's views on what were for him the crucial questions of the *nature* of revolutionary practice find their most typical expression, if only because of the predominance of contradictions and unanswered questions which for him were of the essence of intellectual reflection.

The only valid form of revolutionary activity, in Toller's eyes, was that which rested on the 'will to power' of the proletariat. The potential power, which in his judgement was objectively available in the period of upheaval after the collapse of the monarchy in November 1918, was not translated into real power because the leaders of the revolution lacked the convinced support of the masses on whose behalf they believed themselved to be acting. Even the 'will to power' is in itself not enough if this will is not driven by what Toller chooses to call the 'spirit of community' ('Geist der Gemeinschaft'). These two terms are in many ways central to an understanding of what we may call the positive *pre*scriptive dimension of Toller's world view and more specifically of his attitude to the question of radical social change. If we turn to him for elucidation of these concepts we shall be disappointed, especially in the case of 'Geist', since Toller's definition is characterised by a lack of specificity not unfamiliar to students of modern German intellectual history. Nevertheless it is important to consider the following statement, since it is the nearest approximation to a definition he offers:

Geist: the synthesis of emotion and intellect, the possession of sceptical awareness and the readiness for complete submission, the courage of the believer to say no with complete determination, the ability to perceive limits, to bear and put up with even the harshest realities without suffering pain.[42]

Here Toller seems to be advocating what Roy Pascal has described, with reference to Kurt Hiller, as 'a curious alliance of the intellect and emotion' which reflects 'a persistent awareness of the sterility of the analytic intellect that ... cannot provide motivation for action and, as it analyses reality and uncovers hidden processes and laws, lays bare man's chains, not his freedom'.[43] This at least equal emphasis on the role of emotion in the process of intellectual enquiry goes a long way to explain Toller's misgivings about the ultimate validity of orthodox dialectical materialism, since this approach lacked the indispensable element of 'creativity'.[44] 'Creativity' here is meant as a necessary prerequisite or quality of any political action, without which action will be condemned to the 'sterility' to which Roy Pascal refers. As Toller writes in the speech in question:

Power alone is not sufficient for action and construction. The creative element of the spirit of community ['Geist der Gemeinschaft'] is a vital prerequisite.[45]

It is precisely this 'creative element' which in Toller's aesthetics is provided by literature:

There is a sphere in which one is able to perceive problems with synthetic clarity, where this clarity is not open to rational examination. It is in this sphere alone that the creative element operates.[46]

In accordance with his own observations about the role of the creative element Toller invests even his political speeches, which for him are the legitimate sphere of 'action' for the intellectual, with a considerable degree of highly poetical formulations. One quotation from the speech in question will suffice as an example:

A revolution without 'Geist' can be likened to a flame which rears up, only to flicker and die, because it lacks vital sustenance.

However, despite the apparent similarity in the use of the term 'Geist'[47] by both Kurt Hiller and Toller, in that for both the concept appears to connote a synthesising sphere of intellect and emotion, it would be wrong to equate absolutely the respective positions of the two intellectuals purely on the basis of this superficial similarity. For whereas both writers share the belief that it is the intellectual, the man whose sphere of philosophical enquiry ultimately leads him to look beyond the particularities of conventional political activity, who is best imbued with the powers of 'Geist', there is in Toller's thought no hint of the intellectual elitism which pervades all Hiller's work and which indeed confirms his debt to the work of Nietzsche, as R. Hinton Thomas had indicated.[48] In a letter to Hiller written in the autumn of 1923 Toller reproaches him for this latent elitism, which for Toller implies an unhealthy element of authoritarian imposition of the will of the intellectual on the mass of the population:

You assume that each intellectual ['Geistige'] possesses a priori greater powers of judgement than the man in the street. Let us not forget what powers of judgement the intellectuals exercised during the war. You seek to achieve Logocracy ['Logokratie'], the rule of 'Geist'. How do you propose to achieve the necessary power? You must surely realise that your 'Logokratie' would be a nonsense without the necessary restructuring of society. This power must be struggled for and its achievements must be defended by practical means.[49]

It is above all this emphasis on the indispensability of the restructuring of production relations which differentiates Toller from the idealist school of philosophy. For although Toller uses the term 'Geist' in much the same way as a philosopher would use 'Truth' (indeed, in Toller's thought the two terms often appear as coterminous), Toller is always at pains to stress the material prerequisites for the successful realisation of this moral absolute. 'Geist' is therefore not simply a critical criterion but an ultimate goal, whose achievement is inextricably tied up with the economic transformation of society.

However, 'Geist' is only one of the two concepts central to Toller's thought, and we must now address ourselves to the other, which is no less problematical or significant, namely the term 'Gemeinschaft'. To embark on an exhaustive exegesis of the origins of this concept in German intellectual history would be an impossible undertaking here, and we must content ourselves with a brief examination of the specificity of Toller's use of the term. However, in order to be able to do this successfully we must first of all turn to an intellectual contemporary of Toller who, perhaps more than any other single figure, exercised a profound, though in my submission not decisive, influence on him. I refer to Gustav Landauer, who, like Toller, was deeply involved in the abortive Munich 'Räterepublik' but unlike Toller failed to escape the wrath of the troops who restored 'order' to the city.

In his autobiography Toller makes frequent references to Landauer, calling him at one point one of the revolution's 'purest men, one of its greatest intellects'.[50] He makes it clear that Landauer's work *Aufruf zum Sozialismus*[51] had a great effect on his own thought, and in the letter to Landauer written in 1917 from which he quotes in his autobiography he describes 'the feeling of community' as 'elating and fortifying'.[52] This 'elation', derived from a feeling of common purpose, common endeavour, manifested itself in Toller's life as early as August 1914, when, in common with the great majority of his contemporaries, he greeted the Kaiser's decision to go to war with unquestioning enthusiasm. In chapter three of his autobiography Toller talks of an 'ecstacy of emotion', and in his first work, *Die Wandlung*, the autobiographical central figure, the student Friedrich, anticipates the war as 'liberation from the narrow confines of stultifying torment'.[53] For him the war will impose order and unity on the directionless tedium of an empty existence. Friedrich yearns for a sense of purpose, a goal which will give him the opportunity to 'prove himself' and thereby to overcome his 'fragmentation of the self'. In the initial stages of enthusiasm the 'Fatherland' is the source of this feeling of 'community' both for Friedrich and for Toller himself, but as the reality of the war gradually becomes apparent the abstraction 'Fatherland' is eventually replaced by that of 'Revolution', and the 'transformation' of the title is little more than a transference of allegiance from one abstraction to another. Indeed, it is not until *The Machine Wreckers* that Toller introduces a degree of differentiation into the concept of 'community', and it is in this work that the real implications of the term in Toller's thought emerge and above all that his examination of Landauer's use of the term is fully worked out. By revealing the real implications behind the factory owner Ure's call for 'a living bond of community between entrepreneurs and workers'[54] Toller demonstrates the dangers of a purely formalistic interpretation of the term 'community': unless the nature and ultimate goals of the cause are specified the concept itself is empty and furthermore can be exploited by interests profoundly hostile to the kind of 'community' Toller envisaged. It is precisely this question of specificity which enables us to pinpoint the difference between Toller's understanding of the term and Landauer's. In his excellent study of Landauer Eugene Lunn offers the following illuminating definition of Landauer's conception of community:

a living independent organism and 'personality' which represented something
above and beyond the mere sum of individuals who composed it.... The
community is not a mere abstraction, a construct of the human brain designed to
deal with discrete, individual phenomena ... it is a 'concrete reality' and an
'organism'.[55]

This view of community as an 'organism' whose corporate will
transcends the sum total of the individual wills of its members reveals a
profoundly mystical element in Landauer's thought which is largely
absent from Toller. However, it is with regard to the crucial question of
the translation of this mystical 'community of the living' into political
practice that the most fundamental differences emerge. For Landauer the
only valid form of communitarian democracy was the village
community, since only on such a small scale was 'socialism' as he
understood it possible:

Mankind must have its kernel and its roots in the unique individual, in the
couple, the house, the village ... in the 'Gemeinde'.[56]

Landauer's conception of communitarian socialism involves a wholesale
rejection not only of 'the thin influences of State and society[57] (the
characteristic anarchist rejection of authority per se) but also of
industrial society in toto. The stress is firmly on the individual and the
collective *will*, which if asserted to the full has the power to transcend
and negate economic and social circumstances. As he writes in *Aufruf
zum Sozialismus*:

The realisation of socialism is always possible if a sufficient number of people
want it. The realisation depends not on the technological state of things,
although socialism will of course look differently and develop differently
according to the state of technics; it depends on people and their spirit ...
Socialism is possible and impossible at all times; it is possible when the right
people are there to do it; it is impossible when people either don't will it or only
supposedly will it, but are not capable of doing it.[58]

Whilst it would be misleading to deny the residues of such a voluntarist
approach in Toller (it is particularly apparent in Jimmy Cobbet's final
speech in *The Machine Wreckers*) it would be wrong to see this as the
primary emphasis. The whole import of *The Machine Wreckers* is a
warning against the dangers of an undifferentiated rejection of
technological society, firstly because it implies an idyllic view of a feudal
past, and secondly because it involves a wilful (and ultimately utopian)
negation of the present. It is surely no coincidence that the co-operatives
which Toller's 'entfesselte Wotan' seeks to establish bear more than a
passing resemblance to the supposedly self-sufficient co-operatives which

Landauer, as Minister of Education, attempted to set up during the Munich soviet republic.[59] In other words we find in *Der entfesselte Wotan* and *The Machine Wreckers* an anticipation of the dangers inherent in Landauer's form of 'völkisch' communitarianism, with its emphasis on the fusion of individual and collective will, its desire for a return to pre-industrial forms of existence, and its recourse to rhetoric.

Toller's conception of 'community' is devoid of these regressive and mystical tendencies. Although his use of the term is not entirely free of a certain rhetorical tone, it lacks the kind of a priori abstractional quality prevalent in Landauer and is always linked to an awareness of the importance of economic and social structure. 'Community' is used by Toller both in a prescriptive sense of an ultimate goal and in a descriptive sense as connoting what are believed to be inherent qualities in man which are always striving for realisation but which are stunted by an inhuman environment. These qualities can achieve full expression only in a society which provides the essential preconditions for that self-fulfilment. The mere establishing of a political superstructure of parliamentary democracy with its principle of universal suffrage was in itself not a guarantee of individaul freedom. Indeed, as Toller was to reflect after the collapse of the Weimar Republic, such a conception of individual freedom is vacuous if not accompanied by a 'planned organisation of production and consumption according to the needs of the community'.[60] Only in this way could 'anarchy and the ruthless exploitation of human labour power'[61] be eradicated. The failure of the revolution after the first world war had resulted in the strengthening of capitalism and the increasing disorientation of the individual, a circumstance which is reflected in all his dramatic characters, who seem deprived of the feeling of an active and autonomous membership of a community, a deprivation which Toller always locates in the nature of social circumstances. The practical alleviation of this deprivation was not, as he came increasingly to realise after his experiences in Munich, the prime responsibility of the writer. It was the writer's task to thematicise the dialectics of the relationship between the individual and his environment and thereby to stimulate public awareness. Toller's suicide in New York in 1939 can be seen only as the bitter conclusion that he had failed in his self-imposed task. The closing lines of his penultimate work, in which Marx's eleventh thesis on Feuerbach is quoted disapprovingly by Napoleon, serves as a fitting, if ultimately ironic, epitaph to a man whose life represented a constant sacrifice in the interests of a community which to this day has failed to appreciate the extent of his achievement:

Hitherto philosophers have sought to explain the world. Our task is to change it.[62]

Notes

[1] The following is a selection of work published on Toller since his death.
In English:

W. A. Willibrand, *Ernst Toller and his ideology*, Iowa, 1945.

John M. Spalek, 'Ernst Toller: the need for a new estimate', *German Quarterly* 39, 1966, pp. 581–96.

Richard Beckley, *Ernst Toller, German Men of Letters*, vol. III, London, 1968, pp. 85–107.

Malcolm Pittock, 'Masse Mensch and the tragedy of revolution', *Forum for Modern Language Studies*, vol. III, No. 2, April 1972, pp. 162–83.

In German:

Alfred Klein, 'Zwei Dramatiker in der Entscheidung. Ernst Toller, Friedrich Wolf und die Novemberrevolution', *Sinn und Form* 10, 1958, pp. 702–25.

Martin Reso, 'Die Novemberrevolution und Ernst Toller', *Weimarer Beiträge* 5, 1959, pp. 387–489.

Martin Reso, 'Gefängnislyrik und dichterische Wiederspiegelung in der Lyrik Ernst Tollers', *Weimarer Beiträge* 7, 1961, pp. 520–56.

Jost Hermand, *Unbequeme Literatur. Eine Beispielreihe*, Heidelberg, 1971.

Thomas Bütow, *Der Konflikt zwischen Revolution und Pazifismus im Werk Ernst Tollers*, Hamburg, 1975.

There are, of course, many other works which deal with Toller. A complete bibliography is to be found in J. M. Spalek's *Ernst Toller and his Critics*, Charlottesville, 1968.

[2] J. M. Spalek, 'Ernst Toller: the need for a new estimate', p. 590.

[3] Wolfgang Frühwald, Nachwort to *Hinkemann*, Reclam, Stuttgart, 1971, p. 75.

[4] Martin Reso, 'Die Novemberrevolution und Ernst Toller', p. 409.

[5] *Cf.* Paul Pörtner, 'The writers' revolution: Munich, 1918–19', *Journal of Contemporary History* III, 4, October 1968, pp. 137–53. This, together with Reinhard Rürup's article 'Problems of the German revolution' (pp. 109–37 of the same journal) provides a useful introduction to the Munich 'Räterepublik'.

[6] *Justiz. Erlebnisse*, Berlin, 1930.

[7] Letter to Romain Rolland, 13 December 1921, *Prosa Briefe Dramen Gedichte*. Mit einem Vorwort von Kurt Hiller, Hamburg, 1961.

[8] Letter to Tessa, 14 August 1922, *ibid.*, p. 221.

[9] *Der entfesselte Wotan. Eine Komödie*, Potsdam, 1924. All references are to this edition.

[10] *Cf.* Joachim Fest, who writes, 'The poverty of his [Hitler's] ideology contrasted with the demagogic skill with which he turned to his own ends dissatisfactions sprung from a thousand sources.' Also: 'Hitler never regarded "positive" formulas ... as imposing constructive obligations, but always as slogans to stimulate and intensify resentment and cupidity.' (*The Face of the Third Reich*, London, 1972, pp. 41 and 42.)

[11] The most obvious example is Charles Chaplin's *The Great Dictator*, 1940.

[12] *Cf.* 'Are we responsible for our time?', *Literaturwissenschaftliches Jahrbuch der Görres-Gesellschaft*, 6, 1965, p. 298. This speech, in which Toller emphasises repeatedly the ability of National Socialism to exploit legitimate grievances forms the core of Toller's crusade against Hitler in the United States in 1936–37. J. M. Spalek and Wolfgang Frühwald's research, published in the above mentioned journal, is indispensable to students of this important field.

[13] Hitler's own description of his period of imprisonment in 1924 when the bulk of his work on *Mein Kampf* was done. (Quoted in Werner Maser, *Hitlers Mein Kampf*, Munich, 1966, p. 13.)

[14] *Hoppla, wir leben!* in Günther Rühle (ed.), *Zeit und Theater, Bd. 2, Von der Republik zur Diktatur* Berlin, 1972.

[15] *Cf.* Siegfried Kracauer, *From Caligari to Hitler. A psychological history of the German film*, Princeton, 1947.

[16] Toller's view on 'Neue Sachlichkeit' is perhaps best revealed in the following statement: 'I have the suspicion that a virtue is being made out of necessity and that this is the reason why "Neue Sachlichkeit" was invented . . . The more objective ("sachlich") literature becomes, the more empty it will be. Those who lack ideas resort to objectivity ("Sachlichkeit").' (Reportage und Dichtung, *Die Literarische Welt* XXVI, 25 June 1926, p. 2.)

[17] *Cf.* Franz Neumann, *Behemoth. The Structure and Practice of National Socialism*, London, 1942.

[18] *Cf.* R. Hinton Thomas and Wilfried Van der Will, *Der deutsche Roman und die Wohlstandsgesellschaft*, Stuttgart, 1969, pp. 156–9.

[19] *Cf.* the collection of articles in *Justiz. Erlebnisse, op. cit.*

[20] *Cf.* Karl Thomas's desperate conclusion: 'Is there no difference between a mental asylum and the world outside? . . . The same people who are kept here as insane are running around outside as sane, trampling down the others.' (*Hoppla, wir leben!, ed. cit.*, p. 232.)

[21] *Cf.* Kilman's statement: 'We are agreed about the ultimate goal. It's just a question of method.' (*Ibid.*, p. 182.)

[22] Kilman's assertion that 'violence is always reactionary' echoes one of the central issues of Masse Mensch, namely the justification or otherwise of violence as a means of effecting radical social change. Toller was never really able to resolve this dilemma, although there are indications that after the onset of National Socialism he had serious doubts about the feasibility of pacifism as an absolute moral doctrine. (*Cf.*, for example, 'Are we responsible for our times?' *loc. cit.*)

[23] *Cf.* 'The artist should not aim to prove theories, he should present examples. Many great works of art are political, but political literature should not be confused with propaganda which makes use of literary devices.' (*Eine Jugend in Deutschland*, op. cit., p. 176.)

[24] *Hoppla, wir leben!, ed. cit.*, p. 213.

[25] *Cf.*, for example, the way the 'intellectual workers' ('Geistige Kopfarbeiter') exclude Pickel, a member of the proletariat whose "redemption" they seek, from their private meeting. (*Hoppla*, Act III.)

[26] Piscator, for instance, made changes to the ending of *Hoppla* for the stage version on the grounds that Toller was too 'defeatist'. *Cf.* Erwin Piscator, *Das Politische Theater*, Hamburg, 1963, pp. 146–58.

[27] *Cf.* the Millardärsohn's vain appeal for a return to an agricultural mode of existence in *Gas* I, Act II. (The whole of the *Gas* trilogy is available in B. J. Kenworthys edition, London, 1968.)

[28] *Cf.* especially the articles by Reso and Klein referred to under n. 1.

[29] *Eine Jugend in Deutschland*, Leipzig, 1970, p. 231. (The final chapter, 'Blick heute', is not included in the Rowohlt edition.)

[30] *Ibid.*, p. 231.

[31] *Prosa, Briefe, Dramen, Gedichte*, p. 418.

[32] *Cf.* 'Hinkemann is the tragedy of the individual rejected by society, and for that reason the tragedy of society itself, i.e. of socialist society.' (Wolfgang Frühwald, 'Nachwort' to Reclam edition of *Hinkemann*, Stuttgart, 1971.)

[33] Martin Reso, 'Die Novemberrevolution und Ernst Toller', p. 399.

[34] *Ibid.*, p. 398.

[35] 'Das Versagen des Pazifismus in Deutschland. Ernst Tollers amerikanische Vortragsreise, 1936–37', *Lit. wiss. Jahrbuch* 6, 1965, p. 308.

[36] Letter to Tessa, *ed. cit.*, p. 193.

[37] *Ibid.*, p. 199.

[37] *Ibid.*, p. 203.

[39] *Ibid.*, p. 228.

[40] In many ways Toller's misgivings on the role of the party correspond to those expressed by Rosa Luxemburg. The following passage, written by her in gaol in 1918,

could easily have come from Toller himself: 'The fundamental error of Lenin and Trotsky's theory is precisely that it opposes dictatorship and democracy ... Lenin and Trotsky opt for dictatorship in contrast to democracy and therefore for the dictatorship of a handful of people, i.e. for dictatorship in accordance with the bourgeois model ... The proletariat must exercise dictatorship, but it must be the dictatorship of a class, not of a party or clique, dictatorship in the full glare of public scrutiny, with the active and unimpeded participation of the mass of the people exercising limitless democracy ... It is the historic task of the proletariat upon achieving power to replace bourgeois democracy with socialist democracy, and not to abolish democracy altogether ... Dictatorship, yes! But this dictatorship must involve a particular form of the realisation of democracy, rather than its abolition ... This dictatorship must be the work of a class, and not the work of a small minority assuming leadership in the name of a class.' (Rosa Luxemburg, 'Die russische Revolution', *Schriften zur Theorie der Spontaneität*, Hamburg, 1970, p. 190. The translation is mine.) The affinities between Rosa Luxemburg's and Toller's thought would provide interesting material for a separate study, which might come to the conclusion that Toller's dilemmas in the spring of 1919 in many ways paralleled those which Rosa Luxemburg would surely have experienced had she not been murdered in January 1919. Rosa Luxemburg's 'image', especially in the late 1960s in Germany, seems ironically to have benefited precisely from her unhappy lack of opportunity to translate her theories into practice, an opportunity which in Toller's case has had unfortunate negative consequences for his subsequent reception.

[41] 'Deutsche Revolution', *Quer Durch, ed. cit.*, p. 229.
[42] *Ibid.*, p. 233.
[43] Roy Pascal, *From Naturalism to Expressionism*, London, 1973, p. 302.
[44] *Op. cit.*, p. 233.
[45] *Loc. cit.*
[46] *Briefe aus dem Gefängnis*, Amsterdam, 1935, p. 64.
[47] *Op. cit.*, p. 233.
[48] *Cf.* the following two articles by R. Hinton Thomas which provided the stimulus for this essay: 'Das Ich und die Welt. Expressionismus und Gesellschaft', in *Expressionismus als Literatur*, ed. Wolfgang Rothe, Bern and Munich, 1969, and 'German and English intellectuals: contrasts and comparisons', in *Upheaval and Continuity. A Century of German History*, ed. E. J. Feuchtwanger, London, 1973.
[49] *Op. cit.*, p. 231.
[50] *Op. cit.*, p. 159.
[51] Gustav Landauer, *Aufruf zum Sozialismus*, 2nd edn, Berlin, 1919.
[52] *Eine Jugend, op. cit.*, p. 81.
[53] *Die Wandlung, ed. cit.*, p. 247.
[54] *Die Maschinenstürmer*, Rohwolt, *ed. cit.*, p. 357.
[55] Eugene Lunn, *Prophet of Community. The Romantic Socialism of Gustav Landauer*, Berkeley, Cal., 1973, p. 106.
[56] Landauer, *Rechenschaft*, Berlin, 1919, p. 195. Quoted and translated by Lunn, p. 221.
[57] Landauer, *Skepsis und Mystik*, 2nd edn, Cologne, 1923. Quoted and translated by Lunn, p. 169.
[58] *Aufruf zum Sozialismus, ed. cit.*, p. 61. Quoted and translated by Lunn, p. 212.
[59] *Cf.* Lunn's observations on this question: 'Landauer envisaged a possible return of large numbers of Munich proletarians to the land in the course of the revolution ... In Landauer's view of the Räte movement ... anarchist socialism and völkisch anti-urbanism combined.' (*Prophet of Community*, p. 302.)
[60] 'Sind wir verantwortlich für unsere Zeit?' *loc. cit.*, p. 283.
[61] *Ibid.*, p. 282.
[62] *No More Peace!*, London, 1937, p. 103.

TONY PHELAN

Ernst Bloch's 'Golden Twenties': *Erbschaft dieser Zeit* and the problem of cultural history

Hence, in Hitler's view, propaganda comprised only 'a positive and a negative; love or hate, right or wrong, truth or lie, never half one thing and half the other'. Variations on a theme must not be made a pretext for differentiation, but 'in the end must always say the same thing. For instance a slogan must be presented from different angles, but the end of all remarks must always and immutably be the slogan itself'. [Werner Maser, *Hitler*, citing *Mein Kampf*]

Writing in 1929 in *Die Böttcherstrasse 1* Otto Frenzel quotes as a basis for his reflections on 'Contemporary literature: development and prospects of recent German poetry' the following lines from Stefan Zweig, written two years earlier:

... a condition of illumination dominates nowadays which is thoroughly alien to poetry – or, at any rate, to the poetry created and understood by an earlier generation. And the new expression, the new poetry of the new generation, the metrical sublimation of a sense of life ['Lebensgefühl'] which, within one decade, has changed in an unexampled way – this poetry has, for the present, not yet achieved its full form. All that is clear is that poetry will be different and will have to be different if it is to do justice to this changed, clear-sighted young generation, if it is to create a community ['Gemeinde'], a public for itself once again. Everything in the present time is as yet transition and confusion.[1]

The two major indications of Zweig's account are familiar enough: on the one hand he registers, as a sense of brightness and clarity ('ein Zustand der Helligkeit'), the emphasis on neutral, clear-sighted objectivity associated with the term and the movement 'Neue Sachlichkeit', discussed elsewhere in this volume. On the other hand, and less specifically, the as yet unarticulated transformation is located in the decade which divides the relatively stable middle years of the Weimar Republic from the first world war, 1927 from 1917. This sense of a radical break, a rupture within the continuum of cultural activity, finds its origin in the early '20s, as Horst Denkler has argued, in the deliberate rejection of artistic ideals reflected by the closure of literary journals and the growth of a cultural pessimism or scepticism: thus in 1921 C. G. Heise writes,

One may say without fear of contradiction: everything that there is has found its eulogist. The present task is not to extend but to set limits.[2]

The possible forms which this awareness may take are many. It may lead to a 'retreat from the word', either negatively or with the eloquent silence finally chosen by Karl Kraus ('If anyone has anything to say, let him step forward and say *nothing*'). At another extreme the sense of cultural rupture may lead to the 'Gebrauchslyrik' defined in 1928 by Kurt Tucholsky as 'rhymed or rhythmic party manifesto'.[3]

In general there is much to suggest that, during the second half of the Weimar Republic, writers and critics felt that art and culture, imaged in the traditional supremacy of lyric poetry, had reached a critical point.[4] Contributors to journals as far apart in the ideological spectrum as *Der Gral* and *Die neue deutsche Bücherschau*, Catholic and Marxist respectively, are driven to reflect on the prospects of lyric poetry in the context of the transformed 'sense of life' perceived by Zweig. One of the clearest examples of the problem is to be found in Brecht's 'Brief report on 400 (four hundred) young poets'. The Berlin journal *Die literarische Welt* had initiated a competition in which Brecht was to award a prize for the best poem contributed by a young poet: Brecht decided to award the prize not to any of the competitors but to Hannes Küpper, the author of 'He! He! The iron man', a poem about the racing cyclist Reggie MacNamara which Brecht himself had come across. In his 'Report' Brecht already suggests the terminology of Tucholsky a year later, by proposing that lyric poetry, precisely, must be investigated with a view to establishing its use value ('Gebrauchswert'). What is of particular interest here is not simply Brecht's definition of great poetry as 'document' nor his attempt to restore poetry to its 'original gesture of the communication of thought';[5] rather it is the subliminal uneasiness of his critical tone. He confesses himself to be a critic whose knowledge of poetry is defined by his junior school readers, to be without feeling or sympathy for the work of Rilke, George or Werfel. In a later response to a notice of his competition decision in a literary feuilleton Brecht explains that these three poets name the unsatifactory origins of the young poets he found himself judging. Such poets of the great tradition cannot pass the test of usefulness:

The reflection of a flock of lambs in the pure eyes of a man of great natural stature would have to have great value, so too would the song of a singer immersed in the enjoyment of his own voice. But these people have neither pure eyes nor beautiful voices. And no Nature at all. They are the owners of flocks of lambs or the kind of people who do without the lambs because their souls keep them too busy. The levity of tone with which I make this observation should not conceal the seriousness of the point. It is just that I, like everyone else who writes honestly about these things nowadays, find it embarrassing ['genant'] to be caught giving very serious consideration to unserious things.[6]

Brecht's uneasiness, which he claims to share with anyone writing on similar problems, is neatly caught by the foreign word he uses. The disturbance is a general embarrassment rather than being formulated as a particular difficulty. As he wryly explains, 'In the present intellectual environment it is comic to strike a pathetic note for complaints about the leakiness of umbrellas.'[7]

Brecht's comments and Zweig's prognostications, for all their obvious differences of tone and emphasis, reflect a common problematic: breakdown and possible continuity in the cultural life of Germany under the republic provide the terms in which the question is posed. For Zweig the possibility of continuity depends on the creation not simply of a public for poetry but of a community within which it might once again flourish. 'Community', 'Gemeinde', implies with its religious overtones and its sense of spiritual unity the possible restoration of poetic values, however changed their form may have to be. Brecht, on the other hand, could be recognised publicly (again in 1927) as the final break with the past. Klaus Herrmann, writing in *Die neue Bucherschau*, identified Brecht with 'the end of personality' in the very title of his review of the *Hauspostille*. While Stefan Zweig, then, hopes for the restoration of 'Gemeinde' and the reforging of links with the poetic past, Brecht is made to represent the dissolution of 'Persönlichkeit' – the great natural stature and pure eyes which he himself had been unable to find in the last scions of the tradition, Rilke, George and Werfel. 'Brecht,' wrote Herrmann, 'smashed the smooth form of the Traditional and put the fragments together again in a torso of imposing simplicity'.[8] What is inescapable here is the recurrence of the language of rupture *and* continuity, at the very point where the radical nature of the break is being asserted.

The title of Brecht's rejoinder to criticism of his 'Report' itself gives further evidence of the tension between a radical break and a continuing tradition: 'Neither useful nor beautiful' ('Weder nützlich noch schön') takes up the terms of Classical aesthetics, the 'aut prodesse aut delectare' which had been a stable point of reference for the discussion of poetry in the eighteenth century and after. Brecht insists that he is perfectly well aware that 'there are values in art which are, as it were, no use, especially if one relies on a few concepts, of which there is no shortage.'[9] 'Useful' or 'beautiful' would provide such critical aids – but for Brecht such terms no longer provide an adequate account of the necessary practice of poetry. Instead, of 'nützlich' as a criterion for the judgement of verse he proposes 'Gebrauch', as we have seen. The distinction might, in English, seem tenuous (between 'useful' and 'use'); but in fact it is considerable and important. 'Nützlich' retains a relatively comfortable, 'moral' sense, resting on the classical doctrine that ethical notions can be helpfully ('usefully') communicated through the pedagogically effective aesthetic form of literature; 'Gebrauch', derived from the consumer world, is on the other hand much more aggressive, suggesting the applied and instrumentalised view of literature which Brecht is proposing.

There remains, however, a further indication in the title of the rejoinder: 'prodesse' and 'delectare' had functioned not simply as pointers to the categories of poetic composition, guidelines for the young poet, they had also been essential tools for the judgement of art. By dispensing with these categories and substituting the new standard named 'Gebrauchswert' Brecht disturbs the canons of literary criticism and, as he recognises, overturns the traditional processes of literary *history* itself:

> Even if it is not a Marxist who has the job of separating the wheat from the chaff at the end of this interesting epoch, he will be unable to understand the poetry of, say, Stefan George, Rilke or Werfel (or of almost anyone else) – however vague this may sound today – unless he considers it as manifestos of the class struggle.[10]

It was the first point which was taken up in the course of the Weimar Republic by the 'Bund proletarisch-revolutionärer Schriftsteller', and which has been revived again more recently in the discussion of Marxist and working-class aesthetics. For a development of the problem of literary history, however, we must look elsewhere.

Precisely this problem is taken up by Walter Benjamin with remarkable sensitivity in a review article, based on the symposium edited by Emil Ermatinger under the title *Philosophie der Literaturwissenschaft* (The Philosophy of Literary Studies), which appeared in *Die literarische Welt* in May 1931. Benjamin's argument begins, in his consideration of 'Literary history and literary studies' ('Literaturgeschichte und Literaturwissenschaft'), with the recognition that any attempt to describe the history of a particular field of academic study must temper the autonomy of its subject matter with the need to locate it 'as an element in the total cultural position at any particular time':[11]

> If . . . literary history is in the midst of a crisis, it is only as one part of a much more general one. Literary history is not only a discipline, but in its development it is itself a factor in history generally.[12]

In initiating his argument in this way Benjamin has taken the problem

raised by Brecht's alternative aesthetics of use value, and instead of seeing the necessary consequence of a transformed literary criticism in instrumental terms – Brecht's reflections on 'the end of this interesting
epoch' is, among other things, a hint at the end of the period of bourgeois
dominance – he situates the question in the area of a theory of
knowledge: it is the hermeneutic practice of 'Literaturwissenschaft' and
its epistemological basis which are now centrally at issue.

The crisis identified by Benjamin is interpreted as the decay of a
method derived from the traditions of German literary historiography but
finally formulated in the neo-Kantian terms of a universalist Cultural
Science ('Kulturwissenschaft') by Rickert and Windelband, which – by
an irony which does not escape Benjamin – had even found its way into
the epistemological foundations of the empirical discipline of history
itself.[13] The interpretation of literature as the repository of eternal and universal values transformed all research into the service of a cult in which
they were celebrated 'according to a syncretist rite'. The failure of this
whole procedure, which Benjamin finds reflected in the increasingly
empty phrases of literary history, is inscribed in Ermatinger's symposium; but Benjamin immediately transfers the argument of his critique
on to a new plane. In a curious metaphor the majority of Ermatinger's
contributors are suddenly seen as a company of mercenaries marching
into the House of Literature: far from seeking to admire its treasures,
their intention is to take cover there while they defend an important
bridgehead or railway in the course of a civil war. (On the other side are
the troops of materialist literary historians.) This metaphor both brings
the argument nearer to Brecht's, in that it interprets differing critical
methods as elements in an ideological struggle, but also introduces a distinctive emphasis. It is no longer literature itself which has to be understood, if at all, as ideological manifesto; rather ideology has taken up its
place in the discourse of interpretation. It is now from critics and
historians of literature that we must look for the instrumentalisation required by Brecht.

The metaphor perhaps takes Benjamin further than he had intended,
however; although the problem it raises – the objective neutrality of
literature and its ideological appropriation – is one that will recur: Benjamin's major concern is the return of literary studies to their necessary
historical foundations. This will entail and make possible the destruction
of an illusory participation in the cultural commodities ('Kulturgüter') of
belles-lettres which is fostered 'in certain social strata' by popular literary
history. Precisely what Benjamin had in mind by this shadowy phrase
remains unclear, though there are indications that he is here already
thinking in the terms which were finally formulated in the essay 'Der

Autor als Produzent'('The author as producer') of 1934.[14] Positively, the destruction of the illusion of timeless values enshrined in literature will make possible once again the location of literature in time. This will entail a double-edged method of interpretation which, in Benjamin's view, will revitalise research procedures in literary fields by recalling them to their primary didactic function – the explanation of the past to, and its appropriation for, the present. The final formulations of the essay reveal the dialectical complexity of Benjamin's proposal:

> The whole sphere of their [*sc.* of literary works] life and influence must stand with equal justification alongside the account of their origins – indeed, the former must take pride of place; I mean, then, their fate, their reception by contemporaries, their translations, their glory. In this way the work inwardly takes on the form of a microcosm, or rather of a microaeon. For it is not simply a matter of presenting works of literature in the context of their own time, but rather of presenting, in the time when they were produced, the time which now perceives them – i.e. our own. Thus literature becomes an organ ['Organon'] of history, and it is the task of literary history to ensure that this is so – not to turn written works ['Schrifttum'] into the material of abstract and academic history ['Stoffgebiet der Historie'].[15]

Literary interpretation must thus subordinate itself to the imperatives of the present by restoring and maintaining the dynamic tension between knowledge or understanding ('Erkenntnis') and practice ('Praxis').[16]

The conclusion of a later essay, 'Stefan George in retrospect', makes a similar point, but sharpens it with the edge of aphorism and polemic: George was the poet of the generation doomed to perish in the first world war and, Benjamin argues,

> he was such as the fulfilment of 'la Décadence'. .... He stands at the end of a spiritual movement which began with Baudelaire. It may be that there was a time when this assertion was of no more than literary-historical ['literarhistorisch'] interest. In the meantime it has become an historical ['geschichtlich'] one, and demands its rights.[17]

In one respect this is an example of what Benjamin has in mind at the end of the 1931 essay: what had been a 'literary fact', enabling the critic to situate George in the tradition of European poetry since Baudelaire, has now become an element in the present historical situation. The demands of praxis energise, as it were, what had been a purely abstract 'Erkenntnis'.

These essays of Walter Benjamin transpose the question of continuity and rupture, traced in Zweig's observation of a cultural problem and in Brecht's rejection of any conventional literary criteria, to a world of hermeneutics constrained by the immediate and pressing problems of history itself. In some respects the question of 'continuity' may be seen as one aspect of the wider difficulties which go by the name of modernism: in his recent article on 'The crisis of language' in modernist literature Richard Sheppard, paraphrasing Rilke's *Duino Elegies*, remarks that

many moderns feel that 'man is not very securely at home in the world which he interprets with his intellect'. Because a principle of unity is felt to have been lost, the present seems to lose its organic connection with the past and future. Time becomes a series of fragmented instants, and a sense of continuity gives way to discontinuity.[18]

The origins of this collapse, signposted in Hofmannsthal's *Letter of Lord Chandos*, lie in the loss of 'the essential powers of language and the person, variously described as "the Logos", "the Word", the "Self" ...':[19] these are the values to which Brecht – together with those who shared Klaus Herrmann's response to his work – feels he can no longer appeal; and to the extent that this is true the situation described by Stefan Zweig may be seen as the final echo of that earlier crisis; Walter Benjamin's alternative proposals, on the other hand, represent an attempt to recover the poise and dominance of the intellect, in the reassertion of a practice.

It is against the background of this cultural criticism that Ernst Bloch's reflections on literature, painting, music, journalism, philosophy and politics in the context of Weimar Republic society are of greatest interest. The very title of *Erbschaft dieser Zeit* indicates an awareness of both discontinuity *and* continuity – and Bloch's central purpose in speaking of the 'inheritance' of the time is to complicate the linear model of time and its dissolution attributed to an earlier generation by Sheppard. In a discussion with Rainer Traub and Harald Wieser, 'On dissimultaneity, provincialism and propaganda', which first appeared in *Kursbuch* 39 (1974), Bloch explains his general intentions and the particular emphasis of his title:

I attempted in *Erbschaft*, then, to point up and capitalise on those things from our own time from which one can learn, not just for propaganda purposes. I was particularly interested in what had been abandoned. Above all, absolutely no thought has been given to the fact that a heritage can be taken not only from periods of revolutionary ascendancy (hence the word *inheritance* ['Erbschaft'] in the title – the expression comes from Engels, 'cultural heritage' ['Kulturerbe'], and it is not philistine in origin), and not only from cultural 'golden ages', but that we can and must become the inheritors of periods of so called decadence?[20]

This statement serves to clarify two important aspects of *Erbschaft dieser Zeit*. The first concerns the relation of Bloch's work to the development of an adequate Marxist propaganda in the face of growing fascist power, before 1933, and the proper tools for the analysis of National Socialist ideology thereafter. Bloch's investigation identifies, as he was quick to re-emphasise in 1974, not so much sins of commission in the anti-fascist propaganda of the KPD of the '20s and '30s as sins of omission.[21] In drawing attention to the residually 'progressive' or even 'revolutionary' (Bloch himself uses the word 'rebellisch') elements in what he identifies as a lower-middle-class ideology, increasingly prone to appropriation by National Socialism, he suggests a means by which Communist Party propaganda might extend both its range and effectiveness. The recent volume of studies dedicated to Bloch on his ninetieth birthday, *Es muss nicht immer Marmor sein,*[22] pays particular attention to this aspect of the philosopher's work, commenting on and developing the thesis of the *Erbschaft,* that the revolutionary contents of apparently reactionary ideological formations can be 'taken over' and 'occupied' by revolutionary forces. Helmut Lethen, on the other hand, is critical of Bloch's analysis in his study of *Neue Sachlichkeit 1924–32.*[23] Bloch's project is summarised as a 'strategy which he develops from the collapse of liberalism', a strategy which unites his theory of the cultural heritage with the practice of class struggle and the tactics of the Communist Party. Lethen's criticism questions the status of the 'revolutionary contents' identified by Bloch and stresses in particular Bloch's failure to identify the role of the State and its reactionary exploitation of progressive elements. This analysis of Bloch's work in fact turns on his account of the relationship between the lower middle class and the industrial proletariat, a class analysis which, Lethen argues, was bound to lead to incorrect political action. Criticism of this kind may or may not provide a true reflection of the political necessities of the time; what is missed by Lethen, and to a lesser extent by the authors of *Es muss nicht immer Marmor sein,* is the real complexity of Bloch's account of the culture (in the broadest sense) of the Weimar Republic. Nor does the emphasis on propaganda *as such* allow any scope for detailed reading of his practice, a reading which goes beyond the mere assertion that for Bloch society has become an aesthetic totality. For Bloch's own emphasis on the need for adequate propaganda among the 'proletarianised' middle class, in the 1935 preface to *Erbschaft,* needs to be seen in the light of, and indeed as a version of, Benjamin's restoration of literary history to its didactic function; in propaganda too the pressing claims of history make themselves felt in the hermeneutic process.

The *Kursbuch* interview cited above makes it clear that the analyses and reflections of *Erbschaft dieser Zeit* were *not* conceived solely in terms of propaganda purposes: the second aspect of the work which we may now attempt to clarify is more complex but also closer to Bloch's central concerns. The notion of a cultural heritage which can be appropriated by a projected socialist society is presented here in a more differentiated way: the sense in which the realist novel of the nineteenth century is said to provide a model or point of departure for 'socialist realism' would exemplify the stricter view of Communist aestheticians – and that is, of course, a view which was being developed and debated in the '20s and '30s. Bloch argues, however, that not only the high points of the cultural past can be harnessed to serve in the struggle for a 'progressive' socialist order; rather what are called decadent periods, in the Communist jargon, should also be recognised as having a positive value, and in particular Bloch argued for such an evaluation of Expressionism in his debate with Georg Lukács, and of the 'modernists' Joyce, Proust and Kafka. The interview with Traub and Wieser recalls the particular articulation of Bloch's view in the title of his study: '*Erbschaft* dieser Zeit' – inheritance of this time. The operative distinction is made between 'Erbschaft' and 'Erbe', inheritance and heritage. What Bloch sought to stress by his use of the former term is the concrete, detailed reality of what is inherited. A famous passage from the 1935 preface to *Erbschaft dieser Zeit* illustrates the point of differentiation:

... Die Tendenz vernichtet, was sich ihr in den Weg stellt, sie erbt, was ihr auf dem Weg liegt.

Das war selten fälliger als heute. Gewiss muss die Tante erst tot sein, die man beerben will; doch vorher schon kann man sich sehr genau im Zimmer umsehen.[24]

The political 'tendency' annihilates whatever gets in its way, but it is able to inherit what it finds in its path: in the second part of this assertion there is – in keeping with Bloch's figurative and plastic usage – a hint of word play, suggesting that the things which are found 'on the path' are in fact suitable for or proper to the 'Tendenz', in spite of their superficially random appearance. Such a reflection has rarely been more necessary, argues Bloch; and then, in an ironical image, he adds his distinctive point: an inheritance includes whatever is there in the room of an imaginary aunt – one must wait, of course, until she is dead to inherit it, but there is no harm in having a good look round beforehand! In terms of the distinction between 'Erbe' and 'Erbschaft' this means that the second, the actual inheritance, is what should first be considered, for it is from these particularities that the heritage will be distilled.

This initiative, by refusing the easy abandonment of certain cultural activities as decadent, is deliberately concerned to seek out ambiguity, to recognise the complexity of 'transitional phases'. As Bloch remarks, 'The present work contains its share of the late bourgeois period ['spät-bürgerlichen Zeitinhalts'], for the most part in its ambiguous aspects and therefore rendered dialectical' (*EdZ* 18). In other words, and more simply, '. . . not everything which is as yet "irrational" is a mere stupidity which can simply be resolved' (*EdZ* 19). It suggests a curious misreading of Bloch when Georg Lukács in 'Es geht um den Realismus' – even allowing for the polemics of the 'Expressionism debate' – accuses him of understanding radical change as only 'fissures and catastrophes'.[25] For the critical methods of *Erbschaft dieser Zeit* (which includes Bloch's contributions to the 'Expressionismusdebatte') are supremely concerned to elaborate not the points of total collapse in the culture of the Weimar Republic but the ambiguous moments whose articulation is as yet incomplete. The epilogue which appears at the end of the original preface in the new edition of the work (1962) provides a striking example of the kind of cultural ambiguity Bloch pursues in the remainder of the book, and one to which he has often returned in published discussions. The time from which the book came, he writes, is still in the air:

Indeed, it is there with increasing vitality – particularly among young people who did not experience it, and instead have an almost sentimental sense of its absence. In keeping with the phrase 'the golden twenties' and that other – incidentally older – exaggeration, that Berlin was the intellectual capital of the world up to the night of 1933. [*EdZ* 20]

In isolating the phrase 'the golden twenties' Bloch reveals a largely mythical image of the period encompassed by the Weimar Republic which still commands a kind of credence or at any rate plausibility. Yet against that consciousness of European (cultural) history Bloch sets, as any retrospective consideration of the period must now set, the other compelling aspect of the time: the history of the Weimar Republic is also in a certain important sense the history of the rise of fascism in Germany. Bloch formulates the opposition more sharply: ' "Golden twenties": the Nazi terror germinated in them' (*EdZ* 22). It should not be thought of as a simple contradiction, as though the one must erase the other; rather the '20s represent for Bloch a constellation of forces, constantly interrupting and overlaying one another – a complexity which has by no means been resolved in the post-war period, and one which is dynamically evoked by this juxtaposition.

The central concept with which Bloch will analyse what he defines not simply as a juxtaposition or contradiction in both individual and social consciousness in the Weimar Republic, but rather as the stratification of history into non-synchronised and even syncopated layers of movement forwards, is that of 'Ungleichzeitigkeit', which may be translated as 'dissimultaneity' or 'non-contemporaneity'. Before setting out towards a working definition of this notion, which appears in the central sections of Part Two of *Erbschaft dieser Zeit*, Bloch initiates his reflections and the whole course of his argument with a sequence of brief échapées under the general title 'Dust' ('Der Staub'). These observations, never more than two paragraphs in length and some consisting of only two lines, are written in a highly suggestive and yet severely restrained prose which provokes both puzzlement and thought in the reader. Puzzlement because he is confronted by meticulous observation of the ambiguities in social practice and consciousness; thought, because the resolution of these suggestive contradictions seems only just out of reach. 'Knowing eyes', the fourth of these brief aperçus, concerns the relationship of the 'small man' to both his inferiors and his betters, though in both cases the distinction is presented as a purely financial one. It is curious, observes Bloch, that the small man finds a limited existence not only cheap but right too. There is a characteristic Blochian pun here: 'Merkwürdig nun, dass er das eingeschränkte Leben nicht nur billig, sondern auch recht findet.' 'Billig' must carry the sense of 'cheap', but does so within an inversion of the phrase 'recht und billig', meaning 'just and reasonable' or even 'meet and right': the moment of ambiguity is present even in the substance of Bloch's language (*EdZ* 26). The moderation of the petty-bourgeois is then revealed in a sequence of social relations, turning on money or rather on 'charity' in the first instance:

The kindly benefactor suffers if poor children buy sweets with their penny, woe indeed to the beggar who boozes away the mite which is no match for misery ['ein Scherflein, das keinem Elend gewachsen ist']. For charity demands that the one who receives it should exceed in his moderation the modesty of the gift itself. [*EdZ* 26]

What is registered here is not merely the commonplace observation of a moralist – though the precision of Bloch's aphoristic language suggests, beyond the connections with Voltaire's philosophical 'contes' noted in *Spuren* by Hans Mayer,[26] associations with La Rochefoucauld and even with La Bruyère – rather in the pregnancy of Bloch's notation an aspect of lower-middle-class consciousness is rendered significant and, in its way, symptomatic. As Bloch remarks, programmatically, in the 1935 preface, the book 'limits itself to traits, names, and the symptom which is posited by them' (*EdZ* 18). The same sort of ambiguity is then traced in the attitude of the petty-bourgeois to those 'apparently' better off than themselves:

But even little people notice that they have nothing to laugh about. And they console themselves – with the disease which the others are supposed to get as a result of their pleasure. It's perfectly all right, then, if enjoyment 'revenges itself' on those who have it. The jaded ['verlebt'] young man belongs in this category, and specially the 'knowing eyes'; these usually make their appearance in youths and preferably with black shadows beneath them. As though, of all things, the body should give the moaners ['den Muckern'] the pleasure of doing their job for them. As though the hangover itself came from intemperance and not from cheap schnaps. [*EdZ* 26]

In this example, as in the later one of the dancer who dies not of consumption but of a debauchery which her delicate, childlike body cannot stand, moral aetiologies masquerade as purely physical ones: the value system of the petty-bourgeois mind is naturalised as the revenge taken by the body, its ideological or ethical substance is submerged in an image of what the world is like, and is thus mystified.

Other forms of this naturalisation of ideology, its ascription to the nature of the world and, more radically, to the *world of nature*, will be encountered elsewhere in Bloch's analysis. Prima facie, however, it might be argued that what is in fact uncovered here is not so much an ambiguity as such, as a general state of confusion. It is only at the very end of 'Knowing eyes' that the confusion which interprets one set of phenomena (social deprivation or, more simply, social ills (!), let us say) as another (i.e. *moral* degradation and decline) is revealed as an actual ambiguity or, in the strictest sense of the word, as an ambivalence:

The middle class has less to say of the phthisis of the workers ['Proleten'] than it does of that of the dancer, although the former usually comes to a really sad end. The middle class sees only the chill which is supposed to come from fresh air, from the very thing for which at bottom it really longs. [*EdZ* 27]

Here Bloch finally begins to uncover the transpositions by which the moral explanations encountered earlier come into being: the apparent philistinism described in 'Knowing eyes' is a precise inversion of its real sense, what the epilogue of 1962 calls 'the freedom bell of the old drive, of the implied goal, the heritage of 1789' (*EdZ* 21). The failure of bourgeois aspirations in the century and a half or so since the French revolution, not least – and perhaps even especially – in Germany, has led to their repression. In an essentially Freudian image Bloch argues that these aspirations – the 'old drive' ('Antrieb') – finally re-emerge in distorted form, as *symptoms* of a particular 'unhappy consciousness' in the golden twenties. The symptom may not, however, be taken for the drive, however distorted now, which in fact generates it; and so the contradictions or ambivalences uncovered in Bloch's analysis are not those of classical Marxism between the forces of production and the relations of production. Bloch's work is concerned rather with 'intentional content' ('Intentionsinhalte'), through which a pheno- menology of consciousness in the Weimar Republic can be adumbrated.

Such a project entails above all an interpretative model and procedure which can demonstrate that the apparently irrational elements within a culture and its contemporary consciousness cannot be resolved without remainder into mere stupidity. In its foundation the method adopted by Bloch is, as one might expect, profoundly Hegelian:

Just as the expressions 'unity of subject and object', of 'finite and infinite', of 'being and thought', etc, have the drawback that 'object' and 'subject' bear the same meaning as when *they exist outside that unity*, so that within the unity they mean something other than is implied by their expression: so, too, falsehood is not, *qua* false, any longer a moment of truth.[27]

It is, of course, no accident that this passage from the *Phenomenology of Mind* is cited at the end of the original (1922) preface to Lukács's *History and Class Consciousness*, for although Lukács later insisted that important distinctions would now have to be made between his own work in the '20s, particularly *History and Class Consciousness*, and Bloch's *Geist der Utopie* and *Thomas Münzer*, he generously admitted both his affinity to Bloch then and his continuing sympathy for his utopian system.[28] However, Lukács adds one further extension to Hegel's formulation which is central for the development of his own theory and, it seems to me, for the exposition of history and consciousness undertaken by Bloch in *Erbschaft*:

In the pure historicisation of the dialectic this statement receives yet another twist: in so far as the 'false' is an aspect of the 'true' it is both 'false' and 'non-false'. When the professional demolishers of Marx criticise his 'lack of conceptual rigour' ... they cut as sorry a figure as did Schopenhauer when he tried to expose Hegel's 'logical howlers' in his Hegel critique. ... The logical conclusion for the dialectician to draw from this failure is not that he is faced with a conflict between different scientific methods, but that he is in the presence of a *social phenomenon* and that by conceiving it as a socio-historical phenomenon he can at once refute it and transcend it dialectically.[29]

Erbschaft dieser Zeit avoids the danger of becoming an essay in social psychology by securing the notion of the symptom (which, although it provides a useful expository metaphor, is anyway never stressed by Bloch) and the other units of interpretation, named variously as 'trace' ('Spur') or 'sign' ('Zeichen'), from any purely idealist argument within the limits of its conception as a 'socio-historical phenomenon'. Within that context the dimensions and the dialectics of the 'false', which is mysteriously also the 'non-false', in its relation to the 'true' may safely be elaborated.

The point at which the 'non-false' may be grasped in its dialectical ambiguity is its 'Ungleichzeitigkeit', its dissimultaneity or non-contemporaneity. Traub and Wieser gave an initial definition of the concept, in their *Kursbuch* interview with Bloch, as the 'contradictory coexistence – especially characteristic of German history – of developed capitalist production relations and ideologies with pre-capitalist ones dragged along with them'. [30] Bloch's own initial approach to the idea is inevitably more laconic: in the passage headed 'Early stage' which opens the discussion of 'Ungleichzeitigkeit', Bloch writes simply.

Not everyone is there in the same Now. They are only superficially there – because they can be seen today. But that is not to say that they yet live simultaneously with the others.

They carry much more that is early along with them, that gets mixed in. [*EdZ* 104]

Energies, whose origin lies in the past ('Von ganz anderem Unten her,' says Bloch), remain actually current and in contradiction with the Now, the present age and its social formations. Thus an incompetent man who is left behind by the demands of his job *stays behind* simply as himself. But Bloch insists upon a different question and one which for him is central to the whole issue: what if such a one, apart from his incompetence, does not fit in to a very modern business precisely because through the force of still effective peasant origins he is an 'earlier type'? The class consciousness of such a man would include elements which were at odds with the existing social order not simply because of the classic contradictions defined by Marx (though these might still hold) but because he worked in terms of a residual value system which was at odds with *any* developed capitalist organisation.

Bloch names three social groups of which this might generally be true: the first is the young. The young are at odds with the present time not because they thrive on roots in the past but precisely because of a sense of incompletion which Bloch characterises as a 'hollow youthfulness' ('hohles Jungsein'). This emptiness or absence is filled with dreams; that is, the non-contemporaneous element in the young takes its strength not from the past but from some possible future – and already the argument is set to open into the utopian discourse of Bloch's major thought. In thus establishing the nature of a youth consciousness Bloch provides the basis for a political analysis: he is far from assuming that such a frame of mind, as he sensitively demonstrates it in the 'Bündische Jugend', for instance, will of necessity be progressive. The complex of forces which is uncovered can do no more in the first instance than prepare the ground for a satisfactory solution to a question posed by Lukács in *History and Class Consciousness* which seems to me to provide an exact summary of the project undertaken in *Erbschaft dieser Zeit*:

... we must discover ... the *practical* significance of these different possible relations between the objective economic totality, the imputed class consciousness and the real, psychological thoughts of men about their lives. [31]

Clearly, the particular balance of forces outlined here by Lukács is directed within his own argument towards the definition of that consciousness which is 'neither the sum nor the average of what is thought or felt by the individuals who make up the class',[32] and as I have suggested this would call for clear distinctions between the two writers: yet the sense of a 'tertium datur', of a further concealed meaning, is common to both analytical approaches.

If the temporal structure of the young, as it were, is founded not so much in time, in the ordinary sense of a history, as in an awareness of a possibility which Bloch interprets as an openness to the future, then the second social group to which an analysis of non-contemporaneity might be pertinent offers a precisely inverted case. 'One type' – i.e. the young – Bloch writes, 'always begins from in front' (*EdZ* 105); the second, namely the peasantry 'is from long ago, where it has its roots' (*EdZ* 106). The agrarian economy in Germany has remained free of the immediate effects of capitalism and of capitalisation because it has retained a communal form of production: this has direct consequences for the social and political awareness of the peasantry, which in turn, mutatis mutandis and in the dialectic of country and city, influences the consciousness of the middle class of town dwellers. The peasantry tends to move to the right politically, not just because it seeks security in the agrarian crisis with those who offer tariff controls, but because of what Bloch calls its 'bound existence' ('gebundene Existenz') which in its way recalls Zweig's hope for a cultural return to the values of 'Gemeinde', 'the relatively archaic form of its production relations, its customs, and its calendar of life within the cycle of an unchanged nature' (*EdZ* 107). Thus the social and economic forms of peasant life and the concomitant awareness of the contemporary world enter into an only partial contact: non-contemporaneous layers of time and history exist with only apparent simultaneity in the present, but in fact, by the operation of a shift located in the very structure of history itself, stand in a temporal discontinuity which amounts to a contradiction. That contradiction Bloch sees as productive because it entails a critical relationship to the realities of the capitalist 'present'.

Between these two groups stands, as a third instance of non-contemporaneity, the middle class, with its own particularly urban form of regressiveness. The desire for the social values which came to an end with the first world war emerges as its widespread symptom, transforming insecurity into a certain 'homesickness' for the past and so rechannelling essentially liberal energies into distorted, archaic forms. In this context Bloch provides an illuminating definition of the time structure he has, within a rhetoric of indirection, been describing:

Older forms of being thus return in a precisely urban way, together with older forms of thought and images of hatred, like that of Jewish usury as exploitation itself. There is belief in a break with 'servitude to interest rates' ['Bruch der "Zinsknechtschaft" wird geglaubt'], as though the economy were that of about 1500, superstructures which seemed to have been long since overthrown are thrown back up again, and repose like complete medieval towns ['Stadtbilder'] in the midst of the present. Here stands the Nordic Blood Inn, there the castle of Duke Hitler, there the church of the German Reich, a church of the soil, where the townsfolk too feel themselves to be the fruit of the German earth and honour the earth as holy, as the confessio of German heroes and German history. [*EdZ* 109]

It is in this demonisation of bourgeois values, in the return to a chthonic 'participation mystique', that the dynamic relationship between the country and the town leaves its mark. The establishment of values essentially founded upon a notional or moral 'return to the land' suggests that a pastoral attitude to nature and its relation to the city is here invoked. Such an attitude is repeatedly analysed in Bloch's work, and in particular reference should be made not only to the section headed 'Spirits at large in town and country' ('Rauhnacht in Stadt und Land') in the second part of *Erbschaft dieser Zeit* where the 'völkisch' mythologies of National Socialism are revealed as a 'pastorale militans', but also to the essays included in the second volume of *Verfremdungen* which date from the same period but offer a much more positive exploitation of the pastoral motif. William Empson's discussion of pastoral forms [33] points out the resolution of conflicts which can be enacted by them in the overtly ideological context of literature, particularly when it is viewed as the historical product of a particular class dealing with actual social relations; Bloch on the other hand, while recognising in the non-contemporaneous elements of social consciousness the matrix which provides *in a later mediation or mediations* the substance of ideological formations, insists on a potentially positive, as it were 'pre-ideological' and critical aspect. Thus there can be a *real* 'Ungleichzeitigkeit', which does not necessarily partake of any false consciousness: rather it represents the 'non-false' of Lukács's definition. In such a case

the drives and reserves which stem from pre-capitalist times and superstructures become effective, among them genuine non-contemporaneities, which a sinking class gives currency in its consciousness . . . [*EdZ* 113]

In the definition we have considered the complex reality of 'exploitation' is resolved into the simple image of 'Jewish usury', and the process of simplification is already a pastoral one; it appears more clearly as such in the other figures (in the rhetorical sense) analysed by Bloch: the feudal–'völkisch' imagery of blood and soil ('Blut und Boden'), where Hitler appears as a medieval baron, an image borne out by Nazi portraiture of the Führer, where National Socialist racial theories emerge in the harmless image of drinking companionship; these figures at once mediate and distort, and finally defuse, a potentially critical distance towards developed capitalism, which in essence expresses the tribal socialism of what Engels called the primitive 'gentes'. In more general terms any case of 'Ungleichzeitigkeit' presents a segment of human history which has never been developed and so has never become a part of contemporary experience. In Bloch's own terminology, what is recognised *subjectively*, in the petty-bourgeois or peasant, as a dull antipathy towards the present, as a kind of suppressed anger ('gestaute Wut'), emerges *objectively*, in the investigations of *Erbschaft*, as that which is alien to (even alienated from) the capitalist present. Objectively these residual value systems represent for Bloch a past which has never been 'worked up' ('aufgearbeitet') to attain its sublation in capitalist organisation ('kapitalistisch noch nicht "aufgehoben"') (*EdZ* 117). Crucial for Bloch's position, however, is the further aspect of non-contemporaneity which was considered in his discussion of the young: any segment of the past which is left in such an undeveloped form not only speaks critically of the present, it stands too for a *future* which has been prevented and avoided.

The present discussion has done no more than sketch Bloch's applications of the notion of discontinuous but somehow overlapping layers of time. They entail among other distinctions the need for a multi-level view of time and of social and cultural development which can deal not only with the varieties of non-contemporaneity considered but also with the classical contradictions of Marxist analysis which are experienced directly by the working class and thus represent 'contemporaneous contradictions'. This difficulty raises for Bloch the 'problem of a multi-level dialectics' ('einer mehrschichtigen Dialektik'); it is resolved in the notion of a totality by which the multiple contradictions registered in *Erbschaft* may be grasped. It is in his definition of such a totalised historical thought which must be both critical and non-contemplative that the propagandist element of the work is most to the fore: only such a multi-level approach can avoid the idealist repose of Hegel's monadic 'dialectics of remembered knowledge' (*EdZ* 125), and thus retain an openness to the future. But the word 'propaganda' and Lethen's empirical, political objections to Bloch's strategy should not occlude the significance of the procedure: although the central section of the book – 'Non-contemporaneity and the need for its dialectics' in the second part – is concerned to establish a general model of history, the actual application of this theory is made in Part One, in the remainder of Part Two and in Part Three to aspects of what has been called 'Weimar culture', encompassing everything from the marathon dancing competitions of the Depression to the development of Jaspers' philosophy of 'Existenz'. What results is a mode of cultural interpretation which is sensitive to the need for critical – and, for that matter, political – engagement with its own object: history itself.

It will be apparent that the nature of this object is not finally clear: the problem of *what* Bloch is talking about is signalled not least in the range of terms brought into play in the course of the argument. Thus he speaks of 'productive forces which have not yet been unleashed' and in the same breath of 'intentional content' ('Intentionsinhalte'), and elsewhere of symptoms, symbols, mythologies and dreams. The latter stand in relation to the former as signs to the thing signified, and yet what is thus signified or hinted at is, in itself, disparate: for while 'productive forces which have not yet been unleashed' suggests an essentially deterministic model of historical development, the intentionality of the second phrase suggests an individualist voluntarism. To dwell on this dilemma would in the long run be to lose track of Bloch's actual practice: for the problem thus posed exactly reflects the difficulty of self-engagement in the historical interpretation of culture which, as we noted, Benjamin demanded and which in its way *Erbschaft dieser Zeit* undertakes.

With the complete text of Bloch's major work, the *Prinzip Hoffnung*, now before us, it is of course possible to read his analysis of the '20s and early '30s with hindsight and thus to insert them into the larger pattern of his philosophy. That task will finally be indispensable,[34] but already within the scope of Bloch's writing up to *Erbschaft dieser Zeit* it is possible to see the outlines of what will be worked out in far greater detail later. In particular the parable-like texts of *Spuren*, first published in 1930, suggest the mode of the other investigations collected in *Erbschaft* and in the political essays of 1934–39:[35] habit, Bloch argues in one of the early texts, functions as a very slight narcotic against the frustrations of humdrum work in office or factory. The more extreme case he then describes is much more immediately true of the Marxist philosopher who finds himself living through a period when fascism is ascendant:

If, however, the situation gets really desperate, not simply monotonous but crushingly bad, then a much stronger antidote forms, one from ourselves. Even boys experience a curious intoxication when their school reports keep on getting worse and misery has really taken wing. Adults feel [spüren] this in a different but related way: if someone has risked everything on the last card and lost everything, then sometimes an illusory but very real sense of happiness ['ein ganz täuschendes Glück] will come to him just because he has hit rock-bottom. A soft happiness which absorbs the blows, so that for a time at least they miss or

go awry. No energies emerge from this, but while habituation lets us down gently
and dulls our senses, the small sparkling ecstasy in unhappiness presents the
enjoyment of a defiance, indeed of a defiance which apparently no longer even
needs to be defiant, which makes us strangely free, even if only for a moment.
There a piece of that which has not yet come ['ein Stück Ungekommenes'] lies
hidden, in part as what has been put aside 'for a rainy day' and in part as a lamp
– and not merely an inner one.[36]

In one respect the already encyclopaedic form of *Erbschaft* prefigures the
pattern of *Prinzip Hoffnung* but inverts its stress; for in the earlier work
the sense in which every despair entails a hope is taken from its point of
origin, as an 'Unglück', an unhappiness, rather than being immediately
projected towards its utopian resolution in hope.[37] What helps to clarify
the object of Bloch's analysis, i.e. the nature, in his view, of history itself,
is the final formulation here. At those points where we experience an
element of the past which has not been 'worked up' – the residual pre-
capitalist ideologies of the peasantry, the blood-and-soil myths which
capture the imagination of the petty-bourgeoisie – we find an illumination
of the present status quo, an elaboration of its mere negativity (in a
Hegelian sense), which is certainly intuitive or inward, but which is by no
means *only* intuitive. It can also have objective status as an experience of
the progressive but as yet *incomplete* clarification of the nature of being
human.[38] The gesture which accompanies Bloch's considerations of the
varied aspects of Weimar culture is what the *Spuren* call 'Das Merke',
which might be rendered as 'The *nota bene*': that is to say, engagement in
history can be achieved only by a sharp awareness of the many factors
which interweave to make up the simplified and therefore mystified thing
which is called 'reality' and appears as the immutable. What the
Erbschaft undertakes first is an identification of those moments within
that culture which are despite appearances neither simple nor immutable
but ambiguous and in flux. Bloch quotes an adage from the Arabian
philosopher Ibn Tofail to the effect that 'the living one is the son of the
watchful man' ('Der Lebende ist des *Wachenden* Sohn', *EdZ* 343), by
which is implied his belief that to be truly alive, to be partaking in the
continuing process of human self-definition, and so avoid stagnation in
the mystified form of a non-contemporaneity or, perhaps worse,
limitation to a merely fashionable contemporaneity (as in his account of
Berlin in the *Erbschaft*), it is necessary to enter upon a process of
gathering and reading of cultural signs which alone can locate them in
the totalised system where their ultimate sense is possible and *actively*
achieved.

'The *nota bene*' concludes with a general statement of the practice of
Spuren as 'a reading and gathering of traces in all directions' ('Es ist ein

Spurenlesen kreuz und quer' – again the pun is scarcely representable in English!): the identification of such signs is, as we have seen, intuitive, but also authenticated by an existential necessity. Thus speaking of Kierkegaard in the Hegel critique of *Geist der Utopie* Bloch comments: 'We and we alone are addressed by the Christian parables and curiously illuminated by them within ourselves ("selbsthaft")'; and later in the same work he says that the 'occasions of astonishment' 'bear the imprint of absolute clarity and necessity'.[39] As we have noted, astonishment appears in *Erbschaft dieser Zeit* in inverted form as despair, limitation and the final gamble, yet the same kind of existential authentication operates – which is one reason why a meditative, narrative form is well suited to communicate Bloch's thought to his readers: *Erbschaft* and *Spuren* are a good deal easier to 'get hold of' than *Geist der Utopie*. Yet such traces, signs or figures remain to be read, to be decoded, and one of the early – and non-metaphysical – concerns of *Erbschaft dieser Zeit* is precisely with a failure of reading as such. Thus in 'Dust' and in the first part of the work proper we encounter discussions of the relationship between reality and how it is *read* after what Bloch calls the 'triumph of the magazine'. Behind these down-to-earth reflections we glimpse, it seems to me, Nietzsche's notion of 'interpretation' as opening up a new infinity in the world:

The world has once more become 'infinite' to us: to the extent that we cannot dismiss the possibility that it *contains infinite interpretations.* Once more the great horror seizes us – but who would desire forthwith to deify once more *this* monster of an unknown world in the old fashion? And perhaps worship the unknown as the 'unknown person' in future? Ah! there are too many *ungodly* possibilities of interpretation comprised in this unknown, too much devilment, stupidity, and folly of interpretation – our own human, all too human interpretation itself, which we know . . .[40]

The multiplicity of the world described here has ample room for both the demonic misreading of its possibilities which produced National Socialism and for Bloch's socialist projection. What appalls Nietzsche is, on the one hand, the very endlessness of possible versions of the world, and, on the other, the prospect of deifying that very endlessness in a subjection of the human to some further abstraction. In the final turn of the screw, however, even 'our own human, all too human interpretation' is stripped of its priority. Nietzsche's resolution of this problem is twofold. In the first place he points out that the range of possible versions is not a purely cognitive aspect of human existence but entails a 'willing'. Will and the will to power decisively cut through the apparent endlessness of interpretation, since they represent the bedrock experience which is beyond the palimpsest of tissued commentaries which 'are' the world.[41] The late Nietzsche proposes a further solution, characterised in the often repeated phrase of a lack of, or incapacity for, 'philology'. In a remarkable passage in *The Antichrist* he describes the theologian, representative still of the tendency noted in *The Gay Science* to deify an abstracted infinite world, as being marked out by his incapacity for philology and then defines what has become a key term in the late works:

Philology is to be understood here in a very wide sense as the art of reading well – of being able to read off a fact *without* falsifying it by interpretation, without losing caution, patience, subtlety in the desire for understanding. Philology as *ephexis* in interpretation: whether it be a question of books, newspaper reports, fate or the weather – . . .[42]

Hollingdale translates the Greek word 'ephexis' as 'undecisiveness', but a better rendering would be 'hesitation'. The characteristic of philology as the art of reading well is its resolute refusal to jump to conclusions: it dwells upon the elements of its object, the text, and avoids the immediate interpretation which might be available. Instead the construction of meaning which any hermeneutic activity envisages is delayed or, as it were, 'hesitated' – not least, as the same section of *The Antichrist* remarks, out of a sense of decency.

Apart from *Geist der Utopie*, parts of *Prinzip Hoffnung* and a longer discussion in the third part of *Erbschaft* ('Der Impuls Nietzsche'), Bloch makes only occasional reference to Nietzsche's work. While it would be false, therefore, to speak of any direct influence, two kinds of relation can be proposed between Bloch's philosophy and Nietzsche. First, although Lukács had perceptively observed that Bloch's writing presents a unique mixture of Hebel's *Schatzkästlein* and Hegel's *Phänomenologie*,[43] any fuller attempt to characterise his philosophical style would, it seems to me, have to take account of Nietzsche's work. Secondly, Nietzsche's two resolutions of the interpretation problem, in the notions of the 'will to power' and of a philological 'ephexis', while they cannot be thought of as in any way the 'groundwork' of Bloch's cultural and ideological analyses, may provide nevertheless useful tools with which to elucidate his model of history.

At one point, quite early in *Erbschaft dieser Zeit*, Bloch defines history:

History is not a being which progresses along a single line, where capitalism as the last stage might have transcended all earlier ones; rather it is a *polyrhythmic and multi-spatial thing, with sufficient corners that have not been dealt with* ['unbewältigt'] *and which have certainly not been enlisted, transcended.* [EdZ 69]

The corners or nooks of history which have not yet been mastered by any linear progression are the ideologies and value systems which the remainder of the book seeks out and records: what is of primary interest here is the musical and spatial image Bloch adopts. In both aspects this is a picture of history drawn in physical terms – even a rhythm requires actual sound if it is to be measured at all. Spatiality becomes the dominant metaphor in the remainder of this definition, and there are good reasons for suggesting that it plays an important part in Bloch's construction of history. The account of non-contemporaneity, which has been discussed above as an analysis of pastoral functions, relies to a large extent on geographical models: the clearest case of this in *Erbschaft* is to be found in the essay 'Ludwigshafen – Mannheim', in Part Three, as well as in the reflections of *Verfremdungen II*, significantly subtitled 'Geographica'. From one point of view, then, the construction of the notion of 'Ungleichzeitigkeit' essentially answers the need to see disparate oppositional or reactionary ideologies *not* as merely local, geographically determined 'provincialisms' but as simultaneous moments in a unitary sense of time. In practice the envisaged simultaneity can only be represented spatially, in as much as space is the form of a perceived coincidence of objects or events in time.

The origins of this aspect of Bloch's thought may be found in relatively clear form in *Geist der Utopie*; he is discussing the 'darkness of [immediate] experience' ('Dunkel des Erlebens selber') and comments:

Only when it has passed . . . can what has been experienced be examined, and it takes on a spatial order, in the perceived form of its simultaneity ['seines Zugleich'; literally 'its At Once'], just as it emerged from the flow of the river,[44] half still possessed of the reality of experience and half already resolved into the contiguity of contents now in repose. If what has passed is recognised as such in the grand style, as a world of the no longer conscious, as a world independent of the experiencing, conceiving subject, then it . . . becomes the object of a separate academic discipline. In the half-ordered reality of experience, space – as simply the perceptual form of simultaneity – was still an enclave in time, surrounded by it, behind and before, as the perceptual form of vitality . . . [*GdU* 251–2]

This is essentially an account of the phenomenology of experience and consciousness in the individual: in *Erbschaft dieser Zeit* the same dialectic between space and time is seen as a clue to the historical process. In the existential terms brought into play in the *Geist der Utopie* the spatial form ('contiguity') in which any experienced simultaneity is available for thought and reflection falsifies it. As Bloch goes on to say, however, the philosophy of history and the philosophy of value – which he glosses as 'the concept hope' – restore, in a utopian projection, the possibility of 'das *wahre Zugleich*' (the true simultaneity) of 'absolute vitality and existential revelation' upon which they are centred. An awareness of this utopian prospect will prove finally indispensable, as in all his work, for an adequate account of the construction of history upon which *Erbschaft dieser Zeit* is based.

The musical form hinted at by Bloch's definition of history as 'polyrhythmic' also takes up some of the ideas developed in *Geist der Utopie* under the titles 'The philosophy of music' and 'On the theory of music'. The musical form provides an almost ideal metaphor for the problem of simultaneity and of space: as a sequence of printed symbols, a piece of music obviously occupies a space, a number of pages of score. But because, unlike almost any other art form, music *in performance* crucially occupies time it provides an exactly parallel model for the questions posed in Bloch's work about the nature of history. In very primitive terms, the relation of melody to harmony, depending on which is given more weight, images the notion of a historical progress and its relation to disparate and even contradictory elements within a given society at a given moment. Nor is the utopian prospect neglected in the metaphor; the aesthetic argument is a complex one, but it may be suggested by the question: at what point is a musical work grasped – in the particular moments of harmony, in the development of melody, in the broader movements of harmonic development . . . or finally, only when the last note has been sounded and the final word uttered, as it were?

In the first place Bloch's decipherment of the notation of a complex historical configuration is derived, as a version of *allegory*, from the Church Fathers – in particular Origen's doctrine of the three levels of biblical exposition – and from the contemplatives Richard and Hugo of St Victor. Between these Bloch can develop an expository theory which is applicable not simply to written texts but to empirical experience of the kind recorded in his study of the Weimar Republic.[45] What is literally undertaken, then, is a reading of history in all the signs of disturbance which he sees around him, throwing up the 'dust' of the first few sections of the book. Fredric Jameson has described this hermeneutic procedure as entailing a 'demystification and . . . an essential restoration of access', and this is widely true of his practice. The reading of the allegory of history is not, however, bound to a static, vertical exegesis, as it were; and it is here that Nietzsche's 'ephexis' can re-establish the structural connection between the musical model of history and the practice of a 'Spurenlesen' – a connection which Bloch *never* loses sight of. For the symbolic side of an allegory is always prone to return to its otherness, to its mythical essence, which is neither human nor humane.[46] Only in the case of music do we encounter a 'symbolic form' which, although its language is at present wholly irreducible and therefore entirely 'other', promises to become wholly our own as the exact representation of its object – man himself ('. . . das Symbolische an [der Musik] ist der eigene, sich selber *sachlich* verhüllte Menschengegenstand selber', *GdU* 207).

The more overtly political or at any rate socio-historical notion of 'Tendenz' which underlies *Erbschaft dieser Zeit* in both its propagandist and analytical aspects appears in *Geist der Utopie* as 'das Unterwegs': the 'en route'. In a prior image, as it were, early in the book, this is seen simply as a pathway illuminated by art:

This is the path which Klee and Marc wanted to point out; and it is ... an effulgence of fiery and mysterious signs, a sudden meeting of all paths in that overgrown, insignificant byway which proved to be the high road of human development. [*GdU* 26]

It is this pathway which the reader of *Geist der Utopie* and *Erbschaft* must learn to traverse, with Bloch, by following the signposts available, the cultural signs of the times. In the *Spuren*, perhaps without the wholly optimistic energy of the first book, the 'en route' becomes at times a 'diversion' (Umweg); yet even even this possibility of finally getting lost can, in its very hesitation, loosen the apparently static world. Of the narrator in his parable 'Off the mark: the inn of the madmen' Bloch says

He spoke in images, yet they were not flowery or enthusiastic as though he wanted to prophesy something, rather they were slightly frivolous as though he were trying to loosen something with modest tropes. [*Sp* 138]

The rhetorical figures become the moments of hesitation, of Nietzsche's 'ephexis', on the road to human self-identity, which is to say that the moments of cultural insight recorded in *Erbschaft* may be seen individually as hesitations or diversions in their ambiguous or paradoxical aspect, and that any total reading of them must postpone its judgement, as it were, if it is to satisfy the requirements of philological decency. [47]

This double hesitancy is founded finally in the musical image suggested by the word 'polyrhythmic'. Precisely because of the symbolic opacity of music Bloch attributes major importance to it as the form of a promise as yet unfulfilled. Against other art forms music – beginning with Bach, Bloch suggests – is an extremely *young* phenomenon,

a continuous syncope even in modern history, quite clearly subject to a rhythm quite distinct from the morphologically and sociologically given body of culture to which it belongs. [*GdU* 58]

The history of music not only disturbs the obvious lines of cultural development; by being syncopatedly 'out of step' it provides itself a general model of the kind Bloch wishes to use. As music is itself a constant syncope, so too it gives an heuristic metaphor by which to analyse the 'out of step' non-contemporaneities which Bloch sees around him: Grunsky's definition of syncope, elaborated in *Geist der Utopie*, indicates the precision of the metaphor.

> ... a novel forcing ['Herausholen'] and re-emphasis of those points which in the bar would be unstressed, a novum in the rhythm, a tensing and juxtaposition of the stressed against the unstressed and of the unstressed against the stressed, so that, by means of the frictions caused by the parallel development of differently divided times, it is possible to carry through several rhythms simultaneously, even if they are only perceptible as the thrust at the end of the bar. [*GdU* 101]

This is a precise description of the multiple pattern Bloch envisages, and dispenses for the moment with the additional thickness brought to the metaphor by the complication of harmony. The complexity brought to a linear development by the syncope opens the way for a polyphony which does not simply resolve into what Bloch calls the lyric contrapuntal equilibrium or repose in Bach's art of fugue. The finally adequate model of the historical process in its development towards a utopian goal is the symphony itself. In Bloch's speculation the symphony, objectively and in its very substance, represents the form of history: what unites the musical form and 'the remainder of the historic-productive activity of time' ('das übrige historisch-produktive Zeitgeschehen') in structure is the fact that, in both, what occurs is driven on beyond itself into the far distance, while its end must be derived internally – as a final resolution of musical thematics – from what precedes, and yet comes as a goal. Thus, in a final list of common characteristics, Bloch names the images of time in music – and therefore in his model of history – as 'the persistence of the Before in the Now, i.e. conservation, perseverence, construction, inheritance . . .'. Yet it is only at the terminal point that this growing multiplicity finds its full meaning, when the empirical sequence of events can be understood as a true simultaneity, the single articulation of sense. The philosophical point stressed by Bloch here concerns the need to recognise the unique importance of the totalisation he has proposed: only as the 'luminous and discontinuous historical sphere of a now completed epoch' can the 'meaning' of its signs be articulated. The delays of philological reading are the obverse side of the totality which in all Bloch's work appears as the *Noch Nicht*, the Not Yet.

A final question remains which can be only adumbrated here. There is an odd sense in which the final emergence of the goal of history in Bloch's chiliastic vision seems to take on a deterministic stress. The subject of history, that which drives each individual element beyond itself into the 'far distance', still seems shadowy. Clearly the voluntarist idea of a pure willing is not what concerns Bloch; yet the purely determinist line, derived from a possible philosophy of Nature, would contradict not only the registered ambiguities of the cultural world but also the more substantial ambiguities of social relationship which Bloch sets alongside them. Within the musical model, it seems to me, this difficulty is abrogated even if, qua model, it can hardly be resolved. The symphony is composed, performed and heard: what is directed in the score must be enacted by the musicians and can, finally, be grasped as a totality unavailable to either of the former by its audience. Bloch is both performer and audience. As audience his critical totalising activity must stand for the possible participation of all men, too easily caught up with the intricacies of their own line. The apparent determinism of the model of energies driving on through history, though it remains rooted in the concept of matter which Bloch developed later, resolves itself into the collective hope which in his view has always been a 'horizon' of human existence. And hope alone can enable the active construction of meaning, through the reading of history in *Erbschaft dieser Zeit*, which only becomes really available from the point of view of the totalising *finale*.

The indications catalogued and given new meaning in *Erbschaft dieser Zeit* and *Spuren*, on the foundation of the pattern of history developed in *Geist der Utopie*, achieve the insertion of critical consciousness into history demanded by Benjamin, not simply by transforming insight into propaganda but by showing that just as in music 'the hearer finally receives himself, strengthened and given meaning' so too, through the music of time, the world is the scene of our self-inscription, promising – beyond the partialities and confusions of the present – to return us to our truest 'selves'.

Notes

[1] Cited in Frenzel's article 'Literatur der Gegenwart', *Die Böttcherstrasse 1*, H. 12 (1928–29), pp. 31–2.

[2] Carl Georg Heise, 'Zeitglosse und Beschluss', *Genius* III (1921), p. 355.

[3] Kurt Tucholsky, 'Gebrauchslyrik', in *Literaturkritik*, Reinbek, 1972, p. 159 f.

[4] Articles by various critics, apart from Frenzel, bear titles such as 'Vom Sinn der Lyrik in unserer Zeit' (*Die Horen* 3, 1926–27, pp. 401–4); 'Das Gedicht von Morgen' (*Der Gral* 23, 1928–29, pp. 877–85); 'Bemerkungen über Lyrik' (*Die Kolonne* 3, 1932, pp. 3–4); 'Die Zukunft der Lyrik' (*Das Tagebuch* 13, 1932, pp. 1635–7), etc.

[5] Brecht, 'Kurzer Bericht . . .', in *Über Lyrik*, Frankfurt a.M., 1964, p. 8.

[6] Brecht, 'Weder nützlich noch schön', *op. cit.*, p. 12 f.

[7] *Loc. cit.*

[8] Klaus Herrmann, 'Das Ende der Persönlichkeit', *Die neue Bücherschau*, F. 5 (1927), pp. 68–70, 72–3.

[9] Brecht, *op. cit.*, p. 11.

[10] *Op. cit.*, p. 12.

[11] Walter Benjamin, 'Literaturgeschichte und Literaturwissenschaft', in *Angelus Novus*, Frankfurt a.M., 1966, p. 450.

[12] *Loc. cit.*

[13] Benjamin's remarks on historicism, in a general sense, and universalism both substantiate Köhn's analysis ('Die Überwindung des Historismus', *DVjs* 48, 1974) and

suggest that the complex of emphases cannot be seen simply as a number of modes of 'transcendence'.

[14] In *Versuche über Brecht*, Frankfurt a.M., 1966, pp. 95–116.

[15] 'Literaturgeschichte . . .', *op. cit.*, p. 456.

[16] *Cf. op. cit.*, p. 455.

[17] 'Rückblick auf Stefan George', *op. cit.*, p. 481.

[18] Richard Sheppard, 'The crisis of language', in *Modernism*, ed. Malcolm Bradbury and James McFarlane, Harmondsworth, 1976, p. 327.

[19] *Loc. cit.*

[20] 'Über Ungleichzeitigkeit, Provinz und Propaganda', in *Gespräche mit Ernst Bloch*, ed. Rainer Traub and Harald Wieser, Frankfurt a.M., 1975, p. 201 f.

[21] *Op. cit.*, p. 197.

[22] *Es muss nicht immer Marmor sein*. Beiträge von Horster, Leithäuser, Negt, Perels, Peters, *Politik* 68, Berlin, 1975.

[23] Helmut Lethen, *Neue Sachlichkeit, 1924–32*, Stuttgart, 1970, pp. 109–14.

[24] *Erbschaft dieser Zeit*, Frankfurt a.M., 1962, p. 19. The *Erbschaft* was first published in 1935 by Oprecht & Helbing, Zurich. I have used the Bibliothek Suhrkamp edition, but pagination corresponds with the fourth volume of the *Gesamtausgabe*. The second edition of 1962 includes a number of sections in Part Two which are lacking in the first but which date from the period just after the first publication; the second edition also contains a number of smaller alterations and deletions. Further references will be given in the text as *EdZ* with page numbers.

[25] Lukács, 'Es geht um den Realismus', in *Marxismus und Literatur* II, ed. Fritz J. Raddatz, Reinbek, 1969, p. 83.

[26] Hans Mayer, 'Ernst Blochs poetische Sendung', in *Ernst Bloch zu Ehren*, ed. Siegfried Unseld, Frankfurt a.M., 1965, pp. 21–30.

[27] Hegel, *Phänomenologie des Geistes*, Frankfurt a.M. (Ullstein), 1970, p. 32.

[28] *Cf. Gespräche mit Ernst Bloch*, pp. 33–4. There is not scope in the present essay to consider the particular relations of Bloch's analysis of class-consciousness in *Erbschaft* to Lukács's essays of 1922, but clearly reference would have to be made in the first instance to the notions of 'false' and 'possible' consciousness and to the role attributed by Lukács to 'reification'.

[29] Lukács, *History and Class Consciousness*, trans. R. Livingstone, London, 1971, p. xlvii.

[30] *Gespräche . . .*, p. 196.

[31] Lukács, *op. cit.*, p. 51.

[32] *Loc. cit.*

[33] The techniques and mechanisms of the pastoral, both as a critical potential for 'proletarian literature' and as a bourgeois occlusion of class conflict, were fully described in Empson's *Some Versions of Pastoral*, which, like Bloch's studies of the Weimar Republic, also appeared in 1935.

[34] The best general introduction to Bloch's thought is Fredric Jameson's discussion of 'Ernst Bloch and the future' in Jameson, *Marxism and Form*, Princeton, 1974, pp. 116–59.

[35] *Vom Hasard zur Katastrophe*, Frankfurt a.M., 1972.

[36] *Spuren*, Frankfurt a.M., 1969, pp. 15–16. Further references will be given in the text as *Sp* with page numbers.

[37] *Cf. Prinzip Hoffnung*, Frankfurt a.M., 1959, pp. 353–4; Jameson, *op. cit.*, p. 122.

[38] *Cf.* 'Romantik des Diluvium', in *Erbschaft dieser Zeit*, pp. 334–43.

[39] *Geist der Utopie*, Frankfurt a.M., 1964, pp. 227, 261. Further references will be given in the text as *GdU* with page numbers.

[40] Nietzsche, *The Gay Science* V, section 374. I have slightly altered Common's translation, reprinted by Ungar, New York, 1960.

[41] *Cf.* Karl Jaspers, *Nietzsche*, trans. C. F. Wallraff and F. J. Schmitz, Chicago, 1965, Book II, chapter 5.

[42] Nietzsche, *The Antichrist*, trans. R. J. Hollingdale, Harmondsworth, 1968, section

52, pp. 169–70.

[43] *Gespräche* . . ., p. 34.

[44] There may be a reference here, in relation to the ungraspable 'novum', to the epigraph from Dante which appears on p. 209 of *Geist der Utopie*: 'L'acqua che io prendo/giammai non si corse' (*Paradiso*, II, 7).

[45] Cf. *Erbschaft dieser Zeit*, p. 133 ff.

[46] Cf. *Geist der Utopie*, pp. 206–7.

[47] In relation to the question of 'decency' or 'propriety', compare Bloch's account of what he calls 'das Kählersche' in *Spuren*, p. 168 f.

ROB BURNS

Theory and organisation of revolutionary working-class literature in the Weimar Republic

In the preface to his book *Weimar Culture*, commonly regarded as one of the authoritative overall studies of the phenomenon, Peter Gay writes:

In this essay I have tried to portray Weimar culture as a whole ... What I have done here is to bring together themes that dominated the hectic life of the Republic, and to juxtapose them in ways that will, I trust, permit us to define the Weimar spirit more clearly and more comprehensively than it has been done before.[1]

This claim to comprehensiveness, however, is belied by the omission from his account of a whole dimension of the culture that thrived in the Weimar Republic. For since Gay in effect equates the term 'culture' with bourgeois or 'high' culture, he makes not a solitary reference to the many fertile developments in the working-class culture of the time. And this in a period of German history richer than any before or since in working-class cultural activity. An understanding of the reasons why the Weimar Republic should have produced such an unparalleled wealth of proletarian culture must be related to an analysis of the level of class consciousness of which that culture was, to a certain extent, a reflection, and it is first necessary, therefore, to look briefly at the social and political background against which these particular cultural developments took place.

I

Accumulation of wealth at one pole is ... at the same time accumulation of misery, agony of toil, slavery, ignorance, brutality, mental degradation at the opposite pole, i.e. on the side of the class that produces its own product in the form of capital.[2]

Nothing could demonstrate better the validity of Marx's description in *Capital* of the antagonistic character of capitalistic accumulation than the Weimar Republic. For here the two poles confronted each other in the form of, on the one hand, mass immiseration and, on the other, the acquisitiveness of monopoly capital. Trusts, combines and cartels dominated the entire German economy, and indeed the largest trusts in German history were formed during the Weimar Republic. This continually developing process of monopolisation was stimulated by a series of factors brought to the forefront by the first world war. Industrialisation and the general capitalistic expansion of the economy occurred later in Germany than in other major European capitalist countries. Owing, in general, to the speed with which this process, once initiated, developed, and in particular to the prominence of the armament industry as the consequence of a series of wars, German heavy industry provided an area particularly favourable to the growth of giant monopolies,[3] the prototype of which was the Stinnes empire.[4] This control of the economy by the highly concentrated heavy and chemical industries was further strengthened by two factors: firstly by the large flow of foreign, primarily American, capital into Germany after 1924 which provided German industrialists with the liquid capital necessary to rationalise and enlarge their plants, but more particularly by the raging inflation of the early 1920s which, while bankrupting smaller businesses, allowed the great cartels and banks to discharge their debts in worthless currency. Indeed, inflation rendered the economic structure of the Weimar Republic transparent to such an extent that even a prominent member of the bourgeoisie could say in 1923 that it had 'undermined the political basis of the Republic and concentrated all real power in the hands of a few – namely, the great industrialists ... in no country in the world is capital so strong or politically so despotic. The economic form of society fails to correspond to the political theory: a republic in name, it is a capitalist despotism in fact'.[5]

Consequently, following the period of relative stabilisation from 1924, the means of production were by the end of the 1920s at a more developed stage in Germany than in any other country. But as Kuczynski has shown,[6] there nevertheless remained a significant disjunction between actual and potential production, for at no time in the republic were the productive capacities of German industry fully or even adequately utilised. However, it was not the entrepreneurs but the workers who bore the brunt of this contradiction, for the period is characterised by frontal attacks of capital on the working class in the form of rationalisation, wage cuts, lengthened hours of work and unemployment. In other words, because the contradictions of capitalism revealed themselves at their sharpest in the Weimar Republic, we find there a more intensive and palpable exploitation of the working class than in any other country at that time.

Turning to the other pole in Marx's equation, the working class, we can distinguish three factors which contributed to the marked deterioration in its situation. The first of these was the programme of rationalisation implemented between 1924 and 1932. More important, however, was the rapid fall in the purchasing power of wages. Although at its most evident in the period of inflation, when wages never remotely kept pace with the decline of the currency, significantly even in the so-called 'boom years' the average real wage never reached the official subsistence level (as defined by the Statistisches Reichsamt), while in the years of crisis it sank drastically below it (for instance, in 1932 it stood at almost half the subsistence level[7]). The third factor was the level of unemployment, which between 1926 and 1932 never dropped below 1·3 million, a trend which climaxed in the 1932 figure of over 6 million unemployed. Bearing in mind the attendant phenomenon of short-time work, 1932 thus witnessed the truly astounding situation where only one in three of all workers in Germany was fully employed.

Against this background the Weimar Republic was born in a period of intense class struggle. The 'November revolution' of 1918 was not, it is true, a socialist revolution, for neither was private property expropriated nor the State machine with its bureaucracy 'smashed'. Nevertheless, carried through against the will of the leadership of the socialist parties and trade unions, it not only won for the working class certain immediate gains, such as the establishing of works councils and the introduction of the eight-hour day, but also helped stimulate a period of struggle from 1919 to 1923 which gave rise, for instance, to the Räterepubliken in Bremen and Munich and which culminated in the general strike of 1923 that helped bring about the resignation of the Cuno government. However, with the strengthening of the currency and the economic stabilisation from 1923 the level of class conflict fell, as is best illustrated by the decline in the number of strikes. A major factor in this decline was the right-wing leadership of the trade unions and the Social Democratic Party. The SPD was enmeshed in its own contradictions. While claiming ideologically to be a Marxian party its political practice had long been one of pure gradualism, a development mirrored in the trade unions by their espousal of the theories of revisionism and 'economic democracy'.[8] The politico-cultural position of the SPD was characterised by the fundamental rejection of the idea of a specifically 'proletarian culture', and the newspapers and journals of the party were concerned almost exclusively with the discussion of the modern bourgeois literature of Weimar. It was above all this neglect of a coherent theoretical position that explains why the SPD-orientated 'Arbeiterdichtung', existing as it did in many diverse forms, only rarely gave expression and impetus to the working-class movement of the time.

The other main political expression of the working-class movement was the German Communist Party. Founded in December 1918, it was until the mid-'20s weakened by frequent changes in both leadership and party line – due in part to the murder in January 1919 of its two outstanding leaders, Rosa Luxemburg and Karl Liebknecht – and by the need to establish its mass base. Nevertheless, despite certain erroneous 'leftist' tactics, in particular Stalin's fatal doctrine of social fascism[9] (which viewed social democracy as 'objectively the moderate wing of fascism'[10] and which by the end of the '20s saw criticism concentrated on the SPD almost at the expense of that of the real enemy, the capitalist class and fascism), the significance of the German Communist Party, as Franz Neumann concedes in an otherwise critical appraisal, was that it at least 'gave the working class sufficient critical insight to see through the operations of the economic system and thus left them with little faith in the security promised by liberalism, democracy and reformism'.[11] It was not, however, until the latter half of the '20s that the Communist Party turned its attention systematically to the sphere of working-class culture and concretised its conception of the nature and function of proletarian literature.

II

The theoretical debate on the possibility of a revolutionary literature under capitalism was not peculiar to the Weimar Republic. Its origins can be located in the discussion on Naturalism in the SPD between 1891 and 1896 from which there subsequently developed two diametrically opposed theoretical positions. A central place in this debate was occupied by Franz Mehring, whose work represents the first attempt to found a Marxist aesthetics. He extended his particular criticism of Naturalism into the judgement that the emancipatory effect of any art, whether bourgeois or proletarian, would necessarily be minimal while it operated within a bourgeois culture:

Art can expect its regeneration only from the economic and political victory of the proletariat; it can play little part in the actual emancipatory struggle of that class.[12]

In his belief that 'the fighting class in Germany has no time for writing poetry'[13] Wilhelm Liebknecht, like Mehring, rejected not only the possibility but the desirability of a class literature devoted to the class struggle. This denial of the possibility of proletarian revolutionary literature finds perhaps its definitive articulation in Trotsky's theory of literature and revolution formulated in 1923 in various articles in *Pravda* and appearing for the first time in German in 1924. Although analysing a more advanced stage in the revolutionary process, Trotsky nevertheless considered any artistic participation of the working class under capitalism as a diversion from the primacy of political and economic struggle. Moreover, he argued, the creation of a new class literature would in fact be counter-productive as regards the ultimate aim of the revolution, namely the destruction of class society, for 'the proletariat acquires power for the purpose of doing away for ever with class culture and to make way for human culture'.[14] The consequences this rejection of art as an ideological weapon – what Friedrich Wolf called 'the theory of aesthetic immiseration'[15] – had in Germany have been described by Georg Fülberth as follows:

By excluding art from the realm of the political the SPD missed the opportunity of formulating a coherent literary strategy, that is, of appropriating literature for the cause of the party and using it as a weapon in the class struggle. The result of such a self-imposed restriction was inevitably that this sphere of the superstructure remained the domain of the ruling class – and indeed to such an extent that the working-class literature which began in a real way with the first world war became without exception the vehicle of bourgeois ideology, even in those cases where working-class writers maintained close contact with social democracy.[16]

As a global statement this conclusion has a certain validity but nevertheless contains a certain lack of differentiation, for example, the failure to acknowledge particular areas, such as working-class lay theatre and workers' speech choirs,[17] where the SPD could justifiably claim very real cultural achievements. The misleadingly homogeneous picture Fülberth presents thus invites a mistakenly exclusive identification of the SPD with right-wing, integrationist social democracy.

In fact the first person in the SPD substantially to challenge Mehring's conceptualisation of political art was Clara Zetkin. In her article 'Kunst und Proletariat' (1911) while conceding that only with the destruction of capitalism would complete artistic freedom be attained she nevertheless insisted that art, as an expression of revolutionary consciousness, must of necessity come to challenge the hegemony of bourgeois ideology:

The content of the proletarian class struggle is by no means limited to political and economic demands . . . The more conscious and vigorous its struggle against the capitalist order becomes, all the more sharply does the intellectual content of its activity conflict with the intellectual activity of the bourgeois world. The proletarian class struggle becomes the vehicle of new intellectual and ethical ideals, a new, individual cultural life begins to blossom and thrive among the disinherited.[18]

The clearest formulation, however, both of the necessity of proletarian literature and of the conditions under which it could develop, is often held to be Lenin's article 'Party organisation and party literature', published in Russia in 1905 and in translation in Germany in 1924. In it he criticised as essentially undialectical the view that the sphere of culture could exist independently of the political struggle, whether on the side of reaction or of emancipation. Any postulated notion of neutrality ('Parteilosigkeit') or 'absolute freedom', therefore, objectively imbued literature with a functionalist, crypto-affirmative character, and it was the task of socialism 'to contrast this hypocritically free literature, which is in reality linked to the bourgeoisie, with a really free one that will be *openly* linked to the proletariat'.[19] This was the principle of partisanship ('Parteilichkeit') according to which 'literature must become part of the common cause of the proletariat, 'a cog and a screw' of one single great Social Democratic mechanism set in motion by the entire politically conscious vanguard of the entire working class'.[20] Lenin insisted, however, that his comparison of the writer with a cog in a machine was intended neither to deny the importance of form, fantasy or individual creativity nor to connote a mechanistic subordination of art to some arbitrary party line. Rather the writer should renounce the illusory freedom of bourgeois individualism and unpartisan writing and place his creativity in the service of the revolutionary aims of the working class. The task was therefore:

to organise a broad, multiform and varied literature inseparably linked with the Social Democratic working-class movement. Every newspaper, journal, publishing house, etc, must immediately set about reorganising its work, leading up to a situation in which it will, in one form or another, be integrated into one Party organisation or another. Only then will 'social democratic' literature really become worthy of that name, only then will it be able to fulfil its duty and, even within the framework of bourgeois society, break out of bourgeois slavery and merge with the movement of the really advanced and thoroughly revolutionary class.[21]

Lenin's article is undoubtedly of importance and was in fact one of the first theoretical articles to be republished in the *Linkskurve*, the journal of the BPRS (Bund proletarisch-revolutionärer Schriftsteller, League of Proletarian Revolutionary Writers). Its central value lies in its crucial problematisation of the relationship between writer and reader, destroying the myth that literature is created and consumed in an aesthetic vacuum independent of any market mechanism and arguing that working-class literature must consequently show itself aware of the need to create its own audience, publication network and means of distribution. The problems arise, however, when it is regarded – as it sometimes still is – as the definitive statement on the political nature and function of literature. For it was written in a particular historical situation, namely at a time when the party to which Lenin belonged had just ceased to be illegal, and he was thus confronting problems of a different nature from those posed by, say, the historical circumstances of the Weimar Republic. Moreover Lenin was clearly referring to literature in all its forms, not merely to belles-lettres. The main problem, however, is a definitional one, for the article operates with terms (particularly the problematical concept of 'partisanship') which are by no means unquestionable and which have subsequently formed the basis of an on-going debate.[22] As we shall see, however, this article and its ideas nevertheless exerted a considerable influence on the development of the BPRS.

It is clear even from this cursory exposition of Marxist literary theory that the relating of the class struggle to the sphere of culture involves two fundamental problems: firstly, the evaluation of the classical 'cultural heritage' and the relationship to progressive bourgeois culture and intellectuals in general, and secondly the problem of actually creating and distributing proletarian culture. In the Weimar Republic the Communist Party never achieved an adequate synthesis of these two crucial questions, emphasising instead one aspect to the neglect of the other. Indeed, it was this change of emphasis which could be said to determine the periodisation of proletarian revolutionary culture in the Weimar Republic, for in general there can be distinguished four phases in the development of a Communist Party theory of proletarian literature which coincided more or less with the different stages in the actual political development of the party between 1918 and 1932:[23] The first phase is that from the 'November revolution' to 1923, when the party's standpoint essentially reflected the pre-war position of Franz Mehring, rejecting the possibility of proletarian literature and being concerned primarily to preserve the progressive bourgeois cultural heritage for the working class and to defend it against the allegedly decadent, modernistic tendencies of Expressionism, Activism and Dadaism. The second period spans the years 1924–28. The rejection of the catastrophist theory of the imminent collapse of capitalism prompted the reorganisation of the party on the basis of factory cells which in turn gave rise to the movement of worker correspondents, thus providing a new stimulus for proletarian literature. In the third phase this anti-traditionalist trend was concretised in 1928 in the BPRS, with its development of a theory of operative literature. The Charkow conference of 1930 introduced the fourth and final phase with the gradual emergence of Lukács's theory of socialist realism which was to triumph finally in the so-called Expressionism and

Realism debate of the late '30s between Lukács and Brecht.

III

The tensions inherent in the 'bourgeois or proletarian culture' dichotomy were best illustrated by the immediate post-war years which evinced two irreconcilable positions. The official cultural policy of the KPD represented an unproblematical continuation of the Mehring tradition. This continuity is largely explained by the influence exerted by Gertrud Alexander, one of Mehring's former pupils and a significant contributor to the KPD's main publication, *Die rote Fahne*, who took over two of Mehring's main ideas, namely that the proletariat was the natural heir of the bourgeois cultural heritage and that with the decline of capitalism the bourgeoisie was no longer capable of great realistic art. Thus her response to proletarian literature – 'art is too sacred a thing for it to lend its name to the most vulgar and clumsy work of propaganda'[24] – was no less negative than her attitude to contemporary bourgeois culture, as exemplified in her critique of Expressionism as 'anti-bourgeois from the bourgeois point of view'.[25]

In opposition to the official position, however, there formed around Wieland Herzfelde a group of young bourgeois intellectuals who, politicised by the first world war and the 'November revolution', identified increasingly with the left wing of the Communist movement.[26] Rejecting centralism and Lenin's theory of the vanguard role of the party in favour of spontaneism and mass action, this wing soon came into conflict with the KPD and after 1920 established its own organisations, chief among which was the KAPD (Kommunistische Arbeiter-Partei Deutschlands). Regarding all bourgeois art forms as inexorably fetishised, these intellectuals demanded a total break with bourgeois traditions and turned instead to the ideas associated with the Russian 'Proletkult'. Thus whereas one wing of the Communist movement in Germany tended to reject all cultural work as deflecting valuable forces from the political and economic struggle, the other wing, while providing almost the sole impetus for proletarian revolutionary literature in this period, nevertheless tended to reduce the broad spectrum of revolutionary activity merely to the cultural sector.

Even in the early years of the KPD, however, there were signs that a less restrictive cultural position would challenge the dominance of Mehring's ideas. As early as 1921 the 'Guidelines to the education work of the KPD' had argued that the victory of the working class was contingent upon the emancipation from bourgeois ideology and upon 'the creation of a higher, socialist culture'.[27] But it was not until the tenth party congress of 1925 that the practical application of these general guidelines became a possibility. The recognition that Germany had entered a 'period of relative stabilisation' was but the concomitant of the realisation that there no longer obtained 'an acute revolutionary situation'[28] and that it was therefore essential to establish the party on a mass basis. This the new central committee under Ernst Thälmann sought to achieve by reorganising the party on the basis of factory cells.[29] With them came the development of factory newspapers as indispensable weapons in the daily struggle, and to this end steps were taken in 1925 to organise a movement of worker correspondents who would write reports either from the shop floor or concerning local campaigns for the revolutionary press. These newspapers were intended to educate the working class in two respects: firstly, the workers should learn how to express themselves in literary form, and secondly, by constantly confronting them with their own experiential problems, it was hoped to raise their consciousness of themselves as a class. The first conference of the worker correspondents took place, in fact, in December 1924, but it was with the tenth party congress that the movement was given new impetus and its tasks were extended: the writers were not merely to describe conditions and events in the factory but were encouraged to give free reign to their literary activity, thus providing the basis for a wider development of proletarian literature. The worker correspondents, who by 1930 numbered roughly 1,500, acted as a link between the party press and the masses, and writers like Bredel, Grünberg, Marchwitza and Lorbeer, who became members of the BPRS, were products of this movement.

The second demand of the tenth party congress was for the broadening of ties with potential allies of the party and working class by increasing the work done in the broadly based mass organisations to which individual members belonged. It was for this purpose that the bourgeois writers in the KPD formed the Arbeitsgemeinschaft kommunistischer Schriftsteller (AKS) within the broader organisation of the Schutzverband deutscher Schriftsteller (SDS). The SDS had been formed earlier as a quasi-trade union so that writers might organise themselves and protect their social and economic position. This came in response to the cultural repression represented, for example, by 'Das Gesetz zur Bewahrung der Jugend vor Schund- und Schmutzschriften' (the Law for the Preservation of Young People from Trashy Literature and Pornography) of 3 December 1926. One specific example of the attempted suppression of literature was the proceedings initiated against Johannes R. Becher in which he was charged with high treason over his novel *Levisite*.[30]

The move to broaden the influence in the cultural sphere received further impetus from the 1927 party conference in Essen, which asserted the need to establish a 'red cultural front line'[31] by extending the Communist Party's involvement in the numerous proletarian cultural organisations already in existence. These organisations, such as the Arbeiter-Theater-Bund Deutschlands and the Deutscher Arbeiter-Sängerbund, boasted extensive membership (600,000 and 375,000 members respectively) but were largely under reformist leadership little concerned with actively creating a mass socialist culture. In November 1927 the KPD set up a specific section of the Agitation and Propaganda Department to encourage and advise on the organisation of working-class literature. The aim was to further the progression of worker correspondents to revolutionary writers, a difference defined later as follows: 'The revolutionary writer should seek to create the general fate from his depiction of the individual fate'.[32] It was the 'Proletarische Feuilleton-Korrespondenz' under the leadership of Becher and Kläber which was to facilitate this progression. Their task lay in helping the worker writers by practical suggestions and 'above all by the effective weapon of collective criticism'[33] to rework their simple reports into short stories or reportage and thereby make their texts accessible to a larger audience.

Thus the main preconditions for the setting up of the BPRS had been achieved: firstly, the defection from their class of a group of bourgeois writers and their alignment with the KPD, secondly the reorganisation of the party for the purpose of winning over the mass of the working class, and thirdly the recognition that the ideological and cultural struggle was complementary to the struggles on the economic and political fronts. A final but no less important factor in the founding of the BPRS was the international context. At the fifth world congress of the Comintern[34] in 1924 it was emphasised that 'artistic literature plays a large role in the struggle for the emancipation of the working class as a powerful means of influencing intellectual life and the consciousness of the masses'.[35] At the suggestion of the Soviet Union of Proletarian Writers (WAPP) it was recommended that writers' groups should be established in all countries, which could unite organisationally politically unaffiliated intellectuals with working-class writers. Thus in 1927 the first international conference of proletarian and revolutionary writers was held in Moscow, which then instituted the International Bureau for Revolutionary Literature. As an over-reaction against the literature of social democracy it claimed that the use of bourgeois literature as an instrument of ideological education in the revolutionary sense was impossible. It stressed the operative nature of proletarian revolutionary literature, its 'value for struggle', and explained that one of the main reasons why revolutionary literature lagged behind the demands of the day was the lack of organisation among writers. Indeed, Johannes R. Becher, who, with three other delegates, represented the AKS at the conference, expressed precisely those sentiments when he complained in 1927 that 'the work of our writers is still to a large extent unorganised',[36] and it was as much as a result of this dissatisfaction as in its role as the German section of the IBRL that the BPRS was founded in October 1928.

In the discussions both immediately before and after the founding of the BPRS the question of the desirability or possibility of proletarian revolutionary literature played no part. In his article 'Unser Bund' Johannes R. Becher – who as early as 1925, in an article representing the transposition of Lenin's principles in 'Party organisation and party literature' on to the reality of the Weimar Republic, had affirmed the need for a Communist organisation of writers[37] – declared that the BPRS was itself proof that such a literature existed.[38] So, too, the Provisional Guidelines for Communist Writers – which were placed before the founding meeting of the BPRS – in explicitly refuting Trotsky's view that the working class was incapable of autonomous cultural production until it assumed political power, proclaimed as axiomatic the need for a revolutionary, working-class literature.[39] In its Programme of Action (published in *Die rote Fahne*, 28 October 1928) the BPRS pledged itself to the pursuit of five aims: the development of both a proletarian revolutionary literature and theory of literature, the critique of bourgeois literature, the organisation and education of all potential working-class writers and the defence of the Soviet Union.[40] Significantly, as regards the development of the BPRS, neither this programme nor others submitted later was ever unanimously agreed on and finalised.

Clearly, however, as regards the realisation of the main aims of the programme, one essential organisational prerequisite was the creation of a forum for debate, and to meet this requirement the BPRS founded its own journal, the *Linkskurve*. It appeared for the first time in August 1929 and continued to appear monthly until December 1932. The contents, which varied from thirty to forty pages, were mostly written by members of the BPRS, although the journal occasionally published previously unknown works by Marx, Engels and Lenin on literary questions. (In March 1932, for example, there appeared for the first time the letter of 1882 from Engels to Miss Harkness in which Engels formulated the oft quoted definition of realism.) Literary works by the BPRS were also featured, and there was a regular section containing messages from the BPRS and IBRL and reviews of bourgeois culture.

The editorial board comprised Johannes R. Becher, Andor Gabor, Kurt Kläber, Hans Marchwitza, Erich Weinert and Ludwig Renn. The financial plight of the *Linkskurve* and the members of the BPRS was never less than precarious, such that by 1930 20 per cent of the BPRS were without work and 80 per cent were living below the official subsistence level.[41] The average circulation of the journal was between 3,500 and 5,000 copies, and according to Renn it had a significant readership in Communist organisations abroad.

The BPRS always insisted that it was not a trade union but a mass organisation of proletarian revolutionary writers. And while, in its statutes, it stated its political allegiance to the KPD, actual membership of the KPD was never a precondition for membership of the BPRS. This fact was reflected in the statistics: in 1930, 40 per cent of the members were also members of the KPD, 1·5 per cent belonged to other parties and 58·5 per cent were not aligned with any party.[42] The link with the KPD was anything but a purely nominal one, however, as is evidenced not only by the fact that Becher, the president of the BPRS, was co-opted on to the secretariat of the Central Committee of the KPD but also by the scope of activities expected of the members in their involvement in the party's propaganda work. These were specified in the statutes as follows:

1. the initiation of and participation in all activities which appear suited to the promotion of proletarian revolutionary literature and art; 2. the organisation of instruction and discussion evenings; 3. the organisation of writers' reading evenings; 4. the contributing to radio talks; 5. the development and publication of a journal; 6. the support of the Workers' Theatre Movement, Workers' Radio Movement and Worker Correspondents' Movement; 7. the providing of propaganda material for particular campaigns; 8. the supplying of speakers, teachers and other specialists for proletarian revolutionary events; ... 10. the taking up and developing of contacts with the literature of other countries.[43]

However, despite this, Helga Gallas has argued that the commitment to the platform of the KPD was not fully reciprocated in the party's support for the BPRS.[44] In 1929 the BPRS produced its 'Report on the activities of the BPRS in 1929', which dealt primarily with the difficulties it had experienced in its relationship with the KPD. On the surface these seemed mainly to concern the Communist Party's publishing policy. Significantly, for instance, the *Linkskurve* was financed originally not by the KPD but by the IBRL.[45] More important, though, the party press, the Internationale Arbeiter-Verlag, published mainly political brochures and bourgeois literary works, and it was mostly private publishers, such as the Malik-Verlag, that brought out workers' literature. (Grünberg's *Brennende Ruhr*, for example, was refused by the party press as being 'too unliterary'[46].) Gallas, however, argues that these difficulties were but the symptom of a more fundamental problem, namely the attitude of the Central Committee of the KPD towards belles-lettres. They remained unconvinced of the value and effectiveness of working-class literature, suspecting rather that the activity of Communist writers among the working class would serve only as a distraction from more important tasks. Writers of bourgeois origin, on the other hand, had a clear value for the party in their capacity as 'opinion leaders'. In other words, how they wrote, whether in new or traditional forms, was entirely of less political importance than the mere fact of their endorsement of the KPD.[47] Whether this assessment of the situation is wholly accurate or not, Gallas's argument nevertheless points to an aspect of the BPRS which proved to be undeniably problematical, namely the exact nature of the 'proletarian' and 'revolutionary' components in the programme of the BPRS, that is to say, the relationship within the group between working-class writers and bourgeois intellectuals.

The term 'proletarian revolutionary' was originally used to denote the revolutionary, as opposed to the reformist, wing of the German working-class movement. Karl Liebknecht, for example, used it at the founding conference of the Spartacus League to differentiate its politics from those of the SPD and USPD.[48] The importance of the term was more general, however, in that it reflected Lenin's conceptualisation of the relationship between workers and intellectuals. Lenin contested the view of social democracy (in particular of Kautsky) which seemed to have merely internalised the division of mental and manual labour in bourgeois society within the socialist movement itself, with the intellectuals – emigrés from the bourgeois class – providing theory and ideology for a mass base of non-intellectuals, i.e. workers. Lenin's view, opposing this division of labour, that in the revolutionary party 'all distinctions as between workers and intellectuals ... must be obliterated'[49] derives from the vanguard role he ascribed to the party. That is to say, as regards the mediating of socialist consciousness to the working class from outside, the agency of that mediation was to be located not in the traditional intelligentsia but in the revolutionary party in which workers and intellectuals of bourgeois origin had been fused into a single cohesive unit. In Germany, however, there was a singular lack of clarity as to how this fusion was to be effected. Clara Zetkin, even in her paper of 1924 on 'The question of intellectuals', was unable to provide a precise definition of their practical tasks within the working-class movement, contenting herself with the somewhat vague assertion that intellectuals could be 'of great importance for the undermining of the capitalist State'.[50] And whereas the supposed alliance character of the BPRS was at least reflected statistically in the class origins of its members,[51] the theoretical statements it formulated in the early years on its attitude to intellectuals were at best ambivalent and at worst counter-productively hostile. It was the main premise of the Provisional Guidelines of the BPRS that 'the literary, just as much as the economic and political, emancipation of the proletariat can be achieved only by the working class itself',[52] but with the qualification that 'working-class origin alone does not suffice to make a proletarian revolutionary writer, since origin in itself does not signify class consciousness'.[53] The guidelines further pointed out that there were indeed working-class writers 'who in their development did not progress beyond the level of social democracy or who fell prey to leftist or anarchist tendencies',[54] whereas, they conceded, the possibility did exist of changing one's class allegiance. These were the 'deserters of other classes who without reservation have joined the revolutionary proletariat and placed their artistic skills completely in the service of the class struggle'.[55] This tone of apparent conciliation, however, was not extended to the plight of 'fellow-travellers' ('Mitläufer'), who were roundly condemned as:

the lackeys of imperialism, the left bourgeois, liberal democrats, sham pacifists, pretend-socialists and pseudo-anarchists of literature who, disgusted and repelled by the increasingly voracious economic forms of accumulation and by the ever more shameless methods of 'democracy', reject capitalism and seek a remedy which they believe they can find or have found in communism in general but not in 'party communism', which is too rigid for them.[56]

This unproductive and alienating mistrust of 'petty-bourgeois intellectuals' – exemplified in Becher's exhortation 'we must distance ourselves from sympathisers'[57] or Andor Gabor's demand 'even more resolutely must we dissociate ourselves from fellow-travellers'[58] – was reflected in the *Linkskurve* in a plethora of polemical critiques of such writers as Ernst Toller, Kurt Tucholsky, Alfred Döblin, Heinrich Mann and Bert Brecht.

This sectarian attitude was not limited to specific personalities but rather was extended to an undifferentiated rejection of bourgeois literature as such. This situation was not peculiar to the BPRS, however, but rather, as with the problem of intellectuals, reflected a general lack of theoretical clarity on the relation of bourgeois and proletarian culture. So Lenin, for example, while insisting in 'The tasks of the Youth Leagues' that the proletariat should understand and reshape bourgeois culture – 'We [must] clearly realise that only a precise knowledge and transformation of the culture created by the entire development of mankind will enable us to create a proletarian culture'[59] – nevertheless claimed in 'The achievements and difficulties of the Soviet government'[60] that the proletariat could take over bourgeois culture lock, stock and barrel and build on it: 'We must take the entire culture that capitalism left behind and build socialism with it.'[61] Thus while Becher could declare in 1928 that 'it was totally obvious that the League must take up the struggle against *all* forms of bourgeois literature',[62] his definition, a year later, of proletarian revolutionary literature as 'literature which views the world from the perspective of the revolutionary proletariat and reflects it accordingly',[63] appeared to stress not the author's class origins but his relationship to reality.

Friedrich Rothe justifies this sectarian phase of the BPRS as an essential precondition for its later development in the sense of constituting a 'process of political education'.[64] The real causes for its appearance, however, must be located elsewhere. Primarily it is explicable in terms of the national and international development of capitalism, the economic crises of which were seen by the Comintern to be leading inexorably towards a revolutionary situation, and of the nature of the German working-class movement, which was split between the SPD, whose leadership, even at a time of acute capitalist crisis, still identified with the Weimar State, and the Communist Party, many of whose energies were channelled into relentless criticism of the Social Democrats. In this context, therefore, even within the newly founded BPRS, literary problems receded before the political task of distanciation from the non-Communist Left. Thus what often masqueraded in the *Linkskurve* as literary criticism of bourgeois authors was not in fact a critique of their works at all but rather an attack on their refusal to renounce the traditional position of the isolated intellectual and join the KPD. Neukrantz's 'review' of Döblin's *Berlin Alexanderplatz*, for instance, restricted itself more or less to the assertion that 'the book merely confirms for us the fact that the so-called 'left bourgeois' writers constitute a political danger for the proletariat'.[65]

More than this, though, the absence of genuine literary criticism in the BPRS was symptomatic of a wider theoretical vacuum. That is to say, the *way* in which literature could become a weapon in the class struggle had not been properly thought through, for in the 'programme of action' any such discussion had been pre-empted by the assertion of the primacy of content over form:

It is not from the revolutionising of form that literature derives its revolutionary significance but the new revolutionary form can and must be an organic product of the revolutionary content.[66]

It may well be that this debate, later initiated by Lukács, presupposed a stage of development which by then the BPRS had not and could not have attained. Nevertheless its absence had evident consequences for a literature in which proletarian revolutionary content was often mechanistically equated with overt political identification with the working class.

The third factor determining relations between writers of working-class and bourgeois origin was the model of the Russian 'Proletkult'. Founded at the end of the 1890s, this had been the first movement collectively to create a proletarian literature. It received further impetus with the February revolution, and between 1917 and 1918 a series of Proletkult conferences took place. The essence of the movement was its stress on proletarian origin in the genesis of revolutionary culture, and its influence was first felt in the BPRS, with the so-called midwife theory ('Geburtshelferthese').[67] This idea, which gained currency largely through Andor Gabor, reduced the role of the bourgeois writer in the BPRS to a sort of literary agent who was to secure publishing facilities for proletarian writers and advise on matters of style and technique. Since, Gabor argued, the experience of the proletarian class struggle was peculiar to the working class, it followed that only they could reproduce that experience in literary form.[68] The pure Proletkult viewpoint, however, was represented by Erich Steffen in an article in *Linkskurve* entitled 'Die Urzelle proletarischer Literatur':

Only the proletariat itself can produce the literature it needs ... The worker is the creator of his own literature in which everything is reflected that the working class experiences. For this purpose he has no need of thick books, he does not fashion beautifully formed words and he is not embarrassed to write down his own language. But what he does express is more provoking, more stirring, more convincing and a thousand times more accessible than the dangerous, convoluted word play of the professional literati ... We do not need to construct a proletarian literature, we have it already.[69]

Steffen's argument, equating proletarian literature with the worker correspondents' movement and soon to be authoritatively refuted in the *Linkskurve*, represented, it is true, an extreme position. But it was nevertheless indicative of the direction in which, by the beginning of 1930, the BPRS was moving. For by dogmatically rejecting all potential non-Communist allies and effectively excluding even Communist intellectuals from actual literary production, the BPRS had reduced Lenin's category of 'partisanship' purely to the level of an organisational link with the Communist Party. It was as yet a long way from the insight of another significant Marxist theoretician, Antonio Gramsci: 'One of the most important characteristics of any group that is developing towards dominance is its struggle to assimilate and conquer "ideologically" the tradition intellectuals'.[70]

chose to publish Erich Steffen's article his views therefore represented the official position of the BPRS. Indeed, the editors expressly labelled the article as a contribution for discussion. Nevertheless the fact that the reply to Steffen in the very next number was written by a member of the Central Committee of the KPD, Josef Lenz, (under the pseudonym of N. Kraus) gives some indication of the official unease at the course the BPRS was pursuing. Lenz's reply, entitled 'Gegen den Okonomismus in der Literaturfrage', rejected any incipient Proletkult tendencies and argued for closer co-operation between workers and intellectuals who were envisaged not as literary 'midwives' but in terms of cultural 'pioneers'. More important, however, the article began tentatively to extend the concept of proletarian literature itself:

The proletarian literature that we need must reflect the entire life of human society, the life of all classes, from the perspective of the revolutionary proletariat ... that is not the perspective of a worker dissatisfied with his wage and work conditions, but the perspective of a Marxist–Leninist, who clearly comprehends the internal mechanism of the existing social order, the causes of its contradictions, of its outrages and of its barbarities and who perceives the inevitability of its collapse. The reflection of all events – not only of the everyday events at the workplace – should, regardless of Steffen's disparaging reference to 'the exalted standpoint', nevertheless proceed from an exalted standpoint, namely that of the scientific knowledge of Marxism–Leninism.[71]

In addition to eliminating the relevance of the writer's class origins Lenz was thus also attempting to redefine proletarian revolutionary literature in such a way as to counteract the tendency to fixate on the industrial proletariat as the sole object and target of working-class literature. Futhermore his stress on the role of scientific Marxism could be seen as re-emphasising the dialectical relationship of theory and practice, that is, as an allusion to the need for Marxist literary theory to keep pace with proletarian literary practice.

This need was partially satisfied by a series of seven articles by Karl August Wittfogel. One of the repercussions of the attempt to combat Proletkult tendencies in the BPRS had been the replacement of Andor Gabor by Wittfogel in the editorial team of the *Linkskurve*, which now published his essay 'Zur Frage der marxistischen Asthetik'.[72] Beginning as a reappraisal of Mehring's aesthetic writings and rejecting Kantian in favour of Hegelian aesthetics, the essay culminated in the call for the proletariat, as the ascendant class of history, to assume the bourgeoisie's mantle of creator of revolutionary literature. Wittfogel's articles exerted very little direct influence on the BPRS in themselves.[73] Nevertheless their publication coincided with the second international conference of proletarian and revolutionary writers in Charkow in November 1930, which welcomed the rejection of sectarian tendencies in Germany,[74] and together these two events marked the beginning of a new stage in the development of the BPRS.

The developments of the next two years, however, were not occasioned simply by internal debate within the BPRS; rather they were determined by changes both in the general political position of the KPD and in the cultural policy of the Soviet Union. The year 1930 brought an end to the period of relative stabilisation experienced by Germany in the latter half of the '20s as acute economic depression once again set in. The resulting disaffection of the middle classes did not, however, prompt an identification with the working class but was exploited by the NSDAP, which in the elections of September 1930 increased its vote by over 6 million. In response to these advances the KPD called for a concerted effort to win over the petty-bourgeoisie in order to establish a united front against the threat of fascism. This affected the BPRS in so far as it redefined both the target audience and the subject matter of their literature, for in order to address themselves to the problems of the petty bourgeoisie they had to extend their literary focus beyond the industrial struggles of the working class. No less significant were developments in Russia which culminated in Stalin proclaiming the victory of socialism in the Soviet Union, that is to say, marking the end of the period designated as 'the dictatorship of the proletariat'. Such a declaration could not be without consequences for literature in the sense that a truly socialist society no longer required a literature dedicated to the class struggle. This logic led in 1932 to the dissolution of the Soviet Organisation of Proletarian Revolutionary writers (RAPP) and the emergence of the theory of socialist realism.

These fundamental changes in direction first received expression in the *Linkskurve* in a long critical article in October 1931 by Becher entitled 'Unsere Wendung'. In it he criticised the literary production of the BPRS for remaining behind the stage of politics which the KPD had reached. The orientation towards the factory, which he himself had advocated in 1930, he now denounced as restricting the links of the BPRS to the vanguard of the working class, whereas what was needed was an appeal to 'all sectors of the class in its entirety' and 'an organic link with the everyday life of the entire working class',[75] in short the creation of a mass literature. Constructively Becher put forward two concrete suggestions: firstly, the BPRS should turn its attention to developing 'a creative literary method ... since for the dialectical-materialist proletarian writer the question of "What" is inseparably bound to the question of "How?" '[76] – a demand which modified the earlier insistence of the primacy of content over form – and secondly, he urged the BPRS to undertake a serious review of the quantity and quality of its criticism. Having overcome the inaugural difficulties of its early phase, when, he argued, criticisms would have been inappropriate, the BPRS could now only benefit from concrete and systematic critiques which could be applied to specific works.

This challenge was taken up in the next issue of *Linkskurve* by Georg Lukács. Becher had been at some pains *not* to exempt from his criticism of 'lagging behind' ('Zurückgebliebenheit') the series of novels published by the KPD under the title of the 'Rote Eine-Mark-Roman'.[77] Lukács now, quite pointedly, selected as the object of his critical scrutiny two novels, *Maschinenfabrik N & K* and *Die Rosenhofstrasse*, by the most successful author in the series, Willi Bredel. While conceding that the novels marked a progression from the point of view of their content, Lukács defined their weakness as the contradiction between the broad epic framework of the novels and the mode of narration. The predominant style of the novels, redolent of journalistic reportage, he held to be incompatible with a breadth more akin to the traditional 'Entwicklungsroman'. This inadequacy was epitomised for Lukács in the language and attributed to Bredel's 'lack of dialectic in his literary creation',[78] which prevented him from encapsulating in his novels the totality of social experience. Bredel's reply to this article showed him ostensibly in contrite agreement with Lukács's criticisms, but it is perhaps an index of the political considerations involved that Bredel considered the main weakness of his novels thematically to be the failure to show the 'determination of the German working class to form a revolutionary united front'.[79] The actual defence of Bredel came, therefore, not from the author himself but from Otto Gotsche, who accused Lukács of a 'pernicious method of criticism'[80] and called for the readers themselves to express their views instead of the intellectualised criticism from above à la Lukács. In a short reply Lukács dismissed these points as politically naive and spontaneistic.[81] One could argue, as Bernd Witte has done,[82] that in specifically choosing to criticise the most prominent representative of proletarian revolutionary culture Lukács was already implicity rejecting the very idea of a literature written by workers. In truth, however, these early articles were, relatively speaking, a mere foray into a theoretical area which, from now on, in the *Linkskurve* Lukács was to dominate almost unopposed.

The main exposition of Lukács's theory of literature was contained in an article entitled 'Reportage der Gestaltung' which, as its subtitle made clear, was nominally intended as a critique of Ernst Ottwalt's novel *Denn sie wissen was sie tun*. Clearly, however, this analysis merely served Lukács as a springboard from which to criticise other bourgeois writers, of whom Ottwalt was representative in his use of 'a quite distinct type of creative method which is nowadays in common usage internationally. That is to say, he works with the means of reportage in place of the "traditional" "antiquated" "bourgeois" means of the "invented" plot and "created, well drawn characters".'[83] Lukács began by establishing a relationship between the emergence of the documentary form and the development of the late bourgeois novel. He argued that the ever widening dichotomy of the individual and society had led the bourgeois novel to concentrate on individual psychology and left it incapable of relating this to the wider configuration of social relationships. Reportage, with its fixation on the factual, was thus held to be a further manifestation of this tendency: 'The fetishistic dissection of reality, the inability to perceive in the phenomena of social life relations between men (class relations) is thus present in them to the same extent as it is in their artistic antipode, the psychologists, only from the other side.'[84]

Crucial to an understanding of Lukács's writings is the concept of totality[85] which he had introduced into dialectical philosophy earlier in the '20s. Essentially this is an epistemological category based on the distinction between the isolated fact and overall reality, that is to say, between the empirical existence of an individual fact and its meaning within a network of relations. For, Lukács had argued in *History and Class Consciousness*, 'only in the context which sees isolated facts of social life as aspects of the historical process and integrates them in a *totality* can knowledge of the facts hope to become knowledge of *reality*'.[86] From this relationship of the individual fact to the totality he developed the category of 'typicality' in which the individual fact, seen from the perspective of the laws and relationships in which it is embedded, acquires a status which raises it from the individual and empirical level to a position where it is seen to contain within itself the laws and relationships which are external to it or seen to be an illustration of those relationships. The part becomes, as it were, the mirror of the whole.

In 'Reportage oder Gestaltung' Lukács distinguished two forms of typicality, scientific typicality ('wissenschaftlich-typisch') and artistic typicality ('dichterisch-typisch'). The former he described in the following terms:

The better the reportage, the more apparent it is that the cited examples are precisely only that, namely only examples and illustrations of the relationships perceived and revealed.[87]

That is to say, scientific typicality serves to enlighten the relationships surrounding the individual fact and makes this individual fact an example

or illustration of them. In artistic typicality, however, the individual is not
an example of general laws but contains them:

In literary creation ['Gestaltung'] the individual, and his fate, must be seen to be
typical, that is, the characteristics of the individuals depicted must embody the
characteristics of their class.[88]

The essential thing about these two forms of typicality, Lukács insisted,
is that they are not mutually interchangeable but are restricted to their
respective spheres of science and art:

As much as their ulitmate basis of inquiry is the same (the ideational
reproduction of reality) the basic representational methods of science and art are
nevertheless mutually exclusive . . .; and artistic representation with scientific
aims will always be both a pseudo-science and a pseudo-art and a 'scientific'
solution of specifically artistic problems produces similarly a pseudo-science in
terms of content and a pseudo-art in terms of form. But it is precisely this for
which – consciously or unconsciously – reportage, when aspiring to be the
creative method of literature, strives.[89]

Moreover this was what Ottwalt had attempted. His preoccupation with
the factual had revealed only surface reality and concealed the 'real and
essential driving forces of social reality in its totality'.[90] He had thus
failed to satisfy the necessary preconditions for true realism, for, Lukács
argued:

The literary expression of the historical process as a totality is the precondition
for the correct composition of the novel. Why? Because only the literary
expression of the historical process as a totality can dissolve the fetishism of the
economic and social forms of capitalist society and make them appear as they
are in reality, as the (class) relations of men to each other.[91]

As Helga Gallas has rightly pointed out,[92] the significant thing about
Lukács's analysis is that what he was criticising was not the *way* in which
Bredel or Ottwalt had applied the new forms of literary construction such
as montage or the documentary. Rather he was criticising as abstract,
scientific and ultimately unliterary any technique which destroyed the
illusion of the closed fictional world, that is to say, he rejected the use of
open forms as such. Moreover his insistence on the distinction between
science and art was a somewhat arbitrary and mechanistic one which
entailed a discussion of literary form more or less divorced from
historical content. It was, therefore, the tradition of late nineteenth-
century bourgeois realism, of which Tolstoi was the supreme practitioner,
that Lukács appeared to be advocating as *the* aesthetic model for
proletarian literature.[93] Nowhere in Lukács's analysis, however, was
there any discussion of the political function that literature should fulfil or
of the extent to which, by virtue of its class standpoint, literature should

be related to the real historical perspective and the concrete political praxis of the working class. Indeed, it was on this basis that Ottwalt, in his reply to the article, criticised Lukács:

It is not the creative method which is object of the analysis but the functional significance which a book has in a quite specific reality that has been formed by quite specific economic and political determinants.[94]

In short, Lukács denied both the functionality of literature and the historical specificity of literary forms. Basically he was attempting to construct an essentially abstract system of aesthetic categories from which the way in which literature mediated reality could be deduced. That he considered the quality of this mediation to be not necessarily contingent on the author's class standpoint was evident from another article, written in the same year, entitled 'Tendenz oder Parteilichkeit'. In it Lukács explicitly rejected the category of 'Tendenz', which, he argued, merely preserves the bourgeois distinction between pure art and political propaganda. Instead the true work of art seeks to portray reality dialectically as a totality, that is, as a process of historical change. The writer's partisanship consists, then, according to Lukács, in:

... the perception and expression of the whole historical process as the condensed totality of its real driving forces, as the constant, heightened reproduction of its underlying dialectical contradictions.[95]

This definition, which bears little resemblance to Lenin's concept of partisanship in 'Party organisation and party literature', is ultimately identical with that of 'Gestaltung' provided in the essay on Ottwalt. The two terms, therefore, could be seen to represent not so much absolute concepts as particular literary methods, 'Parteilichkeit' being identified with the nineteenth-century realistic novel, 'Tendenz' with such techniques as reportage, montage, alienation effects, etc. To what extent Lukács's terminology and the ideas associated with it informed the official literary theory of the BPRS was evident from the changes of perspective adopted by certain of its leading figures. Thus, when asked in an interview with Gottfried Benn in 1930 as to what form of literature he represented, Becher, for example, could answer, 'Dichtung als Tendenz',[96] only to insist two years later that it should be partisan ('proletarisch-revolutionäre Literatur ist keine Tendenzliteratur sondern eine parteiliche').[97] Lukács's theories, however, had implications that clearly went beyond the internal debate within the BPRS. For they were obviously aimed at the only systematically developed alternative to the soon officially to be declared doctrine of socialist realism, namely the theory and practice of open forms as exemplified primarily in the 'epic theatre' of Bertolt Brecht. The discussions in the BPRS thus provided merely the prologue to the Expressionism and Realism debate that was enacted in the late '30s between Lukács and Brecht himself.[98]

IV

Although the *Linkskurve* ceased publication after the issue of December 1932, the BPRS continued as an illegal group of seven or eight members until 1935, when it was officially disbanded following the dissolution of the IVRS (Internationale Vereinigung revolutionärer Schriftsteller). Views as to the level of achievement of the BPRS vary. Schonauer, for example, maintains that it achieved little of significance largely because of what he calls its subservience to and domination by 'Moscow'.[99] Helga Gallas, on the other hand, while accepting that developments in the BPRS were primarily determined by the influence of the Soviet literary organisations, nevertheless argues that 'the actual significance of the BPRS ... lies in the attempt to oppose the prevailing theory of literature with a Marxist one'.[100] To point to the highly developed sense of proletarian internationalism existing at the time and to illuminate the interrelationship of events, both political and literary, in Germany and the Soviet Union, as, hopefully, I have done, is not, however, to portray the BPRS in Schonauer's terms of monolithic Soviet hegemony. Helga Gallas's conclusion, on the other hand – although her research has been of vital importance in initiating the recent debate in West Germany on Marxist aesthetics – is nevertheless susceptible to the criticism that the method from which it derives is tendentially that of the history of ideas and as a result does not concretely locate the history of the BPRS within the historical context of the KPD and the working-class movement in the Weimar Republic.[101] That is to say, Gallas overemphasises the theoretical contribution of the BPRS, and in particular the role of Georg Lukács, and underplays the extent to which the BPRS existed on the basis of fundamental contradictions in German society and of the struggle to remove those contradictions. While, in retrospect, the theoretical debate within the BPRS may be said to have shown the need to determine any aesthetic in the last resort by the demands of a given political situation and not by any rigid, normative aesthetic theory, in its practice the BPRS demonstrated the possibility of working-class literature and culture under capitalism, and in this above all lies its major achievement. The formation of Worker Writers' Workshops ('Werkkreise')[102] in the Federal Republic, while arguably continuing the tradition of the BPRS, demonstrates furthermore that working-class literature will never merely assume one particular form, but rather will and should always represent a particular response to specific historical conditions.

Notes

[1] Peter Gay, *Weimar Culture*, London, 1969, pp. xiv–xv.

[2] Karl Marx, *Capital*, vol. I, London, 1974, p. 604.

[3] *Cf.* Jürgen Kuczynski, *Studien zur Geschichte des Kapitalismus*, Berlin, 1957, p. 113.

[4] For details on Stinnes see Jürgen Kuczynski, *Die Geschichte der Lage der Arbeiter unter dem Kapitalismus*, vol. 16, Berlin, 1964, pp. 45–80.

[5] Brig.-Gen. J. H. Morgan, in a lecture at London University 1923, quoted in E. J. Passant, *A Short History of Germany, 1815–1945*, London, 1966, pp. 163–4.

[6] Jürgen Kuczynski, *Die Geschichte der Lage der Arbeiter unter dem Kapitalismus*, vol. 5, Berlin, 1966, p. 9. *Cf.* also K. Mendelsohn, *Kapitalistisches Wirtschaftschaos oder sozialistische Planwirtschaft*, Berlin, 1932, p. 15, and R. A. Brady, *The Rationalisation Movement in German Industry*, Berkeley, Cal., 1933, pp. 336–40.

[7] Kuczynski, *Die Geschichte der Lage der Arbeiter unter dem Kapitalismus, op. cit.*, pp. 219–22.

[8] For a differentiated analysis of the dichotomous nature of the SPD see Georg Fülberth and Jürgen Harrer, *Die deutsche Sozialdemokratie, 1890–1933*, Darmstadt and Neuwied, 1974.

[9] See Siegfried Bahne, 'Sozialfaschismus in Deutschland. Zur Geschichte eines politischen Begriffs', *International Review of Social History*, vol. X, Amsterdam, 1965, Part 2, pp. 211–45.

[10] Joseph Stalin, *Werke*, vol. 6, Moscow, 1950, p. 253.

[11] Franz Neumann, *Behemoth. The Structure and Practice of National Socialism*, London, 1942, p. 26.

[12] Franz Mehring, 'Kunst und Proletariat' (1898), in *Gesammelte Schriften*, vol. XI, ed. Höhle and Koch, Berlin, 1960–67, p. 449.

[13] Wilhelm Liebknecht, 'Brief aus Berlin', 17 February 1891, *Neue Zeit* 9, 1, pp. 709–11.

[14] Leon Trotsky, *Literature and Revolution*, Ann Arbor, Mich., 1968, p. 186.

[15] Friedrich Wolf, 'Proletarische Kunst in Deutschland' (1932), in *Aufsätze uber Theater*, Berlin, 1957, p. 11.

[16] Georg Fülberth, *Proletarische Partei und burgerliche Literatur*, Neuwied and Berlin, 1972, p. 126.

[17] For discussion of these areas see Gerald Stieg and Bernd Witte: *Abriss einer Geschichte der deutschen Arbeiterliteratur*, Stuttgart, 1973, pp. 100–13; Frank Trommler, 'Das politisch-revolutionäre Theater', in *Die deutsche Literatur in der Weimarer Republik*, ed. W. Rothe, Stuttgart, 1974, pp. 77–113; Jon Clark, 'The relevance of postgraduate research in literature', in *The Study of German in England*, conference held in London in December 1974, (DAAD), Bonn, 1976, pp. 40–8.

[18] Clara Zetkin, *Ausgewählte Reden und Schriften*, Berlin, 1957, p. 469.

[19] Vladimir Lenin, *Selected Works*, Moscow, 1971, p. 151.

[20] *Ibid.*, p. 151.

[21] *Ibid.*, p. 154.

[22] *Cf.* my discussion below of Lukács's concept of 'Parteilichkeit'. For the contemporary debate see Hans Christoph Buch, *Parteilichkeit der Literatur oder Parteiliteratur? Materialien zu einer undogmatischen marxistishen Asthetik*, Reinbek, 1972, and Werkkreis Literatur der Arbeitswelt, *Partei ergreifen*, Cologne, 1974.

[23] This periodisation substantially follows that given by Bernd Witte, with the difference that Witte identifies only three phases, seeing the four years of the BPRS as constituting a complete phase. See Stieg and Witte, *op. cit.*, p. 70.

[24] Gertrud Alexander, 'Proletarisches Theater', in *Die rote Fahne* 3, 17 October 1920, No. 210, in Walter Fähnders and Martin Rector, *Literatur im Klassenkampf*, Munich, 1971, p. 197.

[25] Gertrud Alexander 'Literaturbesprechung', in *Die rote Fahne* 4, 13 June 1921, No. 264, in Fähnders and Rector, *op. cit.*, p. 89.

[26] For analysis of this movement and its relationship to literature see Walter Fähnders and Martin Rector, *Linksradikalismus und Literatur. Untersuchungen zur Geschichte der sozialistischen Literatur in der Weimarer Republik*, 2 vols., Hamburg, 1974.

[27] Quoted by Elisabeth Simons, 'Der Bund proletarisch-revolutionärer Schriftsteller Deutschlands und sein Verhältnis zur Kommunistischen Partei Deutschlands', in Alfred Klein, *Literatur der Arbeiterklasse*, Berlin and Weimar, 1974, p. 123.

[28] *Bericht über die Verhandlungen des X. Parteitages der KPD*, Berlin, 12–17 July 1925, ed. Central Committee of the KPD, Berlin, 1926, p. 194.

[29] To be absolutely precise, however, the decision at the party congress should be seen as setting the official seal on previous developments, for even by 1924 there were already a large number of factory cells in existence.

[30] For documentation and analysis of this case see *Aktionen Bekenntnisse Perspektiven. Berichte und Dokumente vom Kampf um die Freiheit des literarischen Schaffens in der Weimarer Republik*, Berlin and Weimar, 1966, pp. 23–127.

[31] *Thesen und Resolutionen des XI. Parteitages der KPD. Essen 2–7 March 1927*, p. 96 f.

[32] Werner Hendson, 'Der Arbeiterkorrespondent', *Linkskurve* 3, Berlin, 1931, No. 8, p. 17.

[33] *Ibid.*, p. 18.

[34] The third Communist International (Comintern) was an international revolutionary proletarian organisation which united Communist Parties of different countries. It was in existence from 1919 to 1943.

[35] 'Resolution der Delegierten des V. Weltkongresses zur Frage der künstlerischen Literatur in Deutschland', in *Internationale Pressekorrespondenz* 135, 1924, p. 1973.

[36] Johannes R. Becher, 'Uber die proletarisch-revolutionäre Literatur in Deutschland' (1927), in *Zur Tradition der sozialistischen Literatur in Deutschland*, ed. Deutsche Akademie der Künste, Berlin and Weimar, 1967, p. 33.

[37] Johannes R. Becher, 'Bürgerlicher Sumpf, revolutionärer Kampf', in Friedrich Albrecht, *Deutsche Schriftsteller in der Entscheidung*, Berlin and Weimar, 1970, pp. 570–83.

[38] J. R. Becher, 'Unser Bund', in F. Albrecht, *op. cit.*, p. 591.

[39] 'Entwurf von Richtlinien für kommunistische Schriftsteller', in Alfred Klein, *Im Auftrag ihrer Klasse*, Berlin and Weimar, 1972, pp. 630–41.

[40] Aktionsprogramm des BPRS (1928), in *Zur Tradition der sozialistischen Literatur in Deutschland, op. cit.*, p. 118.

[41] Simons, *loc. cit.*, p. 180.

[42] *Ibid.*, p. 178.

[43] *Zur Tradition, op. cit.*, pp. 114–15.

[44] Helga Gallas, *Marxistische Literaturtheorie*, Neuwied and Berlin, 1971, p. 27.

[45] For discussion of the financing of *Linkskurve* see Gallas, *op. cit.*, pp. 45–6.

[46] Quoted by Karl Grünberg, 'Wie ich zu tausend Zungen kam', in *Hammer und Feuer. Deutsche Schriftsteller aus ihrem Leben und Schaffen*, Berlin, 1955, p. 133.

[47] See Gallas, *op. cit.*, p. 27.

[48] *Ibid.*, p. 206, n. 1.

[49] V. I. Lenin, *What is to be done*, Moscow, 1973, p. 109.

[50] C. Zetkin, 'Die Intellektuellenfrage', *Ausgewählte Reden und Schriften*, Berlin, 1960, vol. 3, p. 46.

[51] According to Ludwig Renn (in a discussion contribution at the Charkow conference, quoted in *Zur Tradition, op. cit.*, p. 264) the social make-up of the BPRS was as follows: 30 per cent. of the members were manual or office workers, 25 per cent. editors and journalists, 9 per cent. theatrical and other artists, 3 per cent. students, teachers and doctors, 1 per cent. freelance writers and 32 per cent. 'Halbexistenten' (i.e. people who had more than one profession without being able to support themselves from one of them).

[52] 'Entwurf von Richtlinien für kommunistische Schriftsteller', in A. Klein, *Im Auftrag ihrer Klasse, op. cit.*, p. 635.

[53] *Ibid.*, p. 637.

[54] *Ibid.*, p. 637.

[55] *Ibid.*, p. 636.

[56] *Ibid.*, p. 635.

[57] J. R. Becher, 'Einen Schritt weiter', *Linkskurve* 2, 1930, No. 1, p. 2.

[58] Kurt Kläber, 'Zwei Jahre', in *Linkskurve* 1, 1929, No. 5, p. 4.

[59] V. I. Lenin, *Selected Works, op. cit.*, p. 610.

[60] The device of quoting a person against himself can be methodologically dangerous if it runs the risk of being ahistorical. These two articles, however, were written between March 1919 and October 1920 and do illustrate a genuine problem as regards the question of the 'bourgeois heritage'.

[61] V. I. Lenin, *Collected Works*, vol. 29, Moscow, 1965, p. 70.

[62] J. R. Becher, 'Unser Bund', in F. Albrecht, *op. cit.*, p. 593.

[63] J. R. Becher, 'Unsere Front', *Linkskurve* 1, 1929, No. 1, p. 1.

[64] Friedrich Rothe, 'Die Bündnispolitik der Kommunisten mit fortschrittlichen Schriftstellern im Spiegel der Linkskurve', in *Kunst und Gesellschaft* 11–12, Berlin, 1972, pp. 38–9.

[65] Klaus Neukrantz, *'Berlin Alexanderplatz'*, in *Linkskurve* 1, 1929, No. 5, p. 31.

[66] 'Aktionsprogramm des BPRS', in *Zur Tradition, op. cit.*, p. 119.

[67] For the origins of the 'Geburtshelferthese' see Gallas, *op. cit.*, p. 193, n. 46.

[68] Andor Gabor, 'Über proletarisch-revolutionäre Literatur', *Linkskurve* 1, 1929, No. 3, p. 6.

[69] Erich Steffen, 'Die Urzelle proletarischer Literatur', in *Linkskurve* 2, 1930, No. 2, p. 8.

[70] Antonio Gramsci, *Prison Notebooks*, London, 1971, p. 10. Gramsci distinguished two types of intellectual: the 'traditional' professional intellectuals (literary, scientific and so on) who *appear* to exist as a category independent of class (but who are in reality linked to various historical class formations) and the 'organic' intellectuals, the thinking and organising element of a particular social group. It was the responsibility of the political party, Gramsci argued, to weld together the organic intellectuals of a given group and the traditional intellectuals. Clearly this too was a crucial task of the revolutionary party. Although Gramsci formulated these ideas while the BPRS was in existence (i.e. during his imprisonment from 1929 to 1935) they were, of course, not accessible until much later.

[71] N. Kraus, 'Gegen den Okonomismus in der Literaturfrage', *Linkskurve* 2, 1930, No. 3, p. 11.

[72] Karl A. Wittfogel, 'Zur Frage der marxistischen Asthetik'. The first article appeared in *Linkskurve* 2, 1930, No. 5, and the series continued until June 1931.

[73] Indeed, it is all too easy to overemphasise, as I think Helga Gallas does, the role the *Linkskurve* played within the BPRS as a whole, in the sense that many of its members were happily oblivious to what they regarded as the esoteric theorising of the journal's contributors. For some revealing critical remarks on this and other aspects of the BPRS see a recent interview with Franz Krey (a former member of the BPRS who worked in Essen) in *Kunst und Gesellschaft* 11–12, *op. cit.*, pp. 55–62.

[74] 'The congruence of its ideational content with the most highly developed forms of proletarian ideology and the actual support of the proletarian class struggle in its developed form is the basic characteristic of proletarian literature. It is neither the author's origin nor his intention which constitutes the basis for criticism of his work but his relationship to reality [. . .] A proletarian literature can develop only where the writer stands firmly based on the philosophy of the revolutionary proletariat, dialectical materialism.' ('Durchbruch der proletarischen Literatur. Bilanz der Charkower Tagung', in *Linkskurve* 3, 1931, No. 2, p. 2.)

[75] J. R. Becher, 'Unsere Wendung', *Linkskurve* 3, 1931, No. 10, p. 6.

[76] *Ibid.*, p. 6.

[77] Between 1929 and 1933 many proletarian revolutionary novels were produced, some without any direct relationship to the BPRS, many as a result of discussions and criticism by the BPRS. The most famous series of novels was the 'Red One-mark Novel'. Between 1930 and 1932 nine novels were published in this series with first editions of between 20,000 and 25,000 and these were intensively discussed and read by workers. The series was as follows: vol. 1, H. Marchwitza, *Sturm auf Essen*. 2, K. Neukrantz, *Barrikaden am Wedding*. 3, B. Orchansky, *Zwischen den Fronten*. 4, W. Bredel, *Maschinenfabrik N & K*. 5, F. Krey, *Maria und der Paragraph*. 6, W. Bredel, *Rosenhofstrasse*. 7, H. Marchwitza, *Schlacht vor Kohle*. 8, W. Schönstedt, *Kämpfende Jugend*. 9, M. Pell, *S.S. Utah*.

[78] Georg Lukács, 'Über Willi Bredels Romane', *Linkskurve* 3, 1931, No. 11, p. 25.

[79] Willi Bredel, 'Einen Schritt weiter', *Linkskurve* 4, 1932, No. 1, p. 20.

[80] Otto Gotsche, 'Kritik der Anderen. Einige Bemerkungen zur Frage der Qualifikation unserer Literatur', *Linkskurve* 4, 1932, No. 4, p. 28.

[81] Georg Lukács, 'Gegen die Spontaneitätstheorie in der Literatur', *Linkskurve* 4, 1932, No. 4.

[82] Stieg and Witte, *op. cit.*, p. 125.

[83] Georg Lukács, 'Reportage oder Gestaltung? Kritische Bemerkungen anlässlich des Romans von Ottwalt', *Linkskurve* 4, 1932, No. 7, p. 23.

[84] *Ibid.*, p. 25.

[85] For discussion and analysis of the concept of totality, particularly as developed in Lukács's *Asthetik*, see Roy Pascal, 'Georg Lukács: the concept of totality', in *Culture and the Division of Labour*, Occasional Papers in German Studies, No. 5, University of Warwick, 1974, pp. 63–105.

[86] Georg Lukács, *History and Class Consciousness*, London, 1971, p. 8.

[87] Lukács, 'Reportage oder Gestaltung', *loc. cit.*, p. 26.

[88] *Ibid.*, p. 27.

[89] *Ibid.*, p. 27.

[90] *Ibid.*, p. 28.

[91] *Ibid.*, p. 29.

[92] Gallas, *op. cit.*, p. 129.

[93] From the perspective of the present it may appear an exaggeration to interpret Lukács in this way. There can be little doubt, however, that this was how his criticism was received at the time of writing. *Cf.* Ernst Ottwalt: 'I would like to point out that it would have been more appropriate to have illustrated the question "Reportage or literary creation?" with an example in which Comrade Lukács sees his demands of the proletarian revolutionary work of art actually fulfilled. Since he does not do this, it may be assumed that he does not know such a work. He has therefore failed to provide the evidence that in his theory of literary creation with the means of the traditional novel form such a work can be written at all' (p. 26).

[94] Ernst Ottwalt, 'Tatsachenroman und Formexperiment', *Linkskurve* 4, 1932, No. 10, p. 22.

[95] Georg Lukács, 'Tendenz oder Parteilichkeit?', *Linkskurve* 4, 1932, No. 6, p. 20.

[96] J. R. Becher and Gottfried Benn, 'Rundfunk–Gespräch 1930', in *Literatur in Klassenkampf* (ed. facit e. V.), Dortmund, 1973, p. 139.

[97] J. R. Becher, 'Kühnheit und Begeisterung', *Linkskurve* 4, 1932, No. 5, p. 10.

[98] See Hans-Jürgen Schmitt, *Die Expressionismusdebatte. Materialien zu einer marxistishen Realismuskonzeption*, Frankfurt a.M., 1973.

[99] *Cf.* 'In the five years of its existence the League (BPRS) had not achieved all that much ... The BPRS was the victim of its own ideological narrowmindedness and of the resultant confused, illusionary and non-autonomous literary politics; the dream of the revolution and of the imminent Soviet Germany made its functionaries blind to the political facts of the Weimar Republic,' in Wolfgang Rothe (ed.), *Literatur in der Weimarer Republik*, Stuttgart, 1974, p. 138.

[100] Gallas, *op. cit.*, p. 11.

[101] *Cf.* Georg Fülberth, 'Zur historisch-materialistischen Methode' (Correspondence with Helga Gallas), in *Alternative* 84–5, 15. Jg., Berlin, 1972, p. 132.

[102] For a brief summary of the development of the Werkkreise see Stieg and Witte, *op. cit.*, pp. 138–46 and 152–8. For detailed analysis, see Peter Kühne, *Arbeiterklasse und Literatur. Dortmunder Gruppe 61, Werkkreis Literatur der Arbeitswelt*, Frankfurt a.M., 1972.

HUGH RIDLEY

Tretjakov in Berlin

'It remains to determine whether the function of clercs is to secure empires.'
[Julian Benda, *La Trahison des clercs*]

By the last years of the Weimar Republic the ideological and political divisions which had been present since its inception had become extreme. In politics, only the extremes thrived; in intellectual life too the voices of moderation became less audible. Not only the split between left and right exploded in bitterness. On the left the Bund proletarisch-revolutionärer Schriftsteller (BPRS) engaged in a series of feuds against the unattached intellectuals of the left, and reflected in its own life something of the turmoil through which culture was passing in the Soviet Union. It was to a divided and troubled Berlin that Sergej Tretjakov,[1] a Soviet playwright and essayist, came to lecture in January 1931. Compared with other visitors to and from the Soviet Union, Tretjakov seemed both minor and unofficial, but his visit was to have an impact on intellectual life and was to focus attention on issues in a way which outweighed its original significance.

Tretjakov (b. 1892) had an interesting but far from unique pedigree. An early member of the Futurist movement (he was associated with the Tvorchestvo group in Vladivostok), he had progressed like many of his generation from Futurism to wholehearted support for the revolution. He formed with Mayakovsky and others the left wing of the cultural front in the 1920s. On the editorial board of the important periodical *Novyj Lef* (Pasternak once referred to him as the 'only honest and consistent member of this group'), he was closely associated with the 'literatura fakta' school of documentary writing and remained in the forefront of literary debate (as well as writing poems, plays and sketches) throughout the decade.[2] A teaching post at the University of Peking had made him something of an expert in Chinese affairs, while his period as associate producer with Meyerhold's theatre had given him the chance to experiment with dramatic forms which combined political propaganda with Futurist style. In 1930 his play *Roar, China!* had been performed in Berlin by the Meyerhold theatre on its triumphant European tour. Herbert Ihering had written that certain of its scenes (those free from what, in Germany, seemed merely clichéd Expressionism), which portrayed the awakening of the Chinese people to political consciousness, were 'among the most extraordinary I have ever seen on the stage . . . We see here a style with potential for development.'[3]

Yet it was neither as a Futurist nor as a playwright that Tretjakov came to Berlin in 1931. He came to lecture on the achievements of the Five Year Plan and of his part in them, of which his work *Feld-Herren* (published in December 1931 by the Malik-Verlag) was to give a fuller account. His lecture was entitled 'The writer and the socialist village'.[4]

Tretjakov's lecture gave an account of the time he had spent on a collective farm. He saw his experience of collectivisation as symbolic of the encounter of writers with the new Soviet society, and generalised from his experiences to a picture of a new style of writing and a new social role for the writer. Only within this style and this new role could a writer do justice to the subject matter of socialist society.

Tretjakov began his lecture with a discussion of the nineteenth-century Realists. He showed the inability of their methods to cope with the changes in Russian society since 1917. Their works were too concerned with individuals and their interaction in society, too unable to grasp the statistical and economic data relevant to planned change, too little interested in man at work.[5] The very language of Soviet society – the grating acronyms so beloved by Five Year Planners: Rabfak, Isspolkom, Udarnik – would in their works be a pistol shot at a concert. The Realists might well manage to depict the evolutionary changes of their own time; their famed 'epic breadth' depended on and corresponded to a social situation of 'stability and the slow change of social forms'. But, Tretjakov argued, revolutionary and technologically planned change (such as the Five Year Plan) lay outside the scope of the Realists' method. Inspiration, the devices of plot and characterisation, the idea of a hero – these and all the other Realist techniques had become inappropriate, and the writer who wished to deal adequately with Soviet reality would have to revolutionise his literary techniques as well as his subject matter.

For many years Tretjakov had insisted – like many of the Lef group – upon the need for writers to see the revolution not simply as a subject matter for their works but as an event which would profoundly alter the structure and self-understanding of that writing. 'The Revolution was not simply a theme, or an episode, for the Futurists', he had written in 1923, 'but the only reality.' Two years later Boris Arvatov (fellow member of Lef) had written of the need for art to be revolutionary in its technique as well as its subject: 'innerkünstlerisch revolutionär'.[6] At a time when many campaigners for proletarian literature saw themselves merely as folk-lore collectors, taking down beggars' songs in shorthand, the Lef group had looked forward to the emergence of a technologically sophisticated art, adapted completely to the production relations of the new age: what came to be called 'Produktionskunst' (production art). It was with this concept and its implications practically (rather than theoretically, for the theory had been the subject of many essays) that Tretjakov's lecture in Berlin was concerned.

His audience was familiar with the starting point at least in the novel and drama. That the traditional Realist novel was being eroded by technological developments in social and personal life had been observed by, among others, Simmel, Spengler and Döblin. The early attempts of Meyerhold's theatre to reform traditional acting style in accordance with a system of eurhythmics based on the technically streamlined movements of production-line work were also known in Germany. Meyerhold's 'biomechanics' – the style under which Tretjakov had worked in the early 1920s – used theories of time and motion study and the 'Produktions-training' (developed by Gastev at the Central Institute of Work in Moscow) in order to bridge at least partly the traditionally separate spheres of technology and art. Fülöp-Miller's widely read *Geist und Gesicht des Bolschewismus* (1928) devoted much space to the subject, albeit from the negative angle that the Soviet Union was producing a robot-like 'machine man'.[7] However they may have reacted to it, therefore, Tretjakov's audience would have certainly been familiar with the presuppositions and some of the practice of 'production art'. But as he went on to discuss the effect of this view of art on the status and function of the intellectual Tretjakov was entering new territory.

His lecture explained that the experience of collectivisation had transformed him as a writer. In the first place, his relationship to his material had been transformed. Because of the factual and technical significance of what he had to describe (acres sown, yield, productivity of labour force, etc) knowledge rather than insight became important. No longer could the writer claim to have a special relationship to the world. As he gathered and collated information from other technical experts the individual element in his collecting and evaluating of the material became irrelevant. Stripped of its 'professional mystique' and its 'fetishes', of everything which previously had kept art different from life, 'writing has ceased to be an unusual individual skill and has become part of communal education'.

This 'deprofessionalising of literature' reflected, Tretjakov argued, the new relationship between writer and public established in the Soviet Union. His own experiences had shown the inadequacy of the writer who tried to stay at a distance from the society of which he wrote, whether merely keeping to his desk and observing without participating or paying merely brief visits to the society he was to portray and returning as soon as possible to the more 'literary' life of the metropolis.[8] The people who had supplied information to Tretjakov wanted to see what he had made of it. (No fewer than 181 members of the kolchos bought his book.[9]) He himself wanted to see whether his interpretation of events and facts was right or not – right, that is, neither in an abstract way nor by its artistic success but in a very practical sense: did his ideas work or not? He was obliged to participate directly 'in the life of the material'. He summed up the development of literature as follows:

To put it simply: to invent an important theme is novelistic belles-lettres; to discover an important theme is reportage; to contribute constructively to an important theme is Operativism.

In *Feld-Herren* Tretjakov reiterated his theory of the 'operative writer' and gave a fuller account of the way in which a particular job he was commissioned to do as a reporter (which had led to his original encounter with the kolchos) led him to realise the need for 'permanent observation' of the subject matter and this in turn led him to undertake binding cultural and organisational responsiblities there: *in the long term.* In the late nineteenth century groups of intellectuals (the 'Narodniki') had taken to the land out of the 'idealistic impulse to work . . . "on the soil", "with the people" '. They had been replaced by the 'writers of informative sketches' (the reporters), of whom the worst merely collected local colour for village love stories and the best turned from reporters into the new type of ' "operating" ["operierende"] sketch writers'.[10] In recognition of this change in his role and nature Tretjakov had withdrawn from all literary groups, regarding them as 'specialist corporations . . . unfit for organized activity'.[11]

It is hardly surprising that Tretjakov's lecture should have had a considerable impact, quite apart from the obvious sympathy which existed in Germany both for his works and his person.[12] The documentary was the dominant literary style of the period in Germany, and a lecture on the direction which literature would take *beyond* reportage was bound to be of great interest. The works of Heinrich Hauser, E. E. Kisch, Leo Lania, Stenbok-Fermor and others had created a vogue for the fact-orientated work, free from personal bias or misleading authorial presence, let alone stylistic pretensions – 'artistic dodges', as Ernst Glaeser had called them. In general, the writers and works of 'Neue Sachlichkeit' shared Tretjakov's contempt for the literary and his desire to be useful: it was anything but unusual at that time for novels and even (somewhat ironically) collections of poetry to be published with 'instructions for use'.[13] Tretjakov was interesting to such writers not simply for his prognosis of future developments; his past held for many a model of a development which they themselves had had to make. Tretjakov had passed through a process of depersonalisation, breaking the magic staff of poetry and adapting his originally highly colourful style to the impersonal demands of reportage and 'production art'.[14] That he had been able to make this transition without the simultaneous and stress-laden experience of a political conversion (such had been the fate of the German Expressionists who had found their way to the KPD) added to his interest. There was every reason why he should have been listened to.

Even more relevant to contemporary intellectual discussion in Germany, however, was Tretjakov's account of the function of the intellectual in society. Wooed from left and right, uncertain of the very basis of their art, German writers debated nothing more avidly than their role in society. Periodicals such as *Die literarische Welt* and *Die neue Rundschau* devoted much space to their debates. A characteristic essay, written under the evident influence of Tretjakov's lecture, was Siegfried Kracauer's 'Über den Schriftsteller'.

Kracauer began by claiming that, 'with the pressure of economic and social conditions', both the writer and the journalist were abandoning the functions which they traditionally filled in society: the writer unable to sustain his devotion to a transcendent aesthetic vision, the journalist no longer free to express his opinions openly in the face of the power of capital and party. Both professions were moving, Kracauer argued, towards a new type of existence, in which their service of ideals – Truth or Art – and ideologies would be abandoned. Echoing almost exactly Julien Benda's account of the 'treason of intellectuals', while refraining from personal judgement, Kracauer saw two significant aspects of this transition: 'The writers' lack of interest in ideal values is as pronounced as their anxiety to be absorbed into the here and now of society'. However neutrally he tried to portray intellectuals' readiness to abandon transcendent values and to become identified with purely social issues, Kracauer revealed his own feelings clearly enough when he turned to Tretjakov's lecture. With regret he pointed out that the developments Tretjakov had described, appropriate though they were to the Soviet Union, could not as yet be envisaged in Germany:

Our economic anarchy, the resistance of archaic ideologies, and the inflexible structure of our intellectual class still keep the intellectual in Germany in isolation for the time being.[15]

Later in that year Kracauer formulated more positively his view of the role of the intellectual and revealed how close he was to the purely practical role Tretjakov had envisaged:

It is not, however, the task of the intellectual merely to uphold the ideal – even the socialist ideal – but to engage and commit it in a dialectical relationship to the actual possibilities for its realisation.[16]

Two years previously Karl Mannheim – observing similarly the tendency of intellectuals to desert their role as upholders of the ideal – had attacked such a position, and had expounded at length the value of a 'utopian' element in society. Kracauer's position was symptomatic of many of his generation: he had lost the belief in the importance of the intellectual's independent position but had not found a social order or ideology in which the intellectual might be re-integrated with society. His arguments reveal an open-mindedness characteristic of the late years of the republic – certain only of the destructive function of the intellect 'as an instrument for the destruction of all mythical remnants in us and in our environment', yet longing for a system in which a more positive role would become possible.[17]

It was this attitude for which Kracauer was criticised at the end of 1931 by Alfred Döblin. In the course of a series of polemics following the publication of his essays on the state of society, *Wissen und Verändern* (1931), Döblin turned to Kracauer's argument. He insisted that the intellectual had a role which was more than destructive; the intellect was 'first and foremost an instrument for the implementation of a purpose'. *Wissen und Verändern* had argued for the commitment of intellectuals to the cause of humanistic socialism, to the fight against the erosion of individual values and against the merely economic socialism of the KPD, what he called 'collectivism, the ideal of men as ants or machines'. Intellectuals no longer had any enthusiasm for ideals, Döblin complained, and they tried to make up for this lack by fanatical political commitment. In this spirit Döblin explicitly criticised Kracauer for his impatience with the ideal and his anxiety to relate it directly to 'the actual possibilites for its realisation'. Yet Döblin's own arguments had a circular quality not dissimilar to Kracauer's. He objected both to commitment and to intellectuals' traditional disengagement from politics, and he revealed in this an ultimate pessimism about the effectiveness of ideas in reality which was in striking contrast to the apparent optimism with which his argument had begun. 'Intellectual attitudes work in the long term, working often fruitlessly for long periods on reality,' he wrote, outlining a minimal position very similar to that of Julien Benda, whose ultimate justification of the social function of the intellectual was not that he should alter reality but that he should prevent society justifying to itself the misdeeds it perennially committed.[18]

It seemed a much more consistent argument against Tretjakov's lecture when Gottfried Benn started from an acceptance of that minimal position. In a broadcast in the autumn of 1931 reviewing 'Die neue literarische Saison' Benn devoted much time to a critique of Tretjakov. He portrayed him as 'a literary Tscheka type, who cross-examines, interrogates, condemns and then punishes anyone who thinks differently', and regarded his lecture as 'a propagandist exercise in new Russian imperialism'. Yet there is little doubt that he took Tretjakov seriously, as a kind of absolute opponent. While he was merely amused at Tretjakov's suggestion that bourgeois writers wrote out of a craving for money – Benn was aware that fifteen years of writing poetry had brought him precious little money[19] – he took absolute exception to Tretjakov's view of the relationship between art and society. The socialist man Tretjakov aimed to produce ('the balanced happy collective man with no daemon and no impulses') was the very negation of cultural values. The marriage of aesthetic and practical thinking which Tretjakov and the sycophantic 'Tretjakov group' in Berlin aimed at was merely pathetic. 'Those who organise life will never create art,' Benn concluded, 'and can have no relationship to it.'[20]

Such pessimism about the social possibilities of art was much closer to Döblin's position than Benn realised. Elsewhere he too had argued that intellectual activity filters through public consciousness and affects social practice with extreme slowness; not even an intellectual of the shattering importance of Nietzsche could be said to have intervened at all in the development of society.[21] Materialist in one sense – his feeling for the biological determinants of thought was already well developed – Benn was also close to the traditionally humanist defensive stance which Döblin had taken up in combating the 'Tretjakov group'. Yet it was characteristic of the polarisation of intellectual life in Weimar that Benn failed to see in Döblin anything other than a doctrinaire Marxist. Benn assumed that the left wing were all of a kind and – as Klaus Mann wrote in explanation of Benn's support for Hitler in 1933 – became so angry with them 'that he eventually became a Nazi about it'.[22] In so doing, Benn himself took over many of the tenets of his opponents of 1931. In 1934, for instance, as he greeted in Berlin Filippo Marinetti – himself a Futurist poet in the service of a political system, but one from whom the Russian Futurists were careful to distance themselves – Benn spoke of his eagerness to make 'the step from art into the excitement of history' and to establish a harmony between his artistic visions and 'the ideal of history'.[23] The man who had sneered at the Tscheka types sat down to help purge the Academy.

Had he bothered to listen Benn might have been encouraged by reactions to Tretjakov's speech from the official left. Tretjakov's attacks on the Social Realist novel, his sneering suggestion that it was pointless for the Soviet Union to await the emergence of a 'new Leo Tolstoy', his assent to an anti-literary style of writing, boded ill for the BPRS's attempts to create inside Germany 'a great proletarian work of art'. His influence on left-wing intellectuals, in particular Ernst Ottwalt and, of course, Brecht (whose work he translated and with whom close personal links of friendship tied him), was regarded with great distaste by the leadership of the BPRS. Becher, for instance, in summarising the year 1931 spoke of the mischief ('Unfug') Tretjakov had created among the left wing with his talk of the 'end of literature' and his prediction of the need for the writer to adapt himself to the technical processes of society.[24] It is no coincidence that Tretjakov's name was constantly invoked by Lukács in his campaigns against the avant-garde in the early 1930s, campaigns which have been the subject of numerous studies in recent years.[25]

Already in 1930, in the course of an attack on the Agitprop theatre and on 'the new-fangled "Tendenz" ' introduced by Russian and German experimenters, O. Biha had said of *Roar, China!* and other experimental plays that they had nothing in common with the proletariat: 'These experiments are formal-aesthetic concerns of the rebelling petty-bourgeoisie' – sentiments which he was later to apply to Brecht's didactic play *The Measures Taken*.[26] Much more acceptable than the stylised evocation of the masses achieved by Tretjakov were the techniques used by Friedrich Wolf in his play on a similar theme, *Tai Yang erwacht*. Here the revolutionary impulse is portrayed in a conventional, psychological presentation of one character who, as an individual, awakens to the cause of the masses. The BPRS had followed with interest and no small relief the victory of the Socialist Realists (represented by the All-Russian organisation of proletarian writers, RAPP) over its opponents on the left, and it obviously annoyed them intensely to find Tretjakov creating such a following in Germany at a time when the movements he represented seemed to have been defeated in his home country.[27]

A decisive influence of Tretjakov was on Walter Benjamin. He had know of Tretjakov's theatrical work for some time and placed him with Brecht at the centre of his celebrated essay 'Der Autor als Produzent' (1934), in which – contrasting them favourably with the outmoded attitudes of Döblin's *Wissen und Verändern* – he praised them for rescuing art from consumerism and giving it a new theoretical basis.[28] In 1930 he had reported a meeting of Russian intellectuals in Germany at which the discontent of the radicals with the literary achievements of the Soviet Union was clearly expressed. In a discussion of the development of literature in the Soviet Union, a Soviet intellectual had made it clear that the total surrender of individual creative freedom was being offered by intellectuals in a progressive, not reactionary, literary cause. Benjamin reported his words as follows:

We are ready to surrender the individuality of the poet, to give up literature's claim to a validity outside its age, to abandon objective depiction. But not in order to swop them for a literature operating by primitive suggestiveness and slogans, but in order to make way for an authoritarian literature. We want to see a consumer attitude toward reading replaced by a learning one, a training one, but not by brainless reaction.[29]

With this Benjamin was in agreement. He too was quite prepared to abandon a whole series of positions which had previously been regarded as essential to the intellectual in order to get rid of the kind of second-rate 'archaic' literature of emotional identification which, in common with Tretjakov and Brecht, he thought unworthy of the socialist State. His horror at the kind of literature represented by Socialist Realism, for instance Gladkov's novel *Cement*, which was enjoying something of a vogue in Germany at the time, was genuine. Yet it was characteristic of the age that Benjamin should combine a certain relish in abandoning traditional intellectual values with a susceptibility to authoritarian solutions. Döblin had referred to just this tendency of the intellectual, having lost confidence in intellectual values, to clutch at the straws held out to him by political parties. But Benjamin found the authoritarian less in parties than in technology itself, and his combination of an almost masochistic self-denial with an apparently objective analysis of technology also belonged to its age.

The belief had spread in Germany during the years of economic and political stabilisation that the technical sophistication of economic life would by itself solve political and social problems. Mass production would alleviate the hardships of manual labour and increase working wages to the point at which the working classes would merge with the bourgeoisie. The technical rationalisation and planning of capitalist industry would, it was argued, increasingly approximate to a planned socialist economy. Ideological differences would be erased by the spread of technical rather than ideological solutions to problems. It was in this context that Mannheim had suggested that society was moving towards a 'tensionless' situation. Such thinking exercised much influence on the writers of 'Neue Sachlichkeit'; and, even after the economic crisis and the rise of the political extremes had made absurd the idea of a situation without tension, there remained a widespread tendency to identify the conflict in society as being that between an authoritarian, technological system and an individualistic, liberal world order, rather than between various camps within the liberal system. Such thinking was behind many movements on the left wing of the extreme right: the so-called New Nationalists, National Bolshevists, etc. It was not at all unusual to find writers adopting a position which seemed to unite Mussolini, Stalin, Hitler and the Prussian tradition as allies against the liberal system. Among those who attacked Döblin's view of the intellectual in 1931 had been, for instance, Klaus Mehnert, something of an expert on the Soviet Union. In his article 'The collective on the march' Mehnert flatly rejected Döblin's humanist ideas and welcomed 'the Komsomols in Russia, the Fascists in Italy, the anti-fascists or SA or the *bündisch* youth movements' as representatives of a new, more authoritarian system – an idea which he followed up in his other works of the period.[30] But the discussion of a new technological authority in intellectual life, such as one finds in Tretjakov or Benjamin, took place most extensively in the circles round Ernst Jünger, and it is to these that we now turn.

A characteristic member of these circles was Arnolt Bronnen. Among the wilder of the Expressionists and still notorious in the early 1930s for a number of crass provocative actions, Bronnen had cultivated in the mid-1920s a fascination with technology and Americanism typical of the shallow and brittle anti-intellectualism affected by his close friend Brecht. Selecting his best books of 1927, Bronnen had chosen Gladkov's *Cement* (the very work to which Benjamin's report was to refer with such contempt), precisely because of its analphabetic illiteracy and clumsy attempts to make emotional heroes out of Soviet bureaucrats. It was an extreme example of an admiration for the non-literary which had caused Brecht to award a poetry prize to Hannes Küpper's poem 'He! He! The iron man!'.[31] Yet, like Brecht, Bronnen developed away from a merely provocative relationship to the technological. Particularly through his work in the technical medium of wireless, Bronnen found a new language and a new, positive content in technology. He believed that wireless would bring about a decisive break with the isolation of the artist, that it would replace individual with collective work, communicating directly and continuously, and that wireless would be its very nature undermine attitudes to art which saw it as an object to be possessed, enjoyed, consumed. He saw wireless as a contribution to the 'de-conservation' of art. (He was writing in a time when broadcasting was live.) These opinions exactly mirrored Tretjakov's playing the newspaper off against the novel: *Pravda* against *War and Peace*. As a novelist also Bronnen had experienced the difficulites of adapting literature to the portrayal of the 'Freikorps' characters who were to be his heroes. He searched, during the writing of his novel *'OS'* (Oberschlesien), for what he called 'the literary formula' for a hero who was not to be an individual in a traditional sense but was to be linked to his society by technological rather than personal ties: he was to be one of 'a group of young men interested in technology and electricity and the pulsating energies of their nation in a new way, and linked to each other by this interest alone'.[32] Once again there are uncanny resemblances between this programme and Tretjakov's vision of the productive spirit breathing through the Five Year Plan, for which no individualised, psychological study of what Soviet traditionalists called the 'living man' could ever be an adequate expression.

Bronnen found his 'formula' neither in Tretjakov, nor in Brecht, to whom he had been so close, but in Ernst Jünger and the unmistakably fascist language of *Der Arbeiter* (1932) and the essays which preceeded it. Recent study of Jünger's work has drawn attention to the parallels between Jünger and Benjamin in their understanding of photography and film as 'assassins' of traditional art. In photography Jünger found that ability to typicalise, to capture the collective essence of the soldiers and of the technical processes of trench warfare which no literature could achieve. In his study of the technocrats (the 'Workers') Jünger gave Bronnen the language and insights he needed. Like Benjamin, Jünger looked forward to the emergence of a new authority through technology, to the death of 'bourgeois individualism' and the ending of the impartiality, eternal values and unique insights of the free intellectual. In the 'totale Mobilmachung' (Jünger's celebrated phrase for the technological revolutionising of society) all art and intellectual activity which resisted its incorporation in the work process, all 'museum art', would be destroyed. It was no coincidence that Jünger's work anticipated in almost every respect the Nazi State established only a few months later. But the book, characteristically, did more than anticipate and fatalistically accept events. It added to the masochistic language of intellectual self-destruction when it numbered among 'the sublime and cruel pleasures of our age' none more appealing than 'der Hochverrat des Geistes gegen den Geist', the high treason of spirit against spirit.[33]

It is not clear whether Jünger actually knew of or read Tretjakov. The periodicals for which he wrote (particularly the National Bolshevist *Widerstand*) studied events in the Soviet Union closely, and it is likely that Jünger had encountered Tretjakov's ideas. But, like the majority of right-wing radicals, Jünger was more concerned with stealing the Soviet

Union's thunder than with identifying or commenting on its intellectual accomplishments. It was customary to regard the disciplined Prussian State as a far more effective technological collective than the Soviet Union. Often the 'proletarian communist way of life' was contrasted with the 'military collective', and obedience to the latter was presented as the authentic German response. Spengler, for instance, in his *Jahre der Entscheidung* (1933), contrasted the surrender of self to the State or the army (of which he approved) with the anti-individualism which led to surrender to mass or party, and which Spengler contemptuously dismissed as 'the fashionable theory of the moment'.[34] Apart from the different labels it was hard to see differences between the sacrifice, and however much Jünger and his circle – in contrast to Tretjakov, Benjamin, Bela Balázs and others, who saw technology as an essentially socialist force in society – might protest that technology was 'beyond ideology', they noticeably and nationalistically denied to the Soviet revolution any technological status. In this they were helped by the many studies of the Soviet Union published at this time in Germany. Fülöp-Miller's account of the cult of technolgy in the Soviet Union not only argued that the technical revolution was floundering on the unchanging conservatism of the Russian peasant but also presented the surrender of the individual to the collective as a mystical quasi-religious experience rather than as a genuine encounter with technology. Waldemar Gurian, although he saw the USSR as 'the nation of total mobilisation', suggested that, in intellectual life at least, the signs were of a return to conservatism. Jünger himself believed that, with Trotski's exile, Russia had reverted to the 'Asiatic' (a synonym for the anti-technical, mystical side of the Russian character), and his last essay on the Soviet Union before the Nazi take-over reported, not without satisfaction, that the Soviets were unsuitable material for the technological revolution, and that the home of the total mobilisation would be Germany, its complexion fascist, not socialist.[35]

To all these arguments Tretjakov's language and ideas related, even if the echoes were not direct. He, far more than the right wing of the KPD, spoke to the German situation and he, far more than they, understood the pressures of the age upon intellectuals. Few intellectuals indeed were free of the suspicion of intellectualism, the fascination with the collective and its most recent voice, technology; few did not experience the temptation to bring together the intellectual and social worlds. On right and left, conservatives and radicals alike had little to put in place of a humanist tradition which had seemingly been discredited. Only a small group of writers, trying pragmatically to reawaken humanist values and to recall intellectuals to a more traditional relationship with human values, can be regarded as a legitimate opposition to the Tretjakov position. It highlights the situation of the intellectual in Weimar to conclude our survey with a brief glance at the attitude of the intellectuals round the SPD to the relationship between art and technology.

There is little doubt of the importance which the SPD attached to this subject. Technology was constantly under discussion in party newspapers, and although there was sympathy for the 'neusachlich' streamlining of life there was no enthusiasm at all for the activity of the 'revolutionary anti-aesthetes', those 'over-clever techo-maniacs, snobbish America-worshippers and fanatical utilitarians'. They were regarded with disfavour, not least because they seemed ready to discard the cultural goods of the nation before the proletariat had the chance to enjoy them.[36] It was also an important factor in their discussions that they took seriously (in marked contrast to many of the intellectuals with whom we have been concerned) the actual threat to cultural and intellectual liberty inherent in fascism. The regime of Frick and Schulze-Naumburg in Thuringia had made plain, for those who wished to see, the precise nature of totalitarian repression of culture, in comparison with which discussions of the uncertain freedoms of the intellectual paled into insignificance.[37]

In this spirit two articles appeared at the end of 1931 in the *Sozialistische Monatshefte* under the titles 'Art and reality' and 'Art and technology'. Both were concerned to defend art against those social pressures which were undermining it and against those theoreticians, like Tretjakov, to whom art was merely 'an obedient and cheap servant of some immediate social goal'. Ernst Kallai was concerned to establish that the human imagination was always in advance of technological progress, and that 'its distance from technologically dominated reality is the realm in which art can thrive'.[38] Art depended on being removed from the technical, therefore. It was possible, individually and generally, even in a technically sophisticated society such as the Weimar Republic, and it was socially important that art should remain possible, not least because it was a spring from which flowed the cultural products on which the masses fed. If art (by which Kallai obviously meant 'great art') ceased to be possible, 'mass production and mass consumption of our art surrogates would get into the same plight as our moribund European *Volkskunst*'.[39] Once again, Kallai's argument implied a criticism of intellectuals for ignoring their social responsibility to those further down the cultural ladder.

If Kallai revealed the educational motivation of his belief in art there was much less reason for him to underpin his understanding of art in the way he did. So anxious was he to insist on the distinctness of the artistic and the technical that he was prepared to move a long way towards the irrationalism of the extreme right. There were overtones of Expressionism, very few of socialist theory, in his plea that art should be allowed to make its way, with the full support of the emancipatory political movements, 'to the daemonic, irrational sources of existence'. This pilgrimage (not dissimilar to that which many writers wished art to make to the 'blood') was to take place in the name of the liberation of man from the machine:

In creating symbols and visions of this irrational realm, modern art reaches out to a new life order, which can control the murderous expansion of mechanistic, quantitative forces in economic and technical life and which can lead man to a spiritual and intellectual self-awareness.[40]

The substantive defence of art against technology had brought Kallai to an idealistic and imprecise humanism more likely to find its allies on the right than on the left.

Tretjakov's visit and ideas revealed, therefore, the uncertainty which characterised many German intellectuals' view of their social position. His commitment highlighted the desire for commitment of many of his German counterparts; his apparent victory over the cultural pessimism of a technological age was bound to be impressive inside Germany at a time when economic and political collapse seemed imminent. His visit revealed the shortage of sure platforms from which to oppose collective thinking such as his. What were the chances for a 'committed humanism'? E. R. Curtius, warning in 1932 against all that Tretjakov stood for ('German culture in danger'[41]), called for a new 'initiative of humanism', yet in ways he seemed closer to the initiative of the Nazis than to the human values he had defended. His case was typical of many, and those intellectuals who instead tried to assert the human values, ignoring an immediate social relevance, often found themselves forced, like Kallai, into a mysticism and irrationalism regrettably similar to that what was preached on the extreme right. Such irrationalism was, frequently, merely a further expression of the pessimism of the intellectual in the face of historical developments he could neither understand nor influence.

As for Tretjakov himself, he went home and eventually vanished in Stalin's purges.[41]

Notes

[1] His name is variously transliterated. I use here the form in which he is discussed in current Federal German literature. Standard British transliteration gives Tret'yakov.

[2] A selection of Tretjakov's writing can be found in two recent anthologies: *Sergej Tretjakov. Die Arbeit des Schriftstellers*, ed. H. Boehncke, Reinbeck, 1972, and *Sergej Tretjakov. Lyrik, Dramatik, Prosa*, ed. Fritz Mierau, Leipzig, 1972. *Novyj Lef* is available in reprint (The Hague, 1970) and thus most of Tretjakov's articles of the 1920s

are easily found. His 'Bio-interview' *Den Schi-Chua*, first published by Malik in 1932, is also readily available (Neuwied, 1974). An account of the literary movements in which Tretjakov was involved will be found *inter alia*, in V. Markov, *Russian Futurism*, London, 1969; E. J. Brown, *The proletarian episode in Russian literature*, New York, 1953; G. Struve, *Russian literature under Lenin and Stalin*, London, 1971; Harriet Borland, *Soviet literary theory and practice during the first five-year plan*, New York, 1950. Pasternak's comment in *An essay in autobiography*, trans. M. Harari, London, 1959, p. 100.

[3] Reprinted in H. Ihering, *Von Reinhardt bis Brecht*, 3. Bd., Berlin 1961, pp. 57–8.

[4] Printed in *Das neue Russland*, 7. Jg. Hf. 2/3, March 1931, pp. 39–52. Reprinted in *Die Arbeit des Schriftstellers*, pp. 117–34. Unless otherwise identified, all quotations from Tretjakov are from this speech.

[5] *Cf.* 'Die Biographie des Dings', *Die Arbeit des Schriftsellers*, p. 81 f.

[6] S. Tretjakov, 'Woher und Wohin? Perspektiven des Futurismus', *Ästhetik und Kommunikation*, 2. Jg., 1971, p. 86; B. Arvatov, *Kunst und Produktion*, ed. H. Günther and K. Hielscher, Munich, 1972, p. 77.

[7] *Geist und Gesicht des Bolschewismus*, Zürich and Leipzig, etc, 1928, p. 281f. For Meyerhold's theories see *Meyerhold on theatre*, ed. E. Braun, London, 1969, pp. 181–206. Tretjakov discusses Gastev in 'Woher und Wohin?', *loc. cit.*, p. 89.

[8] *Feld-Herren. Der Kampf um eine Kollektiv-Wirtschaft*, Berlin, 1931, p. 226.

[9] L. Fischer, *Machines and men in Russia*, New York, 1932, p. 266. Other examples in Borland, *Russian literary theory* ..., p. 40 f., and F. C. Weiskopf, 'Ein paar Bemerkungen über Autor, Buch und Publikum in der SU', 1929, *Ges. Werke*, 7. Bd., Berlin, 1960, p. 13 f.

[10] *Feld-Herren*, p. 23. See also *Russian literary theory* ..., p. 46 f.

[11] Letter to *Literaturnaya Gazeta*, 2 December 1929, quoted from W. Woroszylski, *The life of Mayakovsky*, trans. B. Taborski, London, 1972, p. 473.

[12] A selection of favourable reviews: G. Schwarz, 'Der Sendbote', *Die Literatur*, 33. Jg., 1930–31, p. 303; *ibid.*, 34. Jg., 1931–32, p. 588 (*Feld-Herren*); Balder Olden, 'Die Memoiren eines jungen Chinesen', *Das Tagebuch*, 13. Jg. Hf. 34, August 1932, pp. 1307–10; 'Der Schriftsteller und das sozialistische Dorf', 'Unterhaltungsblatt', *Vossische Zeitung*, 31 January 1931; R. Huelsenbeck, 'Tretjakov: *Den Schi-Chua*', *Die literarische Welt*, 8. Jg. Nr. 32, August, 1932, p. 6.

[13] E. Glaeser, *Fazit*, Hamburg, 1929, p. 7; E. Reger, *Union der festen Hand*, Hamburg, 1932, p. 6; and, of course, Brecht's *Hauspostille*, 1927.

[14] *Cf.* V. Shklovskij, 'A few words about the four hundred million', *Novyj Lef*, 2. Jg. 3. Hf., 1928, p. 43, in which Shklovskij criticises Tretjakov for using a literary device – imagery. *Cf.* F. Mierau, 'Tatsache und Tendenz. Der "operierende" Schriftsteller Sergej Tretjakow', *S. Tretjakow. Lyrik, Dramatik, Prosa*, p. 437 f. It is interesting to note how much less rigorous Arvatov was in this matter. ('Kunst und Organisation der Umwelt' (1926), *Kunst und Produktion*, p. 62.)

[15] 'Über den Schriftsteller', *Die neue Rundschau*, 42. Jg. 1. Bd., pp. 860–2.

[16] 'Minimalforderung an die Intellektuellen', *ibid.*, 2. Bd., p. 74.

[17] *Ibid.*, pp. 72, 75. Kracauer's views merely echoed Tretjakov's demands that the intellectual should destroy false consciousness (e.g. 'Wohin und Woher?', *loc. cit.*, p. 88).

[18] A. Döblin, 'Nochmals *Wissen und Verändern*'. *Schriften zur Politik*, Olten, 1972, pp. 272, 287; *Wissen und Verändern. Offene Briefe an einen jungen Menschen*, Berlin, 1931, p. 62 f. *Cf.* J. Benda, *The great betrayal*, trans. R. Aldington, London, 1928, p. 111.

[19] G. Benn, 'Summa summarum', *Ges. Werke*, 4. Bd., Wiesbaden, 1959, p. 15.

[20] 'Die neue literarische Saison', *ibid.*, 1. Bd., pp. 433–9.

[21] 'Zur Problematik des Dichterischen', *ibid.*, p. 72.

[22] Letter quoted by Benn in 'Doppelleben', *ibid.*, 4. Bd., p. 77. When Benn's position in the Third Reich became, predictably, untenable he tried to use his controversy with the Tretjakov group as proof of proper nationalist sentiments, only to be told that his

argument against Tretjakov had been 'conducted so completely in the language of your opponent . . . that it can give scarcely any pleasure to the Movement.' (Letter of 14 August 1937 from J. F. Lehmann, quoted in J. Wulf, *Literatur und Dichtung im 3. Reich*, Gütersloh, 1963, p. 118.)

[23] 'Rede auf Marinetti', *Ges. Werke*, 1. Bd., p. 480.

[24] J. R. Becher, 'Unsere Wendung', *Die Linkskurve*, 3. Jg. Nr. 10, October, 1931, p. 5. Perhaps Tretjakov's most relevant essay on literary technique was 'Der neue Lev Tolstoi', *Novyj Lef*, January 1927, reprinted in both recent anthologies.

[25] *Cf.* Helga Gallas, *Marxistische Literaturkritik*, Neuwied and Berlin, 1969.

[26] 'Wsewold Meyerhold', *Linkskurve*, 2. Jg. Nr. 5, May 1930, pp. 15–16.

[27] *Cf.* Becher's various reports from Charkhov, and, for example, the extremely right-wing article by N. Nowitsch, 'Die schöpferische Methode in der Sowjetliteratur', *Linkskurve*, 2. Jg. Nr. 8, August 1930, p. 20 f. *Cf.* Gallas, *op. cit.*, p. 97 f.

[28] Reprinted, *inter alia*, in *Versuche über Brecht*, Frankfurt a.M., 1966, pp. 95–116. Criticising those who wanted 'eine Herrschaft der Geistigen', Benjamin had pointed to Döblin's *Wissen und Verändern* and 'die Konzeption des "Geistigen" als eines nach seinen Meinungen, Gesinnungen oder Anlagen, nicht aber nach seiner Stellung im Produktionsprozess definierten Typus' (pp. 102, 104).

[29] 'Russische Debatte auf deutsch', *Die literarische Welt*, 6. Jg. Nr. 27, 4 March 1930, p. 8. Further discussion of the episode in H. Brüggemann, *Literarische Technik und soziale Revolution*, Reinbek, 1973, p. 148 f. Brüggemann discusses at length the intellectual links between Brecht and Tretjakov (pp. 139–64).

[30] *Die neue Rundschau*, 42. Jg. 2. Bd., 1931, p. 84. Also *Die Jugend in Sowjetrussland*, Berlin, 1932.

[31] *Cf.* K. Schumann, *Der Lyriker Bert Brecht*, Munich, 1971, p. 172 f.

[32] A. Bronnen, *gibt zu protokoll*, Hamburg, 1959, p. 191. The Jünger circle's view of Bronnen (Brack) as a 'Techniker' in F. G. Jünger, *Spiegel der Jahre*, Munich, 1958, p. 81 f. Bronnen's opinions echo those of Mayakovsky on the radio as a technical medium (*cf. The life of Mayakovsky*, p. 375).

[33] E. Jünger, *Der Arbeiter*, 3. Aufl., Hamburg, 1934, p. 40. *Cf.* also p. 195 f.

[34] O. Spengler, *Jahre der Entscheidung*, Munich, 1967, p. 187 f. *Cf.* also N. Götz, 'Proletkult?', *Widerstand*, 7. Jg. 4. Hf., April 1932, p. 101 f.

[35] *Geist und Gesicht des Bolschewismus*, p. 271; W. Gurian, *Der Bolschewismus*, Freiburg, 1931, p. 320; E. Jünger, 'Trotzkis Erinnerungen', *Widerstand*, 5. Jg. 2. Hf., March 1930, pp. 47–51; and 'Ein neuer Bericht aus dem Land der Planwirtschaft', *ibid.*, 6. Jg. 9. Hf., October 1931, pp. 279–83.

[36] A. Behne, 'Die Kunst im Trommelfeuer der politischen Parteien', *Sozialistische Monatshefte*, 37. Jg. 74. Bd. 8. Hf., August 1931, p. 781; and E. Kallai, 'Kunst und Wirklichkeit', *ibid.*, 10. Hf., October 1931, p. 1001. On SPD cultural policy see Cherry Sewell, 'The *Kulturwille* . . ., M.A. thesis, Canterbury, 1976.

[37] *Cf.* A. Behne, 'Die Kunst im Trommelfeuer . . .', *loc. cit.*, p. 779 f.

[38] E. Kallai, 'Kunst und Technik', *Sozialistische Monatshefte*, 37. Jg. 74. Bd. 12. Hf., December 1931, p. 1096 f.

[39] 'Kunst und Wirklichkeit', *loc. cit.*, p. 1002.

[40] *Ibid.*, pp. 1003, 1005.

[41] *Deutscher Geist in Gefahr*, Stuttgart, 1932, p. 103 f. *Cf.* also pp. 18 f, 41, 43.

[42] How much Tretjakov's fate was due to the mindless denunciations characteristic of the 1930s, how much to the residual offence his theories and works had caused, will perhaps never be known. Certainly his outspoken play on women's emancipation *I want a child* (translated by Brecht as *Die Pioniere*, otherwise only partially in *Novyj Lef*, 1. Jg. 3. Hf., March 1927, but published in full in Fritz Mierau, *Erfindung und Korrektur. Tretjakows Ästhetik der Operativität*, Berlin, 1976, pp. 179–247) had raised intense reaction from the establishment, *inter alis* from Lunacharski, and was frequently the subject of adverse comment from outside observers of the Soviet Union's morality. I would like to record my thanks for their help to Fritz Mierau, Peter Meades and Edward Greenwood, all of whom helped me with material for this essay.

JOST HERMAND
Translated by PETER and MARGARET LINCOLN

Unity within diversity? The history of the concept 'Neue Sachlichkeit'

The concept 'Neue Sachlichkeit'[1] is generally attributed to Gustav Friedrich Hartlaub, who sent out a circular on 18 May 1923 announcing his plan to stage an exhibition in the Mannheim art gallery, of which he was director at the time, and to give it the title 'Neue Sachlichkeit'. By this he meant paintings which have the appearance of being neither 'impressionistically dissolved' nor 'expressionistically abstract' but rather 'in an almost proclamatory way remain loyal or rediscover their loyalty to a positively tangible reality'. After careful preparation the exhibition took place in the summer of 1925 and gave the concept 'Neue Sachlichkeit', which had already been in the air for some time, the impetus necessary to establish itself.[2]

After the 'death of Expressionism', which according to many journalists had occurred in the years 1920–21, a new collective concept for the post-Expressionist tendencies of the most recent art was generally sought after.[3] Nearly all serious art critics considered this type of concept to be absolutely essential. For thirty years each 'ism' had been immediately followed by a new one – from Naturalism via Symbolism, Impressionism, Neo-impressionism, Expressionism, Cubism, Futurism, right up to Constructivism and Dadaism. In the absence of such a concept one felt incapable of moving forward. Even Dadaism, which in fact had wanted to put an end to this merry-go-round of 'isms' and styles, was itself, within the context of this art industry, immediately marketed as one more short-lived 'ism' in the general world of 'isms'. Hence a sequence of new 'isms' was tried out on the new trends since 1920–21, and among these were 'New Naturalism', 'Neo-realism' and 'Magical Realism', until eventually the term 'Neue Sachlichkeit' was hit upon. Thereupon justice had finally been done to the general requirement. The only thing lacking was the customary 'ism'. 'Neue Sachlichkeit' did indeed possess a modernistic ring, a 'new' one, that is, but more in the sense of a distinct 'trade mark' (Friedrich Ahlers-Hestermann) than of a fashionable, futuristic-sounding 'ism'. Therefore this concept, which was really intended to continue the old merry-go-round of styles, finally put an end to it. For with it the period of styles and 'isms' finally comes to a close. While Expressionism and Dadaism are still generally recognised as 'movements' today, 'Neue Sachlichkeit', however strongly it might have been proclaimed at the time, was never really viewed as one. It remained an incomplete concept.[4]

This designation had anyway something defeatist about it from the outset. In contrast to Expressionism, at the heart of which had lain many bourgeois artists' illusion that they could radically transform the world by means of art, 'Sachlichkeit' primarily signified resignation. Central to this concept is no longer the age of the November revolution, the Spartakus uprising, the Munich Soviet Republic, the conflicts in the Ruhr, or inflation, but rather the age of the 'relative stability' of the Weimar Republic, beginning with the currency reform, the Dawes plan and thus the consolidation of the basic capitalist order. After a time, therefore, of ecstatic, utopian, visionary, and social-revolutionary art forms, a type of painting develops of considerably more subdued content and form, seeming in many respects to be a readoption of the older realistic tendencies of the nineteenth century. Thus in 1925 Franz Roh in his book *Nach-Expressionismus* claims that *Magischer Realismus* sets off the post-Expressionist, that is, 'Neue Sachlichkeit', tendencies against previous ones by means of the following pairs of opposites: sober instead of ecstatic, quiet instead of loud, cool instead of warm, static instead of dynamic, smooth instead of roughened, objective instead of subjective, and so on.[5] He maintains, moreover, that this development exists not only in German but also in European painting as a whole and numbers as its major representatives painters such as Severini, Carrà, Chirico, Schrimpf, Mense, Davringhausen, Brotnyik, Kanoldt, Dix, Grosz, Scholz, Beckmann, Hubbuch, Miro, Metzinger, Picasso, Derain, Togores and Kisling. While Hartlaub had divided these artists chiefly into left-wing 'Verists' and right-wing 'Classicists', Roh indicates some seven subdivisions. Both of them, however, emphasise the stylistic common ground between these artists rather than that which divides them politically, and in this way they do set up overall systems based on 'style types'. In Roh's case the common ground is clearly the bourgeois 'middle of the road', which he attempts to distinguish sharply from the abysses on the 'left' and 'right'.[6]

In this form of a unified style complex the term 'Neue Sachlichkeit' caught on in Weimar journalism and was disseminated. With it a catch-word had finally been found which could be used to express the ideological and artistic self-awareness of one's own age. This was not so easily achieved with Expressionism, with its origins reaching back into the Wilhelminian period, and thus 'Neue Sachlichkeit' was the first thing that could be counted as typically 'Weimarian'. Initially the term was understood in the sense of a resigned and yet affirmative 'realism' which renounced all revolutionary tendencies and sought to come to terms with the new actualities of the republic. In the course of the so-called phase of stability there is thus a movement of purely cynical, veristic and crass tendencies which frankly aligns itself with phenomena which previously were as 'alien to art' as sport, technology, jazz – in fact with all forms of modern mass culture and the entertainment business. From now on, instead of pledging oneself to an Expressionist ecstasy, which 'leads nowhere anyway', 'Sachlichkeit' is the order of the day – that is to say, sobriety, realism and good living, and with all the coldness of that stark status quo mentality which for ever lies at the heart of this sort of compromise with grim reality. A similar situation had already come about in the so-called 'Nachmärz' after 1848 when the fervour of the forty-eighters had also yielded to the sobriety of an affirmative realism. In 1923, as in 1850, people were suddenly talking about the absurdity of all ideas of changing the world, the renunciation of utopianism and even the 'end of ideologies'. In place of these there was an effort to see everything in the most sober, factual and sporting way possible, whether it be love, boxing matches, the competition between the parties, the Tiller Girls, one's own job or some motor race built up by the press.

This life-affirming mentality coincided extensively with that of the stabilised middling bourgeoisie and from 1923 onwards also encroached upon the arts of the period. Even the painters and poets suddenly wanted to become factual reporters, newspaper correspondents or editors, each seeking merely to express the 'pulse of the times' beyond all notions of art as something having an aura. Such excursions into the modish and time-bound even found their way into the sacred domain of music. Here it was jazz, popular songs and revue tunes which became the last word. It is hardly surprising that in 1928 a foxtrot called 'Es liegt in der Luft eine Sachlichkeit' (Marcellus Schiffer) became a general favourite as a popular song. Whether from the point of view of the artist or of the bourgeois, 'Neue Sachlichkeit' was understood everywhere as a deliverance from Expressionist revolutionism, whose world-transforming élan was suddenly considered sentimental and even embarrassing. A book such as *Die Überwindung des Expressionismus* (1927) by Emil Utitz serves as proof of this, for it directs itself against every form of spiritual and emotional exuberance and sets its sights instead on a 'Neue Sachlichkeit' 'Classicism' based on the principle of resignation and of 'letting things run their course'.[7] It was mainly after 1929, when the consequences of the world economic crisis caused the so-called period of stability to start crumbling in Germany as well, that the right-wing middle classes endeavoured to cling desperately to the concept of 'Neue Sachlichkeit' merely in order to keep out any new 'revolutionism'. Thus under the title 'Vom Wesen der "Neuen Sachlichkeit"' Heinz Kindermann, later a Nazi, wrote in 1930, 'Enough about war, revolution and world salvation! Let us be modest and turn our attention to other, smaller things.'[8] Of course, he felt himself forced into distinguishing here between a 'radical' (meaning left-wing) and an 'ideal' (meaning right-wing) 'Sachlichkeit'. Only the latter gains his assent – the 'realist–idealist' 'Sachlichkeit' which coincides with the concept of 'poetic realism' in the intellectual history of that time. The same is true of the essay 'Vorläufiges zur sogenannten Neuen Sachlichkeit' by Alois Bauer, which appeared in 1930 in the ominously titled *Zeitschrift für Deutschkunde*. He too sees in the Expressionist desire to change the world nothing more than an 'extended puberty', while he puts 'Neue Sachlichkeit' on the level of positive evaluations such as 'short-term idealism', 'poetic realism' and 'purely humane political neutrality'.[9] Authors like Bruckner, Lampel, Grünberg and Glaeser are relegated to the category of 'unsachlich', while Alverdes, Carossa and Hans Grimm have the predicate of true 'Sachlichkeit' attributed to them.

When therefore the handing over of power to the Nazis was carried out in early 1933 it was first of all Expressionism and not 'Neue Sachlichkeit' which found itself under fire from art critics obliged to follow the party line. While Expressionism was represented as cultural–bolshevist, Jewish or negroid, and was finally killed off in 1937 in the large Munich monstrosity exhibition of 'Degenerate Art',[10] 'Neue Sachlichkeit' was treated with considerably greater tolerance. Its left wing (Grosz, Dix) was naturally attacked straight away; its right wing (Peiner, Dörries), on the other hand, was absorbed into the new tendencies without any loss of continuity. What particularly pleased the Nazis about this movement was its 'clean' realism, which perfectly reflected Hitler's conception of a 'clear German style' that was to try and avoid all subversive or even modish avant-garde tendencies and orientate itself solely around the eternal traditions of all great German art.

As a result of this, the chances of a new interest in 'Neue Sachlichkeit' in West Germany after 1945 were not especially great. The first movement to be elevated at this time was the very Expressionism which the Nazis had felt to be the essence of all cultural-bolshevist and correspondingly of all un-German revolutionary modes of thought. Yet here an important ideological deferment can be observed. With the

Adenauer period of restoration under way it was obviously not the revolutionary character of Expressionism which was newly discovered and rehabilitated with great display, but almost exclusively its avant-garde modernism and ultimately its innovationistic formalism. To this were numbered all tendencies in the direction of abstraction, aesthetic autonomy, hermeticism, rejection of ideology and timelessness. Conversely, people did not have much time for 'realism' in these years as the Cold War led to the popular theory that a red shirt was as bad as a brown one, to which, in the realm of art theory, all forms of the older realism fell victim, whether 'Neue Sachlichkeit', Socialist Realism or Nazi art. Thus Franz Roh writes in 1952 that 'abstraction' is 'the greatest discovery of our century', and that he now 'reproaches himself for not having recognised this' in the '20s.[11] For the same reason Werner Haftmann in his Book *Malerei im 20. Jahrhundert* (1954) – the Bible of abstract painting – gives the 'Neo-realism' of the '20s only five pages out of five hundred, and furthermore qualifies the whole movement as 'thin-blooded' and 'lacking in genius'.[12]

And so even in this respect a totally converse development came about in East and West Germany. While in the GDR the left wing of 'Neue Sachlichkeit' was systematically upgraded right from the beginning, and in the framework of the Dresden successors of Dix was even attributed the cohesion of a school, the painters of 'Neue Sachlichkeit' now living in West Germany such as Dix, Schad or Hubbuch were scarcely, if at all, considered in the '50s. What occurred in the Federal Republic in this period was a thoroughgoing restoration of the modernism which since 1925 had generally been considered dead. Its resurrection in the course of the Cold War atmosphere quickly led to a merciless dictatorship of the totally abstract and to a tyranny of the renowned beams, circles and lines, whose ideological supporting figure is the totally isolated and thus functionless individual artist attempting to keep himself as distant as possible from current mass taste.[13]

A new interest in truly 'realistic' art forms first starts in the West at the beginning of the '60s, when an extremely aggressive controversy about realism was kindled as a result of the first movements towards a conscious transcending of the past, the introduction of North American pop art and the innovation of documentary tendencies in literature. Until then everything had been so ridiculously simplistic. The enemy sat behind the Iron Curtain and painted and wrote 'realistically'. Western artists, however, were glad of the blessings of democratic tolerance and carefully avoided every sort of reality. But to the chagrin of the champions of abstraction there had been in the West since 1960 a series of realist villains for whom the relationship to reality had become a question of ideological judgement.[14] Instead of persisting with the 'modernism' which according to Hugo Friedrich has existed since 1870 and is based on the notion of the now totally 'autonomous' artist, even in these latitudes the 'real' reality was again squarely faced. In this way, as a stimulus to the tendency towards realism, the 'Neue Sachlichkeit' of the '20s once more came within the radius of critical interest, for it was seen to prefigure the same political polarisation and the same direct relationship to reality.

The first to refer back to 'Neue Sachlichkeit' in the wake of this reinforced relationship to reality were the art historians and museum people. Thus painters like Dix, Kanoldt, Schad, Scholz, Radziwill, Räderscheidt, Schrimpf, Mense and others are today no longer such unfamiliar names in the Federal Republic, and their work could be seen at the first retrospective exhibition on 'Neue Sachlichkeit' in 1961 at the Berlin Haus am Waldsee. Since then their paintings have been on show again and again: in 1962 at the Hanover art club, in 1966 at the Zwirner gallery in Cologne, in 1967 in the Wuppertal art club, in 1968 at the Galleria del Levante in Munich, in 1971 at the Stuttgart and Munich art clubs, in 1974 at the Darmstadt regional museum – first under titles such as 'Neue Sachlichkeit' or 'Magical Realism', and then more and more frequently as 'New Realism'. There is also no shortage of scholarly publications dealing with the painting of 'Neue Sachlichkeit'. As always, the well illustrated and richly documented catalogues of the exhibitions listed above are a real mine of information. Independent publications can be added to these, such as *Il realismo in Germania. Nuova oggettività – Realismo Magico* (1967) by Emilio Bertonati, *Neue Sachlichkeit und Magischer Realismus in Deutschland. 1918–33* (1969) by Wieland Schmied, and *Die Malerei der Neuen Sachlichkeit* (1973) by Fritz Schmalenbach, and also in recent years a whole series of essays, special issues of journals and individual monographs (on Dix, Scholz and Grosz among others).

The same is true of literary criticism, which, resulting from the initiatives of the documentary literature of the '60s and the interest which was suddenly aroused in the Weimar Republic, similarly had to come to terms with the concept of 'Neue Sachlichkeit'. In this field it took a little longer, for here the term had never gained such a firm footing as it had in art criticism. Yet since 1967 a number of important essays and compilations can also be found here (Horst Denkler, Reinhold Grimm and Jost Hermand, Karl Prümm, A. V. Subiotto, Bernd Witte and others),[15] of which *Neue Sachlichkeit. 1924–1932. Studien zur Literatur des 'Weissen Sozialismus'* (1970) by Helmut Lethen stands out as the most significant achievement.

As one might expect, these publications bring into relief very clear ideological fronts, reflecting the present-day political and academic theoretical polarisation. On first glance these publications create quite a chaotic impression. On closer examination, however, it is possible to distinguish three main directions: the right-wing middle class, the left liberal and the socialist-orientated voices, thereby expressing the same polarisation as that found towards the end of the Weimar Republic. With regard to 'Neue Sachlichkeit' the right wing is probably the most poorly represented. Such people usually avoid this phenomenon from the outset, and particularly in literary criticism. Even those on the right nowadays find it embarrassing once again to enthuse about Hans Grimm, Carossa or other right-wing Weimarians, and if they nevertheless do so it is in the privacy of their own little studies. For the academic public they prefer to retain the established 'modernism' concepts and extol Benn, Musil or Broch as the truly great figures of the 'Golden Twenties', without venturing into the field of comprehensive style concepts.[16] In the realm of art criticism those who belong to this category are above all the researchers who avoid all group concepts and simply concentrate on individual figures of importance, such as Carl Hofer or Max Beckmann, whenever they deal with the painting of the '20s. Many do indeed yield less secretively to the nostalgia for the 'Golden Twenties' and simply enthuse about the smart, elegant, painted, polished and decorative character of the fashionable paraphernalia which, since the 'Les années 25' exhibition at the Paris Museum of Decorative Art (1966), has been summarised in these circles by the term 'art deco' in order to establish a starting point for a new epoch in cultural history.[17]

Yet alongside such reactionary or purely modish and journalistic labelling of the '20s as the 'Golden Twenties' or the 'Art Deco Era' slightly more liberal scholars have tried again and again to use the term 'Neue Sachlichkeit' for all the art of the so-called period of stability between 1923 and 1929, and have done this irrespective of the extremely disparate political presuppositions of the individual artists and their work. Starting from a liberal concept of tolerance which is anchored in the spiritual superstructure rather than the materialist base, they see in 'Neue Sachlichkeit' a complex of competing artistic tendencies which do indeed differ greatly in their ideological execution but in style and inner bearing have ineradicable points in common, and thus must also be treated as a 'common' group. They start out from a concept of society, and correspondingly of art, according to which everybody really wants the same thing, that is, the permanent reform of all bourgeois capitalist economic, social and cultural assumptions. This reflects their own liberal understanding of democracy, which sees the most important incentive to unflinching progress in the competition between various ideologies of a similar nature.

In art criticism it was Wieland Schmied above all who aligned himself with this trend in 1969 with his book on 'Neue Sachlichkeit'. For him the internal cohesion of 'Neue Sachlichkeit' painting is guaranteed by the following criteria: sobriety, sharpness of perception, a sense of the everyday, banal and ugly, the elimination of all brush marks, and a static image construction within a glassy vacuum.[18] Like Franz Roh before him he carefully analyses the stylistic influences, indicates the international dimensions of the new 'realism', and at the same time clearly distinguishes 'Neue Sachlichkeit' from the left-wing tendencies of the late '20s as well as from the later Nazi painting. In this way he arrives at an image of 'Neue Sachlichkeit' which certainly is extremely well defined but which at the same time creates an extremely sterile impression, for here everything problematical or contradictory is avoided.

A number of the literary critics already mentioned come to similar conclusions. They are likewise concerned with 'saving the honour' of 'Neue Sachlichkeit' following the rediscovery of the Weimar Republic, and emphasise as a result precisely that which is reasonable, well thought out and clearly defined about this group, thereby drawing upon both ideological as well as stylistic criteria in support of this alleged homogeneity. By far the most prominent representative of this trend is Horst Denkler, who, in his 1967–68 essays on the subject of 'Neue Sachlichkeit', isolates group criteria such as contemporaneity, simplicity, partiality, faithfulness to reality, a feeling for science, topicality and a depth of substance, and yet he does this in a realm beyond all party political differences.[19] He claims that the concepts of 'Sachlichkeit' or 'Neue Sachlichkeit' were so vague at that time that they were adopted by nearly every group of artists, and in connection with this he stresses above all the firm break with Expressionism which, after 1923–24, became virtually normative for the art which followed and led to a clear preponderance of 'Neue Sachlichkeit'. In his opinion this style embraced not only the 'bourgeois middle of the road' but also radicals on the right (Jünger, Bronnen) and on the left (Renn, Wolf),[20] and 'Neue Sachlichkeit' disbanded only after 1929 when the left and right suddenly became autonomous. While between 1923 and 1929 the bourgeois middle of the road had largely succeeded in using 'Neue Sachlichkeit' to bind the peripheral groups of radicals to a common line, Denkler claims that a polarisation set in after that which finally led to the dissolution of the Weimar Republic. This conception is probably one of the most positive which have ever been put forward with regard to 'Neue Sachlichkeit', but it nevertheless runs the risk of prescribing the customary totalitarianism theory.[21] A similar attitude predominates in the collection of essays *Die*

deutsche Literatur der Weimarer Republik (1974) edited by Wolfgang
Rothe, in which Thomas Koebner and Hans Dieter Schäfer, as well as
Horst Denkler, extensively use the concept 'Neue Sachlichkeit' in line
with the method that Denkler had already outlined in 1967–68.[22]

Animated dissension from those on the left obviously had to be raised
against this very liberal understanding of the term 'Neue Sachlichkeit'
which works purely on the basis of the bourgeois middle of the road and
thus downgrades all other conceptions as 'radical'. This is exactly what
happened, and in the form of Helmut Lethen's book on 'Neue
Sachlichkeit' of 1970, which is couched in thoroughly critical and
polemical terms. Unlike Denkler, Lethen does not begin with literary
theory but principally with materialist foundations. For him
'Sachlichkeit' is first and foremost a 'normative concept of the ruling
class',[23] which is intended to blur the present class contrasts by reducing
the whole spectrum of political and social thought to purely
'technological' presuppositions. Lethen therefore largely equates
'Sachlichkeit' or 'Neue Sachlichkeit' with terms such as stabilisation,
rationalisation and modernisation which in the '20s manifested
themselves mainly in the form of Americanism, that is, as Fordism and
Taylorism. Thus in the spirit of the so-called 'transcending of the past'
(Vergangenheitsbewältigung) which played a crucial role in the late '60s,
particularly in the student movement, 'Neue Sachlichkeit' comes to be
seen as a decisive stage of development on the road towards a fascism
which then similarly tried to make class contrasts even more
unrecognisable by invoking the theory of the 'beauty of labour'. In this
way the whole concept of the 'bourgeois middle of the road' between
1923 and 1929, which was so carefully constructed by Denkler and
others, is translated into unambiguously negative terms and even loaded
with the reproach of 'pre-fascism'.[24] For Lethen all the talk of
'Sachlichkeit' or 'Neue Sachlichkeit' is merely the strategy of 'White
Socialism', seeking to convince the populace that in advanced
capitalism those inequalities which Marx had rightly criticised in the
nineteenth century had long since disappeared as a result of
rationalisation and automation. Therefore Lethen equates 'Sachlichkeit',
as a structural model of advanced capitalism, with a 'reformist
Realpolitik'[25] – in other words, the expression of the Stresemann period
of stability – which with its exaggerated cult of technology is based on
the capitalist utopia of a Henry Ford, and leads in the sphere of art to
paintings by a city avant-garde and to an Americanised sphere of
production. Thus while Denkler again and again underlines the positive
integrating power of the bourgeois middle of the road, Lethen simply sees
a continuing 'de-ideologisation of liberalism'[26] in the attitudes of this

group, a development which has ultimately contributed to a streamlined society and hence to an internal growth of fascism. As his literary examples he deals almost exclusively with left-liberal authors such as Döblin, Fallada and Reger, and consciously excludes from the concept 'Neue Sachlichkeit' all truly 'left-wing' authors.

Lethen is clearly not alone in holding such views. Almost all representatives of the 'New Left' in German studies today are quite disparaging in their comments about the literature of the so-called 'period of stability ' in the Weimar Republic. They do not, moreover, look merely to Lethen for support but also to the tenth volume of the large *Geschichte der deutschen Literatur* which was published in East Berlin in 1973 and covers the years 1917 to 1945. For here too the concept of 'Neue Sachlichkeit' is used purely negatively and is once more seen as the expression of the so-called 'period of stability' of capital, which led in liberal middle-class literature to a 'technology cult' and a 'renunciation of ideology', and as a result many intellectuals gave way to the deceptive illusion that they could maintain a position 'between the classes'.[27]

In the field of art history this left-wing judgement (or rather condemnation) of 'Neue Sachlichkeit' is represented by the following groups and individual authors. In West Germany the most significant example of this trend is perhaps the volume *Georg Scholz. Ein Beitrag zur Diskussion realistischer Kunst* (1975), which was brought out by a study group from the Heidelberg Institute of Art History on the occasion of the Karlsruhe Scholz exhibition. Here again 'Neue Sachlichkeit' is largely interpreted as the deceptive reflection of the 'relative stability' after 1923.[28] With reference to Lethen, it is mainly concepts like Americanism, the technology cult, Fordism and capitalist 'Sachlichkeit' which are brought to bear, in order to unmask the purely bourgeois capitalist orientation of this movement which was diametrically opposed to the realistic, aggressive art of the ASSO (Association of Revolutionary Visual Artists) then being supported by the German Communist Party (KPD). ASSO paintings were on show in 1971 at a large exhibition in Munich. The East German art historian Wolfgang Hütt represents an almost identical standpoint in his essay 'Neue Sachlichkeit und darüber hinaus', which appeared in *Tendenzen* as early as 1967.[29] Hütt draws a sharp distinction between committed left-wing Verism and middle-class 'Neue Sachlichkeit'. One need scarcely mention that only to Verism is attributed the ability to make social reality really 'transparent'. A similar distinction was made in the 'Realismus und Sachlichkeit' exhibition which was held in 1974 in the East Berlin National Gallery and is generally considered to have been the most exhaustive display of all the realistic trends in the painting of the Weimar Republic. There was no coarse differentation here between the 'bourgeois objectivist tendencies of "Neue Sachlichkeit" ' and the 'progressive realist art' of the same period, but rather a precise subdivision into five groups: Dadaism (Hausmann, Schwitters), Verism (Beckmann, Dix, Grosz, Scholz, Schlichter, Hubbuch, Schad), 'Neue Sachlichkeit' (Grossberg, Räderscheidt, Lenk, Kanoldt, Schrimpf, Mense), proletarian revolutionary art (Griebel, Nagel, Grundig, Querner) and Political Constructivism (Hoerle, Seiwert, Nerlinger, Arntz). This comes considerably closer to the actual group structures than all previous attempts at classification.

Similar voices have of late been heard even in music criticism, which until recently had scarcely touched upon questions of terminological concepts in this area. As a result the term 'Neue Sachlichkeit' had hardly been debated. One of the few people who tried to take the bull by the horns was Hartmut Fladt in his essay 'Eisler und die neue Sachlichkeit', which appeared in 1975 in one of the special editions of *Argument*. Referring unmistakably to Lethen, he defines 'Neue Sachlichkeit' as an aesthetic 'superstructure phenomenon in the capitalist phase of relative stability', whose way was prepared by the Dawes plan, and whose skilful justification of the technological 'pressure of things' had led to a general 'de-ideologisation' of the liberal bourgeoisie, the necessary result of this in the musical sphere being technologism and expressionlessness.[30]

So now the ground has been reasonably clearly mapped out. Alongside the purely liberal voices which stand up for a revaluation of the bourgeois liberal art of the Weimar Republic, more radical ones can be heard urging a revaluation of the really radical art of this era (ASSO, BPRS, *Linkskurve*). Both groups, moreover, rest their case on judgements which were already being advanced in the Weimar Republic. In order to support their theories the liberals refer to statements made by liberals (Döblin, Tucholsky, H. Mann, Kästner and others), and the radicals to statements which are more radical. At first the bourgeois-reformist trend far outweighed the other, but for a few years now the real left-wingers have gained themselves a greater hearing. They no longer base themselves on the well meaning reformists who generally had a very good relationship with 'Neue Sachlichkeit', but on those who were really revolutionary: men of theory and practice like Bertolt Brecht, Hanns Eisler, Walter Benjamin, Georg Lukács and the authors of *Die rote Fahne* and *Die Linkskurve*. These people found no redeeming features in the concept of 'Neue Sachlichkeit' even before 1929, but aligned themselves instead with a 'materialist aesthetic' based on a completely transformed relationship to reality. In other words they no longer took reality as something given but rather as something that could be changed, and thus even in art they sought to develop new strategies in order to change all present conditions and bring about a classless society.

These people reproached 'Neue Sachlichkeit' above all with its objectivism and fetishism, in other words, with its reification of social reality to mere complexes of facts. This left-wing critique of 'Neue Sachlichkeit', moreover, began about 1926 and reached its first peak in 1928. Hence Durus (i.e. Alfred Kemény) published a sharp attack on 'Neue Sachlichkeit' in *Die rote Fahne* on 24 January 1928 in which he reproaches the movement for its 'narrow-minded realism' stemming from a totally fetish-like attitude to reality. In the same paper on 3 July 1928 Hanns Eisler writes, under the title 'Relative Stabilisierung der Musik', that the music of 'Neue Sachlichkeit' suffers above all from 'expressionlessness' and 'objectivisation', and at the same time he passes the following collective judgement on the movement, one which is still valued as a model for Marxist criticism today:

Here an apparently small group of artists wishes to opt out of the present in much the same way as one opts out of school. Their helplessness in the face of the situation of their class has a simply tragic effect. But surely the modern musician affirms all the technical achievements of the present. He uses them. He loves the city, its noise, and is in love with the precise rhythm of the machines. Yet the people who operate the machines are of no interest to him, and in his art he strives towards the highest degree of expressionlessness, of objectivisation. Behind these totally vague phraseologies, behind this apparently radical progressiveness, behind this rejection of the sentimental experience of nature and love, there is nothing but the petty-bourgeois wanting to trick his way into escaping the fate of his class. The bourgeois musician in search of a content for his art and finding none propagates contentlessness as the purpose and meaning of his art. Incapable of understanding the social situation, he writes music which is elevated above everything human.

Similar opinions are expressed in the left-wing papers of the time almost everywhere one looks. There are, for example, the sharp criticisms in *Die Linskurve* of 'Neue Sachlichkeit' authors such as Döblin and Fallada: or there is Brecht's sarcastic attack upon the technology cult of 'Neue Sachlichkeit' in his poem '700 Intellektuelle beten einen Öltank an' ('700 intellectuals pray to an oil tank'), which was published on 11 February 1929. One could also mention the comment of his which has already been quoted hundreds of times to the effect that a 'photograph of the Krupp factory' tells you next to nothing about the place.[31] Or one could mention Walter Benjamin's essay 'Linke Melancholie' which appeared in *Die Gesellschaft* in 1931 and in which left liberal 'political writers in the mould of Kästner, Mehring or Tucholsky' are accused of political inactivity.[32] And one need only think of those all too familiar essays which Georg Lukács published in *Die Linkskurve* in 1932, where he opposes a portrayal of represented reality in terms of mere 'reportage'.[33]

In this way the problem of 'Neue Sachlichkeit' seems really to have resolved itself. After hearing so many authorities, who could still wish to say anything good about this movement without exposing himself as a bourgeois fool? Let us then come to some conclusions. As a result of this survey at least one thing has become clear – 'Neue Sachlichkeit' is by no means the only, nor even the predominant, style of the Weimar Republic, and neither is it the most important style of the so-called 'period of stability'. It is merely the ideological and aesthetic means of expression of a relatively small group from the bourgeois liberal or middling bourgeois sectors between 1923 and 1929 who, partly consciously and partly unconsciously, let themselves be captivated by the deceptive illusion of a new stabilisation of social conditions, basing itself on technology and a higher standard of living. In this way everything seems to be neatly tied up. We now know that the right- and left-wingers should not be thrown into the same basket, even though they display many perplexing similarities in the stylistic embodiment of their aesthetic statements. On ideological grounds one would hardly throw *Biedermeier* and *Jungdeutsche*, or Salon idealists and Naturalists into the same basket either, although similar stylistic parallels are to be found in them. Therefore, neither should one do this with the aggressive Verists and the representatives of the so-called 'Neue Sachlichkeit'. Yet in fact this was already quite evident to Gustav Friedrich Hartlaub as early as 1923. In spite of several tendencies to blur it, the precision of this distinction has increased, to the extent of making a division between cynical and aggressive, anti-bourgeois and pro-proletarian. As a result, the confrontation that is here being pursued and which, viewed purely from without, is founded on the principle of warring brothers, has now taken on quite different political, social and ideological dimensions than one could have foreseen around 1923.

Even the division into a left and a right wing, however, still gives the impression of being rather oversimplified. For in the end the left wing forms anything but a unity, and again and again breaks up into at least two different sections whose relationship to 'Neue Sachlichkeit' varies greatly. Firstly there would be the KPD-supported Worker Correspondents Movement (Arbeiterkorrespondenten-Bewegung), the Red One-mark Novel (Rote Eine-Mark-Roman) and the art of the left-wing 'Agitprop' groups, each of which was concerned with the direct day-to-day struggle and to a certain extent made use of relatively traditional, or bourgeois, stylistic means. To this one could add the art of the so-called 'dialecticians' (Brecht, Eisler), who saw their art against a considerably wider background over and above its momentary reference to daily realities, although they too by no means scorned that which directly 'impinged' but felt it to be equally central, even if they did this in quite a different manner. For where in fact did this group, which endeavoured to operate with non-traditional means, really find its arsenal of forms? Certainly not in the tradition of bourgeois realism and just as little in the tradition of avant-garde modernism around 1900. When considered closely, their parodistically contrived form principles stem largely from Expressionism, or from the constructivist trend of the '20s which directly follows on from Expressionism and is only marginally connected with 'Neue Sachlichkeit'. In this respect their art belongs within the general context of those tendencies which since the late nineteenth century have rebelled against bourgeois 'empathy' ('Einfühlung') in the name of an increasing 'abstraction' ('Abstraktion') – a trend which reaches its first peak in Expressionism. The favourite sequence – first Expressionism, then Dadaism, then 'Neue Sachlichkeit', and then increasing polarisation into left and right – therefore falls well short on this point. For finally, in the course of its advancing process of abstraction from all that is naturally given, Expressionism developed an arsenal of forms which directly and deeply influenced people like Brecht, Grosz, Piscator, Eisler and Heartfield, even if to begin with these artists strongly resisted them as a result of a subjective misunderstanding. In the passionate debate about Expressionism in the '30s it was they who were the first, and not without good reason, to set themselves up as defenders and advocates of this much maligned movement, and thus they indirectly provided proof of the significance of Expressionism for the whole period which followed it.[34]

The reason why this was not recognised earlier is mainly linked with the fact that the word 'Sachlichkeit' contained a perplexing variety of meanings, which played an extremely fateful role in the ideological manipulations of the '20s. Whereas in the free arts, in poetry and painting, which in themselves have scarcely any relationship with technology, the word was used mainly in the sense of the diversionary manoeuvres already outlined, in the field of applied arts and of architecture, which really are related to technology, it often had a completely different function. In this area 'Sachlichkeit' had a positive ring about it as early as 1900 (Hermann Muthesius), and then was played out in the sense of the early work league (Werkbund) tendencies as the main slogan against the old German pomposity of the Gründerzeit and the overloaded ornamentation of the Jugendstil.[35] At that time they understood 'Sachlichkeit' to mean things like defeudalisation and deromanticisation, with the intention of at last breaking out of a mere reproduction of the historically or naturally given and into a productive disposition towards action, which, in the context of its free association of free producers, already grants us a glimpse of a future classless society. The greatest achievements of Expressionism also belong within this tradition: the utopias of a Bruno Taut, the Bauhaus theories, the depersonalising and denaturalising tendencies of many a constructivist painter or writer, whose art set for itself the task of destroying the previous cult of personality and saw this as their contribution to a developing concretely orientated culture, which wished to use advanced technology on a socialist basis in order to liberate man from the previous critical state of society. This 'Neue Sachlichkeit' is therefore the most important achievement of Expressionism. It is its actual telos, one which certainly lives on in the best artistic accomplishments of the '20s and which is put to active use.

The positive element in the art of the '20s is therefore not that which is normally labelled as 'Neue Sachlichkeit', for this is generally neither 'neu' nor 'sachlich', but rather the 'Neue Sachlichkeit' of the Expressionist artistic tradition, whose revolutionary, world-transforming propensity is espoused above all in the greatest achievements of the left-wing materialist aesthetic. Art forms of the 'scientific age' were being developed here which reached beyond the mere technologism of the wrong kind of 'Neue Sachlichkeit', and which have now become famous as the mechanical stage, the epic theatre, photo-montage, re-functioned music, and so on, all containing more elements of Expressionism than of 'Neue Sachlichkeit'. It is here that their prefigurative function is to be found. For although the representatives of this art were against a mere technologism, they were not against a productive application of technology in the sense of social changes which would reach their preliminary goal only in fully developed socialism. Hence it was Expressionism and the left-wing art of the late '20s which were condemned by the Nazis, the most rabid fighting group of all late capitalist ideologies, while 'Neue Sachlichkeit' was to a great extent allowed to flourish even in the Third Reich.

Notes

[1] The phrase 'Neue Sachlichkeit' has no exact equivalent in English, for it implies a new sobriety and matter-of-factness as well as the idea of a new objectivity. For this reason it will be left in German.

[2] On the development of the concept 'Neue Sachlichkeit' see Fritz Schmalenbach, *Die Malerei der 'Neuen Sachlichkeit'*, West Berlin, 1973, p. 9 ff.

[3] On this point *cf.* the chapter 'Der vorgebliche Tod des Expressionismus' ('The alleged death of Expressionism') in Richard Hamann and Jost Hermand, *Expressionismus*, East Berlin, 1975, p. 278 ff.

[4] *Cf.* Helmut Kreuzer on the periodisation of 'modern' German literature in *Basis* 2, 1971, p. 7 ff.

[5] Franz Roh, *Nach-Expressionismus. Magischer Realismus*, Leipzig, 1925, p. 119.

[6] *Ibid.*, p. 35.

[7] Emil Utitz, *Die Überwindung des Expressionismus*, Stuttgart, 1927, p. 3.

[8] Heinz Kindermann, 'Vom Wesen der "Neuen Sachlichkeit"' ('On the essence of "Neue Sachlichkeit"'), in *Jahrbuch des Freien Deutschen Hochstifts*, 1930, pp. 354–86.

[9] Alois Bauer, 'Vorläufiges zu Neuen Sachlichkeit' ('Preliminary thoughts on "Neue Sachlichkeit"'), in *Zeitschrift für Deutschkunde* 44, 1930, pp. 73–80.

[10] *Cf.* Jost Hermand, 'Bewährte Tünlichkeiten. Der völkischnazistische Traum einer ewig-deutschen Kunst' ('Approved antiquities. The Nazi racial dream of an eternal German art'), in *Die deutsche Literatur im Dritten Reich*, ed. Horst Denkler and Karl Prümm, Stuttgart, 1976.

[11] Franz Roh, Rückblick auf den magischen Realismus' ('A retrospect on magical realism'), in *Das Kunstwerk* 6, 1952, vol. 1, p. 8.

[12] Werner Haftmann, *Malerei im 20. Jahrhundert*, Munich, 1954, pp. 311–16.

[13] *Cf.*, for example, Paul Ortwin Rave, *Kunstdiktatur im Dritten Reich*, Hamburg, 1949, p. 5 ff.

[14] *Cf.* Jost Hermand, 'Die 'wirkliche' Wirklichkeit. Zum Realismusstreit in der westlichen Kunstkritik' ('The "real" reality. On the realism debate in Western art criticism'), in *Realismustheorien in Literatur, Malerei, Musik und Politik*, ed. Reinhold Grimm and Jost Hermand, Stuttgart, 1975, p. 122 ff.

[15] *Cf.* Horst Denkler, 'Die Literaturtheorie der zwanziger Jahre' ('Literary theory in the twenties'), in *Monatshefte* 59, 1967, pp. 305-19; 'Sache und Stil. Die Theorie der 'Neuen Sachlichkeit' und ihre Auswirkungen auf Kunst und Dichtung' ('Object and style. The theory of "Neue Sachlichkeit" and its influence upon art and literature'), by the same author, in *Wirkendes Wort* 18, 1968, pp. 167–85; Reinhold Grimm and Jost Hermand (eds.), *Die sogenannten Zwanziger Jahre*, Bad Homburg, 1970; Karl Prumm, 'Neue Sachlichkeit. Anmerkungen zum Gebrauch des Begriffs in neueren literaturwissenschaftlichen Publikationen' ('Comments on the use of the term "Neue Sachlichkeit" in recent academic literary publications'), in *Zeitschrift für deutsche Philologie* 91, 1972, pp. 606–16; Bernd Witte, 'Neue Sachlichkeit. Zur Literatur der späten zwanziger Jahre in Deutschland' (' "Neue Sachlichkeit". On the literature of the late twenties in Germany'), in *Etudes germaniques* 21, 1, 1972, pp. 92–9; A. V. Subiotto, 'Neue Sachlichkeit: a reassessment', in *Deutung und Bedeutung*, ed. Brigitte Schludermann, The Hague, 1973, pp. 248–74.

[16] For an uncritical glorification of this period see Bruno E. Werner, 'Literatur und Theater in den zwanziger Jahren' ('Literature and theatre in the twenties'), in *Die Zeit ohne Eigenschaften*, ed. L. Reinisch, Stuttgart, 1961, p. 339 ff.

[17] *Cf.* Paul Maenz, *Art-Deco, 1920–40. Formen zwischen zwei Kriegen*, Cologne, 1974.

[18] Wieland Schmied, *Neue Sachlichkeit und Magischer Realismus in Deutschland, 1918–33*, Hanover, 1969, p. 26.

[19] Denkler, 'Sache und Stil', p. 167 ff.

[20] *Ibid.*, p. 173.

[21] See the criticism of these theories in Prümm, p. 608, and Helmut Lethen, *Neue Sachlichkeit, 1924–32. Studien zur Literatur des 'Weissen Sozialismus'*, Stuttgart, 1970, p. 184.

[22] *Die deutsche Literatur der Weimarer Republik*, ed. Wolfgang Rothe, Stuttgart, 1974, pp. 19 ff., 143 ff., 359 ff.

[23] Lethen, *Neue Sachlichkeit*, p. 8.

[24] *Cf.* also Prumm, p. 608 ff.

[25] Lethen, *Neue Sachlichkeit*, p. 10.

[26] *Ibid.*, p. 93 ff.

[27] *Geschichte der deutschen Literatur*, vol. X, ed. Hans Kaufmann, East Berlin, 1973, pp. 223, 229 ff., 367.

[28] *Georg Scholz. Ein Beitrag zur Diskussion realistischer Kunst*, Karlsruhe, 1975, p. 108 ff.

[29] Wolfgang Hütt, 'Neue Sachlichkeit und darüber hinaus'(' "Neue Sachlichkeit" and beyond'), *Tendenzen*, No. 46, 1967, pp. 205–8.

[30] Hermann Fladt, 'Eisler und die neue Sachlichkeit', in *Hanns Eisler*, Argument-Sonderband V, West Berlin, 1975, pp. 86–96.

[31] Bertolt Brecht, *Gesammelte Werke*, Frankfurt a.M., 1967, XVIII, p. 161 ff.

[32] Walter Benjamin, 'Linke Melancholie' ('Left-wing melancholy'), in *Die Gesellschaft* 8, 1931, pp. 181–4.

[33] Georg Lukács, 'Reportage oder Gestaltung?' ('Reportage or construction?'), *Die Linkskurve* 4, 1932, vol. 7–8.

[34] *Cf.* Werner Mittenzwei, 'Brecht und die Schicksale der Materialästhetik' ('Brecht and the fortunes of the materialist aesthetic'), in *Dialog 75*, East Berlin, 1975, pp. 9–44.

[35] *Cf.* the chapter on 'Purismus' in Richard Hamann and Jost Hermand, *Stilkunst um 1900*, East Berlin, 1967, pp. 506–40.

RONALD TAYLOR

Opera in Berlin in the 1920s:
Wozzeck and *The Threepenny Opera*

Among the commonplaces of German cultural history in the 1920s – one
which the dedicatee of this volume needs less reminding of than most of
us – is the self-confident, aggressive, irresistible rise of Berlin out of the
ruins of 1914–18. 'This city,' said Carl Zuckmayer, who was living there
at the time, 'ravenously devoured people's talents and energies,
masticated them, digested them – then spewed them out again.' Yet more
and more artists, actors, writers, intellectuals of all kinds masochistically
presented themselves to the monster for sacrifice, unwilling, or unable, to
stay beyond its reach. Max Beckmann, George Grosz, Otto Dix, Ludwig
Meidner, Max Reinhardt, Piscator, Brecht, Heinrich Mann, Döblin,
Gottfried Benn, Stefan Zweig, Erich Kästner, Carl von Ossietsky – their
name is legion. 'There was a taste of the future about Berlin,' Zuckmayer
recalled, 'and this made one willing to put up with the filth and the cold in
the place.' For 'Once you had Berlin, you had the world'.

Musical life in the city throbbed to the same stimulating variety. Never
before had young composers had such opportunities to hear their works
performed, and in spite of inflation and other post-war problems no
expense was spared in the mounting of concerts and operas. Klemperer
came to the Kroll-Oper in 1927; Bruno Walter had returned to his native
city in 1925 to take over the Städtische Oper, two years after Erich
Kleiber had been appointed Generalmusikdirektor at the Staatsoper,
while from 1922 Furtwängler had been conductor-in-chief of the Berlin
Philharmonic Orchestra. Busoni had long lived here; Hindemith became
a teacher at the Hochschule für Musik in 1927, and Kurt Weill, Hanns
Eisler and Paul Dessau – all three remembered chiefly for their
association with Brecht – came to seek their own success in the capital.

Of the famous operatic premieres in Berlin during the 1920s none was
more spectacular – utterly different though they are in intent, in manner,
in technique and every other conceivable way – than those of Alban

Berg's *Wozzeck* at the Staatsoper in 1925 and of *The Threepenny Opera*
at the Theater am Schiffbauerdamm in 1928.

Both works have in common the fact that their historical starting points
– Büchner's *Woyzeck* and John Gay's *The Beggar's Opera* – are
themselves famous moments in literary and cultural history. But that is
about all. Nor do I wish in these remarks to claim the existence of
hitherto unrecognised, more or less implausible links or affinities between
them. I should merely like to offer a few observations on their
relationship to their age, on the way in which their respective sources
have been adapted or interpreted, and on the nature and function of their
music. The spiritual distance between Brecht and Weill on the one hand
and Alban Berg on the other is as great as that between Rilke and
Johannes R. Becher, or between Thomas Mann and Hans Fallada, or
between Gerhart Hauptmann and Ernst Toller. But to identify such
antitheses is only to illustrate the extremes which the cultural life of the
1920s encompassed.

As a work that sets out to entertain through social satire, *The Beggar's
Opera* necessarily owes much of its meaning to personalities,
circumstances and attitudes of the day. Thieves, whores, highwayman,
beggars, informers, corrupt officials – Gay's audience knew them all.
Moreover the apron stage, far from sustaining a dramatic theatre of
illusion, made for an almost conversational intimacy, an identity of
attention and commitment, between players and public. At the same time
the political satire was sufficiently protean to bring Whigs and Tories
together in their enthusiasm for the work, either party finding, to its great
satisfaction, that Gay's wit was really directed at the other. The
foundations of ordered society were firm: what people saw on the stage
before them were familiar but non-substantive infringements of that
order, for which other elements could be held responsible – but never
oneself. Small wonder that *The Beggar's Opera* enjoyed such huge
popularity.

Beyond this, Gay's work, with the music arranged for it by Johann
Christoph Pepusch, was also cast as a parody of formal Italianate
eighteenth-century opera. It was not the first so-called ballad opera, but it
is the only one to have had a real influence in its day and to have
retained its popularity ever since. Upper-class opera seria, with its
artificialities of plot, its rigid conventionalties of manner and the elegant
affectations of its performers, was made to look ridiculous – on the one
hand by the replacement of Handelian emperors, kings and princes from
history by highwaymen, thieves, prostitutes and other characters from
the seamy side of contemporary life, and on the other by having these

characters sing popular ballads, thus parodying the formal arias sung with such pathos and self-consciousness by the interpreters of the great heroic roles. 'I hope I may be forgiven,' says the Beggar–Composer in the Introduction, 'that I have not made my Opera throughout unnatural, like those in vogue.'

Brecht, moving the scene forward a hundred years to Victorian Soho, sees things differently. Robbery, exploitation and prostitution are now props of the social order, integral features of bourgeois capitalism, not temporary and remediable aberrations. Furthermore society is not the product of man's creative efforts, but man is the creature of conditioning social forces. So the centre of Brecht's satire becomes the dehumanised, decaying society of capitalism – implicitly the bourgeois capitalism of the Weimar Republic – with Macheath typified as 'a Burger' and Peachum as 'a businessman'. Morality rests not on the individual conscience and will but on the social order, and in a capitalist society man cannot be good, as Peachum sings:

Of course I know I am quite right
The world is hard and man must fight.
We would be good – but man is low
And the conditions here they are not so.

As with the target of the social satire, so also the function of the music which Kurt Weill composed for Brecht's songs has become quite different from that of the sixty-nine popular tunes and dances – none of them newly composed for the work – which Pepusch had collected for *The Beggar's Opera*, and to which Gay wrote new texts. Weill's original music in *The Threepenny Opera*, as Brecht himself stated in so many words, was to underscore in its own way his presentation of the bourgeois ideology: 'it [the music] became muck-raking, provocative and denunicatory, so to speak'. Certainly the savagery of Brecht's lyrics is perfectly matched by the sardonic sentimentality and acid irony of Weill's tunes in their foxtrotty jazz idiom, with the trade marks of the 1920s stamped all over them – period pieces as bound to their age as the often grotesque distortions of capitalist reality in which Brecht exuberantly indulged.

The reception of *The Threepenny Opera* brought home to Brecht a further and financially very profitable irony, *viz.* that the middle classes were delighted to spend their money on watching entertaining demonstrations of the corruption of their doomed society, and had not the slightest intention of undergoing a Marxist conversion. *The Beggar's Opera* had made no attempt to reform society, and whatever moral content it had was incidental to its entertainment value, right to the very end, when, 'no matter how absurdly things are brought about', as the Beggar says, Macheath is reprieved – 'for an Opera must end happily'.

Yet *The Beggar's Opera*, if produced with this intention in mind, still has the power to involve the audience more directly in its action than *The Threepenny Opera*. The apron stage of the theatre in Lincoln's Inn Fields where Gay's work was first given in 1728 precluded any antithetical thoughts of 'us' and 'them', and *pace* Nigel Playfair's famous revival of 1920 at the Lyric Theatre, Hammersmith, it is through a flexible open-stage production, like that at the Chichester Festival in 1973, with the (middle-class) audience clapping and stamping to the rhythm of 'Lilliburlero', that the spirit of the work is properly captured. *The Threepenny Opera*, by comparison, today in the Berliner Ensemble as at its premiere in the same ornate theatre over half a century ago, is formal and prescriptive, demanding attention rather than participation, presenting the didactic tableau of a dogmatic reformer whose mind is made up, and will remain so.

When one sets these two works side by side – precisely two hundred years separate them – the historical fact needs no labouring that the German *Singspiel*, or opera with spoken dialogue, is descended from the ballad opera. Charles Coffey's *The Devil to Pay* (1728) and *The Merry Cobbler* (1735) were translated by Christian Weisse (*Der Teufel ist los* and *Der lustige Schuster*) and set to music by Johann Standfuss around 1750; shortly afterwards Hiller set the same two libretti and a number of others of the same kind, and in the 1770s the genre spread from Leipzig to Berlin and Vienna. The artistic peak of the *Singspiel* was reached with Mozart's *Die Entführung aus dem Serail* (1782), but the tradition of opera with spoken dialogue continued through *Die Zauberflöte* and *Fidelio* to the Romantic opera of the nineteenth century.

Weill was only one of a number of composers – Stravinsky, Milhaud, Honegger, Krenek, Hindemith, Aaron Copland, William Walton – who indulged in a highbrow flirtation with the jazz idiom of the 1920s. Jagged contours, jerky rhythms, a cultivation of the discrete rather than the coherent, an air of ironic, sometimes supercilious detachment – such characteristics are natural partners of epic theatre, 'Verfremdung' (alienation) and the other values of Brecht's theatre.

The success of *The Threepenny Opera* was not uncontroversial, but it was both immediate and persistent, in a way that avant-garde art rarely is. In the weeks that led up to the first performance, however, sickness among members of the cast, production difficulties and commercial misgivings about the wisdom of the whole enterprise had almost caused the management to cancel it at the last minute.

A similar crisis had preceded the premiere of Alban Berg's *Wozzeck* three years earlier. The manager of the Staatsoper, Max von Schillings – later the Nazi president of the Preussische Akademie der Künste, under whose chairmanship Thomas Mann, Käthe Kollwitz, Heinrich Mann, Döblin, Werfel and many others left, or were expelled from, the academy – resigned a few weeks before the first night. This in its turn raised doubts about the position of Erich Kleiber, who almost two years earlier had staked his reputation on performing the work in Berlin. Then there was the inevitable opposition to the sort of revolutionary, discordant, fiendishly demanding work that *Wozzeck* was rumoured to be: people had already had a foretaste of it in the three concert fragments performed the previous year in Frankfurt.

On the evening itself a near riot broke out at the end of the performance. There was laughter, whistling and hissing, and rival groups of protesters and supporters scuffled with each other in the auditorium. The battle was continued next day by the critics in the columns of their papers. The challenge of so powerful a work had to be faced: one might attack it or defend it, but one could not run away. Before it was banned by the Nazis – who were not the first to brand it as 'degenerate art' – it received two further productions in Berlin and was given in a dozen other cities in Germany; in the four years after its premiere it also had performances in London, New York, Prague, Zurich, Leningrad and other European centres.

Gay's *The Beggar's Opera* is a document of its age, a presentation of certain contemporary social and artistic circumstances; Brecht's adaptation of it is also a social document, and Weill's tunes underline the social message. But Büchner's *Woyzeck* is far more, and Berg pursues the profound spiritual meaning of his chosen source in music whose drama and ruthless intensity have scarcely been equalled in twentieth-century opera. Indeed, even though one may concede that Berg's reduction of Büchner's twenty-six scenes (in Franzo's edition) to fifteen inevitably suppresses certain motifs and alters the balance of those that remain, one comes away from the opera with an even more powerful experience of human tragedy than after reading or listening to the play. And largely, perhaps, because of its terse, utterly undiscursive manner and its unremitting concentration on dramatic essentials, *Wozzeck* can be more immediately felt as 'music drama' than *Tristan und Isolde*, or even *Götterdämmerung*.

The case history from which Büchner chipped out the fragments of his drama belonged to his own age – the historical Woyzeck was of the generation of Büchner's father. Berg, unlike Brecht with *The Threepenny Opera*, left the historical setting where it was, for it was not his concern to produce a work of 'social relevance', still less to preach a doctrine of social revolution. The author of *Der hessische Landbote* had a highly developed political consciousness, but *Woyzeck* is not a call to arms on behalf of the downtrodden and underprivileged. Woyzeck knows that only the well-to-do can afford the luxury of morality, and that talk of right and wrong means nothing to a man with an empty stomach – 'Food is the first thing – morals follow on', as Brecht's Macheath was so delicately to put it. But Woyzeck has no quarrel with the order that distinguishes between officers and other ranks as between human beings and animals. Indeed, it is his dependence upon this order that makes it possible for him to do the only thing that he lives for – to keep Marie and her child.

The fifteen scenes from which Berg fashioned his libretto focus on the human tragedy, and the changes that he made in Büchner's text of these scenes spring from the same dominant concern. When he then casts the music in an atonal idiom, in which the familiar landmarks of key and key relationship are totally absent, his presentation of the life and tragic end of his abused, long-suffering, pathetic hero becomes overwhelming.

Symbolically alone atonality – the rejection of the psychological and structural basis of Western music since the Middle Ages, and the enthronement of the uncertain, the unsettling and the apparently chaotic in its place – is a reflection of the world in which Wozzeck serves his life sentence. Atonality denies tonal relationships and the formal patterns that depend on them. A new basic formal principle was required – which, in the case of Schönberg and his followers, was to be that of the dodecaphonic tone row. But *Wozzeck* is not a twelve-tone work, and cannot have the intellectually generated unity of a twelve-tone work. Nor, whatever may be true on a technical plane, does it draw its unity from the calculated pattern of sonata movements, suite movements, fugues and so on of which the orchestral score consists. Its unity, its spiritual unity, rests on the nihilistic force of atonality itself, which on this one occasion – neither Berg nor anyone else could, or would, achieve anything like it again – becomes so harrowing, so shattering an experience, the epitome in music of the 'expressionistischer Schrei'.

And as though to validate this suffocating atonality, Berg saves for the climax of the whole opera, as Wozzeck drowns himself in the lake, a sudden 'Invention über eine Tonart' – an orchestral epilogue in D minor, an oasis of tonality in the midst of desolate atonal wastes. For Wozzeck's suicide, his solution to the problem of life and his release from torment, is a premeditated act, not the irrational impulse of a madman. In the cruellest of ironies, the almost unbearable tension built up by a remorseless atonality is suddenly relaxed just long enough for the poor wretch to put an end to the pitiful thing that had been his life.

Three years after the first performance of *Wozzeck* Berg wrote an article on 'The problem of opera' in the *Neue Musik-Zeitung*. Of all the ingenuity that had gone into the design of the work, he insisted, with its 'various fugues and inventions, suite movements and sonata movements, variations and passacaglias', the listener should notice nothing. 'Nobody must be filled with anything but the idea of the opera, which goes far beyond the individual fate of Wozzeck.' And Berg's hero does indeed stand, even more helplessly, more poignantly than Büchner's, as a paradigm of abused humanity, the born underdog, tragic spokesman for those who cannot understand why the world treats them as it does, yet whose last thought would be to try and change it.

Wozzeck, 1925 – *The Threepenny Opera*, 1928. The appeal of the two works, as drama, as music, can no more be equated than can their intent. They inhabit different worlds. But both are unmistakably of their age, and the capital of the Weimar Republic could accommodate them both. Zuckmayer was right: 'If you had Berlin, you had the world'.

ROWLAND COTTERILL

In defence of *Mahagonny*

Mahagonny,[1] which has been served admirably by a gramophone recording[2] and at least interestingly in some recent productions,[3] has yet to win the serious critical attention it deserves. In this short essay I hope to discuss some of the objections that have been levelled at the opera by musicians and dramatic critics and to suggest some new lines of approach to the work.

Reviewing the production by the (then) Sadler's Wells Opera in 1963, Arthur Jacobs found the plot unclear. His comments are worth quoting as an example of a response clearly conditioned by an attitude at once timid and dismissive towards the air of "theory" evoked by the name of Brecht:

> And how unsatisfactory is the end! Amid the placarding of contradictory slogans, we are said to be seeing 'the destruction of Mahagonny'. Why? Destruction by whom and for what reason? 'With Jimmy Mahoney's death the fate of Mahagonny is sealed' (H. H. Stuckenschmidt . . .). Why? An earlier 'climax' is equally unsatisfactory − when Jimmy, under threat of a typhoon, arrives at the great, all-sufficing maxim 'Nothing is barred'. Yet it appears that his life, and that of the city, go on just the same after this as before. Anyone volunteering to explain these obscurities to me is requested to do so without using the words 'alienation-effect' and 'epic theatre'.[4]

Even David Drew, the leading English champion of Weill's music and editor of a revised edition of the opera,[5] can mislead his readers: in the synopsis which precedes the English translation of his edition he explains the discontent of Jimmy and his friends in Act I:

> 'They find they are not satisfied . . . in this new city of pleasure, since there are still too many restrictions on the people's freedom to do as they please.'

Drew is presumably interpreting some such passage as the following, from the end of the ninth scene:

Jimmy. Ach, mit eurem ganzen Mahagonny
  Wird nie ein Mensch glücklich werden
  Weil zu viele Ruhe herrscht
  Und zu viel Eintracht
  Und weil's zu viel gibt
  Woran man sich halten kann. [p. 33]
	Ah, a human being can never be
	made truly happy by this Maha-
	gonny of yours: there's too
	much 'Rest', too much 'Unity',
	and there's too much for a man
	to fix himself on.

But Drew's understanding of the situation at this point is distorted by his recourse to a naive liberal notion of 'freedom'. Jimmy's complaint is only incidentally against the direct repression which is seen in the notices hanging in the tavern – 'Do not damage the chairs', 'No singing of rowdy songs'. At a deeper level he experiences the more subtle pressures of a society in which everything is arranged to minister to a sense of social unity and personal contentment. The verse quoted above comes as the climax of one of the most overtly, and parodistically, 'operatic' scenes in the entire work: Jimmy's sense of outrage runs away with him and his heroic-tenor accusations against Widow Begbick are echoed, ironically but in true Italian style, by the full ensemble with chorus. Only after this outburst does he return to the clarity of consciousness in which he can himself echo and with conscious irony distort the earlier verse, from the end of scene 1, in which Fatty and Moses clear-sightedly explain the original motive behind the founding of the city:

Aber dieses ganze Mahagonny Ist nur, weil alles so schlecht ist Weil keine Ruhe herrscht Und keine Eintracht Und weil es nichts gibt Woran man sich halten kann. [p. 9]	But this whole Mahagonny only exists because everything is so bad, because there's no rest and no unity and because there's nowhere for a man to fix him- self.

The city was founded as a bulwark and as a compensation against the general uncertainty of human affairs. As the first act progresses it is demonstrated that it is an over-compensation: the myths of rest, joy and unity no more meet the needs of a fully human being than the uncertainty which they repel. In this act Jimmy functions as the critic of the ordered Mahagonny: his critique issues in the formulation 'Do as you please', or, as the chorus so often repeat throughout the last two acts,

Vor allem aber achtet scharf Dass man hier alles dürfen darf. [p. 44]	But especially notice this clearly: here anyone is allowed to do anything.

The difference between the city of the first act and the city of later acts is the difference between two social programmes: on the one hand the order imposed to conceal the true basis of a consumption-oriented society, on the other the direct encouragement of aggressive individualism in the interests of society as a whole. Brecht's point is that these are equally destructive and stultifying, but quite distinct, programmes. Mahagonny has nothing more creative to offer, and Jimmy's death shows the bankruptcy of all its ideals – its destroyers are its own citizens, and the plethora of placards and slogans in the final processional scene are the sign of its failure in the most basic of social functions – mutual help. As the final procession sings, with Fatty at its head:

Können wohl von seinen grossen Zeiten reden	You can talk about his great
Können seine grosse Zeit vergessen	days, you can forget about his
Können einem toten Mann nicht helfen.	great days: you can't help a
[pp. 79–80]	dead man.

None of this is obscure in the text – though in the cut version which was shown on British television in 1965 it was made obscure by drastic omissions in Act I. The first may have seemed the easiest act to cut because it lacked the pathos aroused by the victim-hero which in the second and third acts Jimmy easily becomes. And the 'fall' of the city can count on arousing an emotional response less readily evoked by the 'rise'. Brecht wanted an audience to understand, not merely enjoy, the fall. To do this is to understand how all the citizens, not Jimmy alone, are caught in the bankruptcy of their own and of all social ideals; and to understand how Jimmy, and not Begbick alone, has his share in the construction of these ideals. Jimmy is not the victim-hero of a tragedy; and if *Mahagonny* is indeed an 'epic', then one of its claims to the title is the clear and equal attention it concentrates on each one of the participants in the action. Arthur Jacobs complained of the intrusion of the terms of theory into the discussion of a plot which – this is his implication – should be 'naturally' and simply comprehensible: but he and others have been misled by their false, however 'natural', assumption that the opera has a hero and points a moral. Brecht's intention may seem more limited than this, but certainly it is different, and it is clearly stated at the introduction to scene 5:

Damals kam unter anderen auch	At that time, among others, Paul
Paul Ackermann in die Stadt Maha-	Ackermann came to the city of Maha-
gonny, und seine Geschichte ist es,	gonny, and it is his story we want to
die wir Ihnen erzählen wollen.	tell you.
[p. 16]	

From this point of view the famous 'discovery of the laws of human happiness' must be understood as one event in a total history. Certainly Brecht does not simply underwrite the discovery – only the 'operatic' heroism of the first act finale could make this seem even momentarily credible – but neither does he condemn it as the origin of all the woes that subsequently descend upon the city: rather the 'discovery' itself is proposed for our understanding, as a consequence of the frustration engendered by the slogans of social unity which pervade the first act.

A different strategy for ignoring the opera may seem able to claim the support of Brecht himself, who, it may be said, dismissed it from serious consideration in calling it 'culinary'. Certainly Brecht's comments[6] reveal his discomfort with the conventional assumptions of opera as a social institution. But it needs no close reading to discover that he set out to make a virtue of the lazy hedonism with which opera was usually approached:

Mag *Mahagonny* so kulinarisch sein wie immer – eben so kulinarisch wie es sich für eine Oper schickt –, so hat es doch schon eine gesellschaftsändernde Funktion: es stellt eben das Kulinarische zur Diskussion, es greift die Gesellschaft an, die solche Opern benötigt . . .[7]

However culinary *Mahagonny* may be – just as culinary as befits an opera – it still has the function of effecting social change: it proposes the culinary for discussion, it attacks the society that necessitates such operas.

As in Brecht's time so in our own the fundamental tactic employed in most histories and analyses of opera[8] is to ignore the content, the actual events represented on the stage, and to concentrate on purely musical style (the analysis of the changes of musical style through history thus becomes incomprehensible in the absence of any parallel analysis of the changing patterns of operatic plot and mise-en-scène) or on an abstract 'dramatic effectiveness'. But Brecht did not so refuse to discuss the substance of *Mahagonny*. For him Pleasure was the substance. As an instance he took the scene where Jakob Schmidt eats himself to death. Brecht risked misunderstanding in limiting himself to this single example: at an obvious level the whole of the second act presents instances of the pursuit of pleasure – in sex, sport and drink as well as food – while it is with a more passively enjoyed form of pleasure that Jimmy's friends tempt him to calmness in the first act. The whole of scene 8 deserves to be understood in this light. Bill, Joe and Jakob enumerate the various pleasures offered by the city: gin, whisky, smoking, sleeping, swimming: each item in the list, though spoken rather than sung, is spoken over a musical accompaniment that abruptly ceases as Jimmy adds his ironic and dissatisfied assent: pleasures such as these satisfy the simple desires of his friends, but his desire is beyond such satisfaction and can only be voiced in the more 'operatic' style of an aria with ensemble refrain. This scene alone suggests the important identification that is sustained throughout the opera between the enjoyment of pleasure, the concept of individualistic heroism, and the forms and style of Italian opera.

In 'Homage to Igor Stravinsky' W. H. Auden wrote:

The golden age of opera, from Mozart to Verdi, coincided with the golden age of liberal humanism, of unquestioning belief in freedom and progress. If good operas are rarer today, this may be because, not only have we learned that we are less free than nineteenth-century humanism imagined, but also have become less certain that freedom is an unequivocal blessing, that the free are necessarily the good ... every high C accurately struck demolishes the theory that we are the irresponsible puppets of fate or chance.[9]

As if to confirm this dictum Weill wrote a sustained high C for Jimmy at the climax of scene 17. Jimmy is in prison awaiting trial. Brecht's sparely written text at this point provides for him no new access of insight into the nature of his subjection: simply he expresses his fear at the coming of day and his vain determination to cling to his already lost freedom.

Jimmy. Wenn der Himmel hell wird	When the sky turns bright,
Dann beginnt ein verdammter Tag.	then begins an accursed day.
Aber jetzt ist der Himmel ja noch dunkel.	But now the sky is still dark.
Nur die Nacht	The night must not stop: the
Darf nicht aufhören	day must not come.
Nur der Tag	
Darf nicht sein. [p. 62]	

Possibly by accident, more probably by design, these images inevitably recall, to the seasoned opera-goer, the second act of Wagner's *Tristan und Isolde*, where the lovers, immersed in night and Schopenhauer's philosophy, fear the coming of the day that will put their heroic passion to the test of survival in an ordered society. Wagner's opera is the greater in that the lovers are indeed put to this test. They are not allowed to claim the listener's undivided empathy any more than is Jimmy Mahoney: Brangäne's voice calls through the gloom in warning of the dawn. Weill has taken the triple time and obsessively chromatic harmony of her warning for his musical setting of Brecht's scene: Jimmy's heroic high C can halt neither the progress of the orchestra against which his vocal line makes such strained counterpoint nor the process of civilised justice in Mahagonny. Such an allusive art is not parody: like Brecht in the text, Weill in the score had written in both the musical representation of heroic passion and the mechanical nature of the social process which at once calls forth and frustrates that freedom. Italianate melody is played off against the regularity of rhythmic pulse which had been the hallmark of German composition since the organ music of the seventeenth century.

Thus in scene 14 the plangent and harmonically rootless melodic lines played by the stage band are set against the soft relentless march rhythms of the orchestra as the men form a queue outside the brothel: the music does not 'accompany' the stage action so much as functioning alongside it, representing in its own terms the same mutual frustration of individual will and social order. In the 'Crane duet' Jimmy and Jenny sing alternately but, apart from the last line, never together: their 'love' can exist only as a chance event, two separate wills coming alongside one another. The individual melodic lines soar and fall to final cadences, points of rest which are systematically denied them by the mechanically shifting harmonies beneath. Weill's technique here is sometimes described as 'neo-Bachian': in fact it is closely related to Stravinsky's exactly contemporary reworking of Bachian counterpoint and Verdian melody in *Oedipus Rex*, where as in *Mahagonny* heroic melodic gestures lose impetus when deflated by mechanised rhythmic figures and harmonies that deny all implied directions.

Oedipus Rex seems to assert the meaninglessness of human freedom: to assimilate its techniques to those of Weill's may seem to imply that Weill was a collaborator Brecht did well to drop as his own dramatic work moved from the nihilism barely staved off in *Mahagonny* to the more positive Marxist stances of middle and later plays. This is to set too low a value on Weill's subtlety, as a comparison with a more recent German composer may suggest. *The Raft of the Medusa*,[10] a 'secular oratorio' with a text by Ernst Schnabel and music by Hans Werner Henze, was first performed in 1967:[11] in style and intention it is significantly comparable with *Mahagonny* at many points. After the wreck of the French flagship *Medusa*, sailing to Africa on a mission of imperialistic reconquest, the slaves on board ship, many of them Africans themselves, build a raft which is eventually cut loose from the lifeboats by the French officers when it hinders their progress. Alone and without propulsion on the open sea, the survivors are in a position to achieve a full and clear consciousness of the nature of their social repression, and to propose for themselves new social bonds: they are adrift from the wreck of a civilisation rather as Begbick, Fatty and Moses are in flight from the law of another civilisation at the start of *Mahagonny*. In both works the possibilities of clear consciousness are set in relief against the dangerous ease with which false consciousnesses offer themselves. 'Peace' and 'Order' are the great myths of the first act of *Mahagonny*: the Christian heaven of Dante seems to beckon the almost dead survivors on the raft. In both works a main protagonist proposes, against these myths, a new law. Jimmy proposes total licence, to do justice to the typhoon-like nature of humanity as he experiences it within himself: the proposal of Jean-Charles in *Medusa* is apparently even more drastic – to kill half the twenty-seven ultimate survivors so that those who are left may have more chance to return to the world with the truth of what they have learnt. In each work the protagonist dies but the meaning of his experience is retained by the survivors.

Schnabel's text carries a directly revolutionary sense: the struggle to free oneself from old ideologies involves a fight against all habits of acquiescence and against many instincts that have claimed the general name of 'humanity': to expose these claims is painful but necessary. Brecht's text must seem more equivocal: social ideologies are criticised, it often appears, precisely in the name of the 'generosity' and 'humanity' against which Brecht directs such sharp questioning a few years later in *Der Jasager (The Yes Sayer)*. But this is to ignore the contributions of the composers in each case. Henze no less than Weill attempts to fuse a German and an Italian tradition, rhythmic force and sensuous, slow-moving harmony: but for Henze the two styles are both used separately and expressively, sensuous harmony for the dying men on the raft who acquiesce in the social fate which has condemned them, forceful brass and percussion ostinato for the emergent revolutionary awareness of Jean-Charles. This minimises the subtlety of Schnabel's dialectic: but there is another and more serious effect – Henze sacrifices the chance of increasing our own awareness of the issues. Through his music Jean-Charles becomes one more in the long line of operatic liberal heroes with baritone voices, fighting for reason against passion: Henze has taken over not merely 'Italianate' sensuousness but, though unconsciously, the dramatic ethos of Verdi. Henze uses the great complexity of his orchestral and vocal resources simply to generalise issues already presented with a fine specificity by his text: his music is culinary in precisely the sense Brecht did well to attack. Weill's music, for all its simpler resources, contains far more internal complexity and unresolved tension: his Italian or mock-Italian vocal style functions simultaneously with his Germanic march rhythms to present the frustrations of Mahagonny. The musical score becomes a résumé of the history of operatic style, nicely in accordance with Brecht's demands for a 'gestic' music that would not 'express' but clearly 'present' the actions of characters. Weill's music is not a 'setting' of Brecht's text: the two exist side by side, each heightening our awareness of the other.

It is perhaps fruitful to set *Mahagonny* at the end of one line of operatic tradition and near the start of an 'alternative', though perhaps stillborn, tradition. From Mozart and Schickaneder's *Die Zauberflöte* of 1791, German opera had set for itself a range of connected themes remarkably far from those of Italian and French grand opera as those forms took shape in the nineteenth century. Italian opera depicted the frustration of human passion (the tenor hero) by blind autocracy (the bass ruler or father figure) or more interestingly by the scepticism and wider perspectives of human rationality (such baritone figures as Posa in *Don Carlos* or Iago in *Otello*). German opera depicted the construction and defence of human civilisation as a whole. In *Die Zauberflöte* we see the persuasiveness with which the youthful and directionless hero Tamino is recruited from impulsive passion (his instinctive love for Pamina on seeing only her picture) and fury (his baseless mistrust of Sarastro, based on the evidence of women and hearsay) to the path of duty and, ultimately, the service of a religion – the religion of true humanity ('Wisdom', 'Love' and 'Virtue'). Similarly in Wagner's *Die Meistersinger* the youthful, impulsive Walther is turned aside from a purely instinctive musical skill and a wilful love and submits to the canons of the Masters. Jimmy and his friends, in *Mahagonny*, are the recruits who cannot be recruited, the potential new leaders who find no social goal worth their pursuit. But the most pervasive connections must be traced from *Mahagonny* back to the *Ring* itself. Brecht and Weill have impudently compressed Wagner's four-evening opera into two and a half hours, but the main lines of the plots remain closely comparable. The gods, like Begbick and her friends, construct a civilisation as a refuge against uncertainty: like her, they have a bad conscience from the start; like her, Wotan needs human recruits to defend his fortress: like her recruits, his disable themselves by their humanity (Siegmund) or threaten him with their disobedience (Siegfried, Brunnhilde): Siegfried, like Jimmy, is destroyed by a corrupt civilisation to whose laws he has voluntarily submitted himself in the pursuit of heroic pleasure. In one respect the two works have even suffered a similar critical fate: the tenor hero has been vindicated – particularly in recent productions of the *Ring* at Covent Garden and Bayreuth – against the founder figure. But Wagner's work has regularly been understood either as metaphysical or as heroic and tragic in purely general and timeless terms, and there is some justice in this: the clear political stances of *Rheingold* become increasingly allegorised, as the work proceeds, into a discourse on the nature of Power and Love. Brecht's work powerfully refuses all reduction to mere allegory. It is reductive to see *Mahagonny* as the Berlin of the Weimar Republic; and it is unnecessary. For Brecht has adequately defined, if not the locale of his action, certainly all the motives propelling his characters, without any recourse to 'general' attributes of human nature. The *Ring* begins, and *Mahagonny* begins and ends, by dealing with the rise and fall of a specific civilisation. And the fall of Mahagonny marks an end of the German tradition of opera: a tradition that from the *Ring* onwards has increasingly devoted itself to the paradoxes and difficulties with which 'civilisation' was sustained. In *Salome* and *Elektra* a relentless will to power (the two heroines, Jochanaan) is set against an inexhaustible but irrational or corrupt instinct for 'life' (Herod, Chrysothemis): in *Ariadne auf Naxos* the opposition between 'will' and 'Life', Ariadne and

Zerbinetta, has become the mainspring of the entire action. And opera, at the same time, has begun to reflect upon the conditions of its own survival.

Ariadne is one of the first operas 'about opera': the juxtaposition on the same stage of a Wagnerian tragic heroine and a Rossinian group of commedia dell'arte players is not so much an attempt to unify the long sundered strands of German and Italian opera as a presentation of the irrationality of either tradition when viewed in terms of the other. But where Strauss and, it seems, Hofmannsthal were content to juxtapose merely musical styles and supposedly general 'attitudes to life', Brecht and Weill penetrate to the content of the two traditions, 'Italianate' passion and 'German' civilised will. *Mahagonny* writes the obituary to these traditions in so far as they might claim to exist separably from one another or assert their total generality as an account of human experience. But they were not writing the obituary for opera as such. And it may be claimed that their work has been at the root of 'music theatre', understood as the contemporary extension of opera or substitute for it.

'Music theatre' is an amorphous concept, and attempts to clarify it at this stage would have to be prescriptive rather than descriptive. Monteverdi's *Combattimento di Tancredi e Clorinda*, Schoenberg's *Pierrot Lunaire* and Alexander Goehr's *Naboth's Vineyard* have all been claimed for it. One common factor in all these dramatic vocal works is the visible presence of a group of instrumentalists: moreover these players function largely as a group of separable soloists rather than as a homogeneous 'orchestra'. An instrumental texture not merely illustrative of a vocal drama but functioning independently alongside it – this is one concept around which future definitions of music theatre might profitably group themselves. In this sense *Mahagonny* could stand as an early example of music theatre extending itself to the length of a full evening – and a clearer example than *The Threepenny Opera*, in that music in *Mahagonny* functions constantly both to lend force to thoughts and to deflate passions. But such definitions fail to attend to the *content* of musical drama. To legislate for this would be out of place: but it would be possible to propose that successful musical drama, since the time of *Mahagonny*, has offered more critical and more specific studies of human social relationships than was the norm at any earlier period. 'Critical': this has involved a retreat from the assumption of a central heroine or hero whose experience was taken as normative for the values of a society: the retreat may be towards a large cast of more or less equal and distinct characters (Tippett's *Knot Garden*) or towards a refusal of moral endorsement for any character at all (Zimmermann's *Die Soldaten*). 'Specific': this does not necessarily involve 'realism' in the sense of stage decor — Maxwell Davies's *Eight Songs for a Mad King* presents the general paradoxes of sanity and madness through a detailed sense of the condition of George III without any stage set at all: nor need it imply 'detail' — in Tippett's *King Priam* the forces that govern Priam's various choices are indicated adequately without any of the conventional detail of 'attendant lords' and minor characters.

Behind these and other musical dramas of our time stands *Mahagonny*. The work of Brecht and Weill invites from its audience specific and critical reflection on itself and on the assumptions of German and Italian opera to that time. It points to a future less in the concrete fate of the characters it represents, rather in the relationship it proposes between performers and audience. But there is one character in the opera who seems capable of the critical reflection Brecht and Weill enjoin on their audience. Pennybanks Bill is not a character who receives much attention in reviews and criticism. But it is he who can distinguish between the claims of friendship and the dictates of reason. He refuses to put his money on Joe, the certain loser in the boxing match: he is unwilling to lend Jimmy the money to pay off his debts; but he argues on his behalf in court against the accusations of Trinity Moses. Explaining himself succinctly to Jimmy in scene 18, he says

Jim, du stehst mir menschlich nah	Jim, you're close to me in a
Aber Geld ist eine andre Sache. [p. 66]	human way: but money's a different matter.

The words are more than a conventional excuse. In scene 11, near the end of the first act, Jim had urged to Widow Begbick:

Siehst du, so ist die Welt:	This is how the world is, you
Ruhe und Eintracht, das gibt es nicht	see: there's no rest and no
Aber Hurrikane, die gibt es	unity: but there are hurri-
Und Taifune, wo sie nicht auslangen.	canes, and where they don't
Und gerade so ist der Mensch:	suffice there are typhoons.
er muss zerstören, was da ist ... [p. 36]	And man is just like that: he has to destroy whatever exists ...

And Jenny at the end of Act II, herself refusing Jim's plea for help, reflects 'Ein Mensch ist kein Tier': a man is not a beast. But it was Jim who assimilated man to a blind force of nature, in his 'discovery of the laws of human happiness''. Brecht's irony is directed against such all-inclusive conceptions of humanity, and Bill becomes the spokesman for that irony when he distinguishes humanity from business sense. Bill is not a 'developed character' — but *Mahagonny* poses, as one of its concerns, the question: under what conditions can truly human character be formed? And the implied answers should encourage us to see, if anywhere here, then in Bill, the focus around whom such humanity can grow.

Human character requires the reflective power to distinguish between different possibilities in specific circumstances. This is a principle which might have been derived from Brecht's dramatic theory: but it is amply exemplified within the action of *Mahagonny*.

Notes

[1] Bertolt Brecht, *Aufstieg und Fall der Stadt Mahagonny. Oper.* The text was written in 1928 and 1929. I have used the Suhrkamp-Verlag edition of 1955 (Berlin). This edition refers to the leading male character as 'Paul Ackermann'. Brecht authorised and even suggested that characters' names should be changed in performances outside Germany to suit the language of performance: in practice many of Brecht's original names have been retained in English performances, while on the other hand 'Paul Ackermann' has become 'Jimmy Mahoney' even on a German recording. I refer to him as Jimmy in my own text: to Brecht's 'Heinrich Merg' as (Pennybanks) Bill – he is Bill in the German recording. Brecht's 'Willy der Prokurist' I call Fatty, his name in the Sadler's Wells production of 1963. All my page references are to the Suhrkamp 1955 edition.

[2] Conducted by Wilhelm Brückner-Rüggerberg, with Lotte Lenya as Jenny: a CBS recording, numbered 77341.

[3] Keith Hack's production at the ADC theatre in Cambridge in March 1967 put the musicians on stage and set the action in a boxing ring.

[4] A. Jacobs, reviewing the Sadler's Wells Opera production of 16 January 1963, in *Opera*, March 1963, p. 201.

[5] B. Brecht, *Rise and Fall of the City of Mahagonny*, revised edition edited by D. Drew, 1969, Vienna; English translation by A. Weinstein and L. Symonette, 1972.

[6] B. Brecht, 'Anmerkungen zur Oper *Aufstieg und Fall der Stadt Mahagonny*', available at pp. 80–96 of the Suhrkamp edition cited above. They were written in 1930.

[7] Brecht, 'Anmerkungen', p. 95.

[8] One salutary exception is J. Kerman, *Opera as Drama*, New York, 1956.

[9] Conveniently available in W. H. Auden, *The Dyer's Hand*, 1963. The quotation is from p. 474 of this collection of articles.

[10] E. Schnabel, *Das Floss der Medusa*; DGG recording with text, 1969.

[11] Or at least given a final rehearsal which became the basis of a subsequent recording: the planned first performance was disrupted by demonstrations.

INDEX